TALKING OF DON MASSON

"Don came late to the international scene but made a huge impact during his three years with Scotland. He was an incredibly educated and talented footballer. He had a terrific football brain and could always see a pass. It's one thing to see it and another to deliver it… he had no problems on that score.

"We shared a great night at Anfield, scoring the goals that beat Wales to clinch our place at the World Cup Finals and that was an amazing achievement for a country with Scotland's population.

"I was always impressed by his desire and determination to make the best of what he had and it's a mystery to me that he didn't play at the top far earlier in his career. Maybe he just felt comfortable at Notts County. There's nothing wrong with that but I hope Notts County supporters fully appreciate what they had. It's a real claim to fame that he captained them from the Fourth Division right through to the First."

SIR KENNY DALGLISH
Celtic, Liverpool, Blackburn & Scotland

TALKING OF DON MASSON

"People talk glibly about the final piece of the jigsaw but Don was absolutely that when he joined QPR. We already had lots of very good players but when he arrived, he joined us all together. He really did make us tick ... a great player."

DAVE THOMAS
Queens Park Rangers & England

"It was all about perfection with Don. He never stopped searching for it and dragged us along with him. He set the standards and could be incredibly intolerant of any player who didn't strive to meet them every single day."

LES BRADD
Notts County

"I met a lot of bad losers in football but Don was in a class of his own. He even used to sulk for days when I beat him at golf - which I regularly did."

IAIN McCULLOCH
Notts County & Scotland

"Supporters voted Don as Notts County's 'Best Ever Player' and I wholeheartedly agree. I never saw anyone better in more than 50 years covering the club."

COLIN SLATER MBE
BBC Radio Nottingham

"I would categorise Don as a supreme play-maker but he also had another string to his bow. He scored more than 120 League and Cup goals and that's a tremendous achievement for an out-and-out midfield player.

"I know it's a cliché but he genuinely made teams tick. Tactics would revolve around his possession of the ball and he had a rare ability to control games. Even at the highest level that was true and one of his great strengths was that he made other players play. We knew that if we made a run, he would pick us out."

"I know he has beaten himself up for years about missing the World Cup penalty against Peru but he really shouldn't do that. He should just remember that in three years playing for Scotland he was a key man in winning the Home International Championships twice and getting us to Argentina."

BRUCE RIOCH
Aston Villa, Derby, Everton & Scotland

"I have the highest admiration for Don for having the courage to take a penalty at the World Cup. No way in the world could I have done that."

MARTIN BUCHAN
Manchester United & Scotland

"He had just about every club in the bag. Brilliant technique, terrific vision, scored goals as well as made them, amazingly consistent performance levels and seldom missed a game. What more could you want?"

HOWARD WILKINSON
Leeds United, Sheffield Wednesday & Notts County

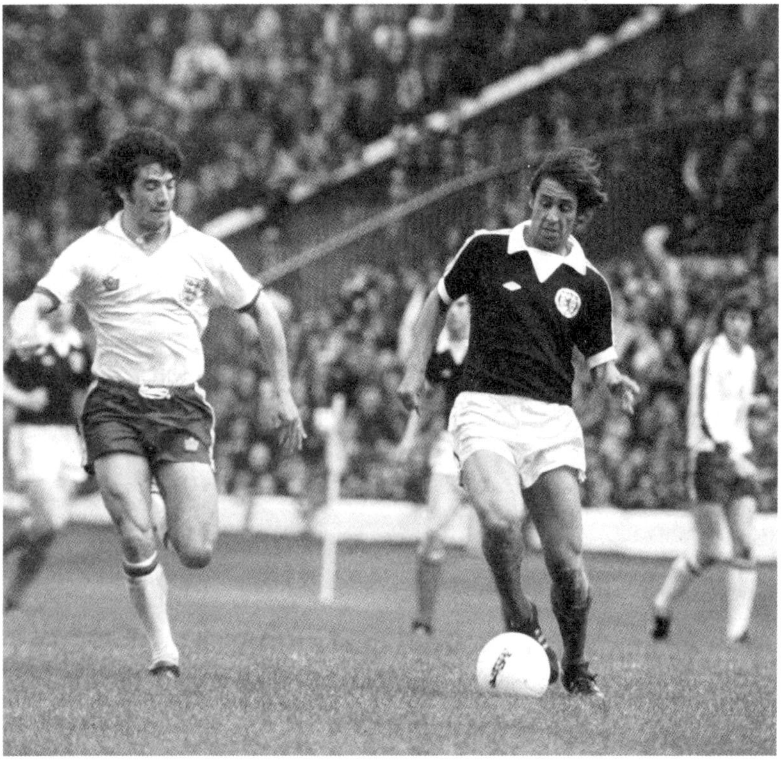

DON MASSON
STILL SAYING SORRY

With
TERRY BOWLES

Don Masson – The Autobiography
Still Saying Sorry

First published in Great Britain
in 2020 by BowlesMasson

Copyright © BowlesMasson 2020

Don Masson and Terry Bowles have asserted their rights under the Copyright, Designs and Patents Act 1988 to be identified as the authors of this work.

Photographs are from Alamy Stock Photo, Getty Images, Notts County FC, Shutterstock & the Masson family's personal collection.

ISBN (HB) 978-1-83853-834-7
ISBN (PB) 978-1-83853-835-4

Printed in Scotland by Bell & Bain, Glasgow

This book is dedicated to Margaret

and my parents, Jock & Barbara

CONTENTS

1	Telling it like it was	19
2	Born in a bothy - but we wanted for nothing	31
3	Whole new world... where do I sign?	39
4	Double-celebration yet the future looks grim	49
5	Starting afresh - things can only get better	61
6	Jimmy's best advice	70
7	"Calling Donald Sandison Masson"	85
8	Pledging to make black & white fashionable	98
9	London bound - but where would I end up?	111
10	Maybe I was the lone ranger... but I loved it	120
11	'Gerry's Gem' launches a special season	137

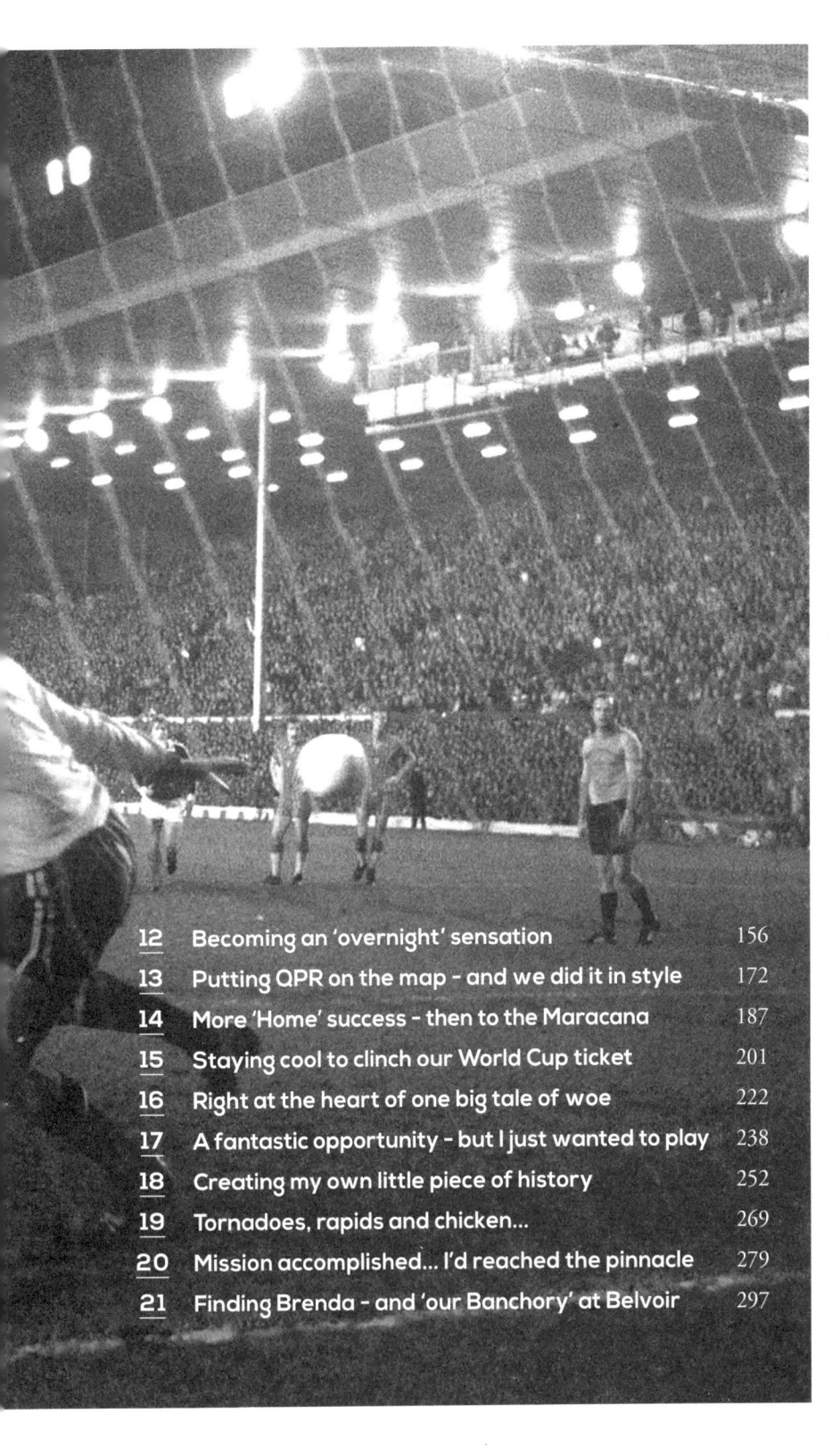

12	Becoming an 'overnight' sensation	156
13	Putting QPR on the map - and we did it in style	172
14	More 'Home' success - then to the Maracana	187
15	Staying cool to clinch our World Cup ticket	201
16	Right at the heart of one big tale of woe	222
17	A fantastic opportunity - but I just wanted to play	238
18	Creating my own little piece of history	252
19	Tornadoes, rapids and chicken...	269
20	Mission accomplished... I'd reached the pinnacle	279
21	Finding Brenda - and 'our Banchory' at Belvoir	297

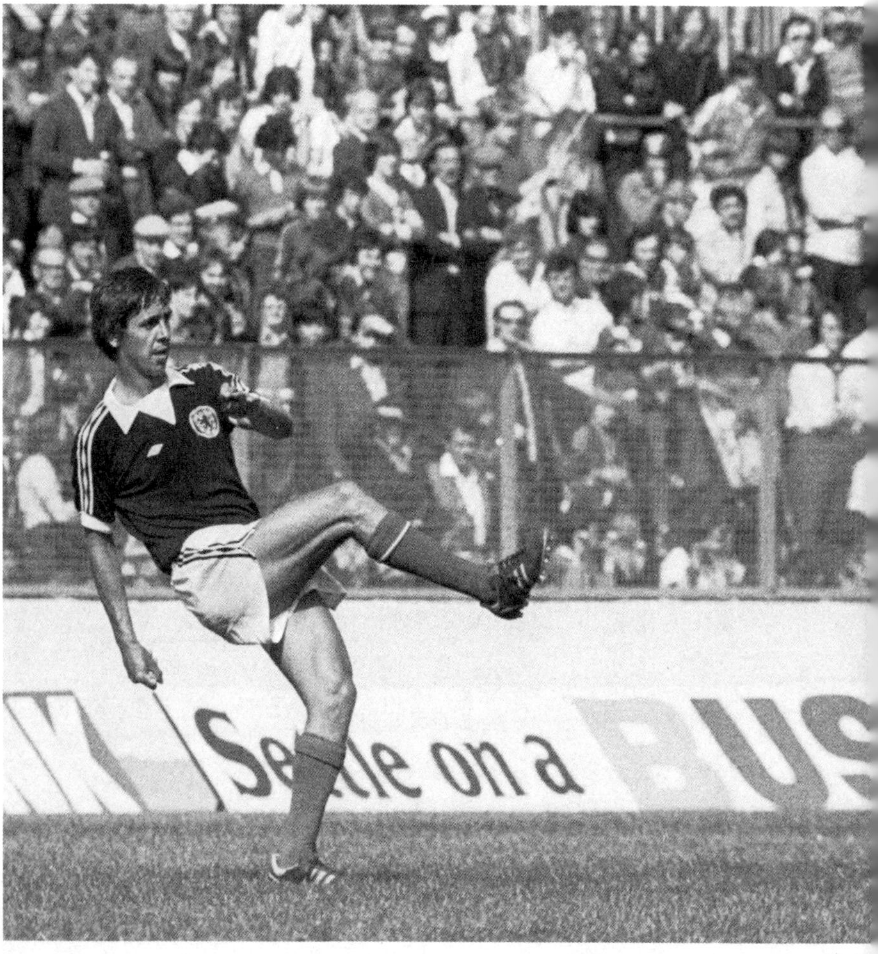
Settle on a
BUS

THANKS

Having spent a large chunk of my playing career doing my level best to steer well clear of journalists and keep a low profile, I still find it difficult to believe I agreed to put my life-story into words. Now that it's done, I feel a huge sense of relief. It has given me an opportunity to off-load baggage I've been carrying around with me for many years.

I'm sure Terry Bowles got the immediate reaction he expected when he suggested we should publish my autobiography but he asked me to think about it. I did just that, tossing and turning for much of that night, before I rang him at the crack of dawn to say: "Let's do it."

Terry's stance was that it would be a shame if the man voted Notts County's 'Best Ever Player' did not put his story on the record in the same way as the likes of Tommy Lawton and Les Bradd had done. More important to me was that it would give me chance to say some things I have wanted to for a long time. My one stipulation was that if I did the book, it would have to be an honest account - no holds barred. Terry said he wouldn't have it any other way. We go back a long way together and there's a mutual trust between us. It's been a rewarding exercise, reliving some great times, and I cannot thank him enough for all his hard work - especially his diligent checking of the facts. When you get to my age, the memory plays tricks and if any of the stories are not quite as you remember them, I can only apologise!

I'm immensely grateful to a whole host of people for their help in putting this publication together. Next on the list of those I must thank is Sam Bowles, who has helped to create a publication that has done me proud. I would also like to thank Ken Jones and Mark Radford for their sterling efforts in proof-reading the book and James Butcher and Richard Pitts, who have been particularly helpful in sourcing old photographs that help tell my story - plus a long list of former colleagues for keeping me on the straight and narrow when it came to the facts.

One of the big bonuses attached to this project is that it has given me cause to catch up with players I hadn't spoken to for years and sharing our memories has been a delight. Among those I especially have to thank are: Martin Buchan, Bruce Rioch and Sir Kenny Dalglish from my Scotland days; former Middlesbrough colleague Derrick Downing; from Notts County - Bob Worthington, Les Bradd, Brian Stubbs, Ray O'Brien, Iain McCulloch and Howard Wilkinson; from Queens Park Rangers - Frank McLintock and Dave Thomas.

My former clubs have been incredibly supportive and I'd like to record my thanks to Lynn Lawson and Nick Richardson (Notts County) and Francis Atkinson, Katie Ashby and Paul Morrissey (QPR). Many others have helped along the way, especially my good friend Denis Frith who has been my 'minder' since we first met in 1974 on the day I signed for Queens Park Rangers. My sincere apologies to anyone I may have missed off the list.

Finally, I did promise members of my extended family that they would get a mention in the book, so - with thanks for all their support and friendship - here goes ...

To my son Neil, who lives in Thailand, and my daughter Jayne, who lives in Spain with her husband Stephen and children Sophie, Ben and Maddie. To my sister Joan, along with her husband Dave who live in Thornaby, their son Dean in Melbourne, Australia with his wife Joanne and twins Maddie and Violet, and also their daughter Emma and husband Rory, along with their children Sonny and Jesse, living in Stockton.

I've dedicated this book to the memory of my first wife Margaret - and to my mum and dad - and I would like to thank Terry, John and Trish, Margaret's brothers and sister, for their friendship over all these years.

How lucky was I to meet Brenda in later life? She has been absolutely fantastic and loving over more than 30 years of marriage and her family - son Mark and wife Jane with children Lawrence, Ashton and Haydn, who live in Nottingham, and daughter Claire with husband Andy and their children Amie, Amber and Layton who live in Daventry - have been great to me.

I would also like to give a very special mention to Sandra Mann and her family who have been my good friends ever since Arthur, bless him, signed for Notts County in 1972.

all the very best

Head and shoulders above the rest – that's how
I like to remember Frank McLintock.

"Who is this bloke?"

FOREWORD

by
Frank McLintock MBE

I have to confess that I was a bit insular as a player. I'd always operated at the top level throughout my career and I'm slightly ashamed to say that what happened beneath that never really interested me.

Consequently, when I was told we were signing Don Masson at Queens Park Rangers I had genuinely never heard of him. I didn't know what club he played for, what position he filled and - until he told me - I certainly didn't know he was Scottish. But like all the lads at Loftus Road, I couldn't believe my eyes when I saw him play for the first time. It was the talk of the dressing room. We were all stunned by his performance and were asking the same questions: "Who is this bloke? Where on earth's he suddenly come from? Why the hell have we never heard about him before now?"

He was 28-years old by that time and once I started digging, I discovered that he'd been regarded for years as the best player in the lower divisions. In those days, before players gained freedom of contract, you were tied to a club as long as they wanted you and Notts County had hung onto Don so he could inspire them to better things. He did that, captaining them to two promotions in three years, but having seen what he could do I was astounded that none of the big clubs had gone in with the sort of bid that County simply couldn't refuse.

Don had a terrific 'football brain' - as good as I've ever known. If there were three or four options available when the ball came to him, he had an uncanny knack of picking the best one. You always had the impression that before the ball arrived, he'd already weighed things up and decided on his next move. Controlling and passing was his bread and butter. He made it look so easy and it amazed me how he was equally effective with both feet. His delivery from free kicks and corners was superb and he would swing the ball in with his left or right foot, whichever was best suited to the situation.

He was already an experienced player when he joined Rangers but even so you would think he'd need some time to settle in, moving to play in the First Division for the first time. Not Don. He was very aware of his own capabilities and he hit the ground running. I cannot pay him a bigger compliment than to say that he was already the complete player.

Over the next few years he was a key man in a very fine Rangers team and it was a real shame that he didn't collect a Football League champions medal in 1975-76. Liverpool pipped us by a point but I felt we were easily the best team in the country that year - and Don was right at the heart of it. Incidentally, he was also runner-up for the PFA's 'Footballer of the Year' Award that season and was selected in the PFA 'Team of the Year'. Clearly, the players with other clubs were just as impressed as we were with the impact he made.

I was delighted when Don asked me to write the Foreword for his autobiography. I knew I'd have no difficulty thinking of good things to say about him. In many ways, he's a man after my own heart. He set himself the highest of standards and demanded the same from his colleagues. That didn't go down well in some quarters but it earned him respect wherever he went.

I remember well the occasion when we were on an end-of-season trip to Israel and our manager Dave Sexton called the players together and said he had an announcement to make: "Don Masson has been selected for the Scotland squad for the Home International Championships." It meant the world to Don, especially bearing in mind that he was a few months short of his 30th birthday, and he was quite overcome. He had to leave the room but I went after him. I wanted to share the moment and tell him how much he deserved it.

A lot of people - especially the Scots - instantly think of the World Cup penalty he missed against Peru whenever Don Masson is mentioned. That's so unfair. What they ought to remember is how he helped Scotland win the Home International Championships two years in a row and how he tucked away the crucial penalty under the most extreme pressure when we had to beat Wales to qualify for the World Cup Finals.

I have great memories of our time together at Rangers - and of the time I went to visit him in Nottingham at the hotel he ran with his wife Brenda. Teddy Sheringham was with me because I was his agent and we'd just been arranging his move from Nottingham Forest to Tottenham. What a night that was!

I hope you enjoy Don's fascinating book. It's a compelling story that covers his humble beginnings, explains how he fought and finally overcame his demons and how tragedy touched his life in a big way. At the heart of it though, is a tale of how talent, coupled with drive, determination and patience, turned him into an exceptional midfield player.

Best Wishes

Frank McLintock

Frank McLintock played more than 700 League and Cup matches in a 20-year career for Leicester City, Arsenal and Queens Park Rangers and was capped nine times by Scotland. He captained Arsenal to success in the Inter-Cities Fairs Cup in 1970 and the following season, to the League & Cup 'Double'. He managed Leicester City and Brentford.

One
TELLING IT LIKE IT WAS

Even now, the best part of 40 years after I retired from playing, I still feel the need to apologise whenever I meet up with former colleagues. Almost without exception, especially those I played alongside in my first lengthy spell with Notts County, they have a story to tell about what a horrible person I was.

Looking back, I can't believe the amount of disrespect I showed them with some of the things I said. That was the root of the problem. It was mainly my mouth that got me into trouble and I have massive regrets about the way I treated people and conducted myself in general.

People said I was arrogant but I'm not convinced that's quite the right word. In my opinion, totally selfish would be a far more accurate description. I certainly was that. I was a driven man, desperate to make best use of any God-given talents I possessed, and very intolerant of anyone who might stop me from achieving it. I guess if I'd sat down in my early days with one of the sports psychologists that are all the rage today they'd have told me to forget about football. I was much more suited to sports like tennis or golf, where you have total control of your own fate.

I did always have a strong inner belief in my ability to get to the top and I make no apologies for that. But I allowed an obsession with seeking perfection to bring out the absolute worst in me. Every day I tried to do my work to the highest possible standards and it used to frustrate me like hell if others didn't adopt the same approach. It's no real defence for the way I acted but what I would say is that

I was a lot harder on myself than I was on others. For example, if ever I saw myself in action during televised highlights of a game, it never occurred to me to look for the good things. I was only interested in what I might have done better. That probably sums up my whole approach to the job.

I've always been a loner, very comfortable in my own company, and part of my selfish trait was that I adopted a routine that set me apart from most of the other lads. In those days, we didn't have anything like the training aides available to modern players but there were some weights in the corner of a grotty storage area beneath the old Main Stand at Meadow Lane. Every day I'd arrive some 20 minutes early to work on those before most of the other lads reported for training. Then afterwards, when they were all heading back to the changing room, I'd regularly stay out to work on set-pieces and some exercises I'd devised to help me develop 'quick feet'.

Even when it came to habits within the changing room, I had to be different. Jack Wheeler, our long-serving trainer/physio and one of the nicest men you would ever meet, used to tell people about how things were when we'd finished training. Most of the muddy gear was just chucked in a heap in the middle of the room. When you got to my changing position, it was neatly placed on a hanger.

I'm not saying this to make me look good, far from it. I'm just trying to paint the picture of how it became inevitable that a 'wedge' developed between me and the other players. I can see now that I just wasn't a team player in the overall sense and under the circumstances, maybe it was incredible that Notts County had as much success as we did during that period. There are countless stories about how one 'bad apple' in a dressing room can ruin the whole thing and when it involves a fairly influential player - as I was - it can be a real problem. But the lads found a way of shrugging their shoulders most of the time, and refusing to let my behaviour get to them.

We were a formidable force, winning promotion twice in the space of three years in the early Seventies, and I was the captain and ringmaster-in-chief in the centre of midfield. But that didn't give me the right to say and do some of the nasty things I did. Most of my actions occurred on the spur of the moment. I would instantly move on after I'd said my piece but I can understand now that those on the receiving end saw things very differently. And as I've already pointed out, it seems that every one of those players has a story to tell.

Mick Jones, for example, has never forgotten what I said to him seconds after he went down injured in only his third appearance after he'd joined Notts County from Derby. Apparently I leaned over him and said: "Get up you soft twat!" Two hours later he underwent an operation on a broken and dislocated ankle and only the brilliance of our surgeon, Peter Jackson, saved his career. Mick still carries that memory around with him to this day and it makes me cringe to think there are plenty more like him. Nobody was spared ... even my best mate Arthur Mann, who joined us from Manchester City. He was so annoyed about some caustic comment I made to him during a match at Aston Villa that he chased me around the pitch while the game was still going on!

One of the worst examples was a training ground incident when we were trying to work out some short-corner routines. I was taking the set-pieces as usual, and as Richie Barker emerged from the pack in the goalmouth and ran towards me, calling for the ball, I just ignored him. When he asked me why I hadn't given it to him I said: "Because you can't f****** play." Richie was understandably furious and when he asked me to repeat what I'd just said, I did so. All hell was let loose and our manager Jimmy Sirrel instantly abandoned the session as the lads made a half-hearted attempt to pull Richie away from me. Just about the worst thing you can say to a professional footballer is that 'you can't f****** play' and I'm ashamed to admit that became a bit of a catchphrase with me. I even used to use it when I went across to the bench on a fairly regular basis and told Jimmy that he needed to bring on a substitute.

A few years further on and Iain McCulloch became a very good friend when I went back to Notts County for a second spell. Yet, as he constantly reminds me, I gave him good reason to instantly dislike me. He signed from Kilmarnock about the same time as I moved back to the Midlands to join Derby County and Arthur Mann was driving him around the area, looking at houses. They made a detour to my house because Arthur needed to see me and as Iain says, I didn't even have the courtesy to walk 10 yards and say hello as he sat in the car. Apparently when he commented on it, Arthur shrugged it off by saying: "That's Don."

What totally baffles me, looking back, is how I managed to get away with it. Meadow Lane was known at that time as the Land of the Giants. We had some really tough lads and they were not averse to dishing out the treatment if a need arose. At 5ft 8in tall and weighing in at 10st 12lb in my prime, I was hardly built for physical confrontation. Yet although I was regularly threatened, I don't recall anyone taking it upon himself to actually teach me a lesson.

The most common response when I've tried to get to the bottom of this conundrum is that they tolerated me because I was influential in earning them lucrative bonuses. In those days, if you wanted a decent wage packet at the end of the week, the best way to achieve it was to do the business on the field. Jack Dunnett, the County chairman and the shrewdest man I ever met, introduced an excellent incentive scheme. On top of our modest basic wage we got a bonus for being in the team, one for drawing or winning, and another for being in the top three places in the League. We even got one if we pulled in crowds above certain levels so it meant that when we were winning games - especially if we played twice a week - we were doing very nicely. The players knew I was doing my bit towards making that happen and that, they tell me, was why they were prepared to put up with my antics.

They all laugh about it now and so do I, but it's not pleasant to be constantly reminded about what a horrible bloke I was. I really wish I could turn the clock back. Only recently I was talking to a County supporter who remembers standing near the front on the County Road side of the ground and being shocked at the way I hurled abuse at Charlie Crickmore when he allowed the ball to sneak under his foot and roll out of play. Charlie was a fine player, a key member of our Fourth Division Championship-winning side, but that counted for nothing as I apparently reminded him sharply that we were not playing a 'pub' match and he should get his act together.

They were a fantastic set of lads and because I was such a loner, I missed out on much of the camaraderie that was right at the heart of making County such a successful club in the Seventies and Eighties. That is one of my biggest regrets. It was standard procedure in those days for the players to get out and about and mix with the fans. Jimmy actively encouraged it and requests would regularly go up on the noticeboard in the dressing room, asking for volunteers to attend a function as representatives of the club. Most of the time only two players were required but because they enjoyed each other's company so much, they invariably turned up en masse ... with one notable exception. It wasn't that I felt it was beneath me. It just wasn't part of my make-up in those days to go out socialising. The lads would come into training the following day and relive all that had gone on the night before, and it didn't bother me. I certainly didn't feel it left a hole in my life but now I can see clearly that I missed out on something very special.

I used to say it was only on the football pitch that I let myself down but that really wasn't true. It went beyond that and inevitably, it was often those who were closest to me who suffered the most. For example, on one occasion, when County were pushing for promotion to the old First Division, we dropped vital points in a New Year's Day fixture at home to Cambridge United as we allowed them to hold us to a goalless draw. I was so angry with myself that within a few minutes of the final whistle I was out of the dressing room door and heading for the car park. I couldn't get away from the ground quickly enough. Halfway back to my home at Burton Joyce I remembered that I'd left my wife and two children behind and hurried back to collect them. Nothing was said when I picked them up. They knew what I was like. It was all about 'me, me, me' and the fact that my wife Margaret was left abandoned at Meadow Lane, wondering how on earth she was going to get home with Neil and Jayne, was of secondary importance to me.

I was actually so self-centred that I totally failed to read the script in 1968 when Middlesbrough, my first club, decided to sell me to Notts County in a £7,000 package deal that also involved big Bob Worthington. I was 22-years-old at the time, had already made 53 first-team starts for Middlesbrough. Almost half of those had come the previous season as we won promotion to the old Second Division so the move didn't make sense. Why would a developing young player suddenly give up the chance to establish himself in the second tier of the English game to join a club struggling near the foot of the Fourth Division?

The memory plays tricks. That was a very long time ago but I'd always told myself I made that move because a fresh start was the best way forward for me. It was all to do, so I thought, with the fact that I was struggling to command a regular place in the Boro midfield. Many years later the real truth finally emerged when I met up with Gordon Jones at a re-union at Middlesbrough. Gordon, a top left-back and our influential captain, pulled no punches. He candidly admitted that I was regarded as such a disruptive figure in the Ayresome Park dressing room that senior players got together and decided they had to do something about it. A 'Round Robin' letter was produced, signed by virtually all the players, saying they wanted me out. As captain, Gordon was then made responsible for delivering it to our manager, Stan Anderson. Looking back, the only saving grace is knowing that I was in good company. Exactly the same thing happened to Brian Clough. He was an absolute legend as a goal-scoring hero at Ayresome Park but I'm assured that most of the players couldn't stand him. Eventually they'd had enough and a 'Round Robin' was delivered.

It seems the dye was already cast for me, long before I arrived at Notts County. And if anyone thinks I'm making it sound worse than it was… it can't get much worse than having most of your colleagues turn against you.

I don't remember my approach to life being quite such a big issue after I moved to Queens Park Rangers and I suggest there were probably two reasons for that. By that time, I was 28-years-old and much more mature. Also, the goalposts had moved completely in the professional sense. All of a sudden at Rangers, the onus was on me to prove myself and show that I was comfortable surrounded by international stars like Gerry Francis, Stan Bowles, Frank McLintock and Don Givens, and that I could make an impact at the top level.

Talking of Stan, although it's nothing like as bad as other examples of me being a hard man to live with, it does make me smile when I think about the time we had a full-scale dust-up on the training ground. It was standard procedure on Friday mornings at Rangers to have a five-a-side session that took the form of England v Scotland & the Rest of the World. On one such occasion, it all kicked off between Stan and me. It was very much 'handbags at 20 paces', just as you'd imagine with us two, and big David Webb eventually pulled us apart. I was furious and stormed off to the dressing room but not before I'd made it very clear that if Stan was playing the following day, there was no way I would be. I just grabbed my stuff when I got to the dressing room and went straight home. I had no idea what the arrangements were for the next day's away game and frankly, I didn't care.

Dave Sexton, our manager, had been standing on the touchline and although he'd seen it all, he said and did absolutely nothing. At around 7.30 that evening our home phone rang and Margaret answered it. "It's Dave," she said, and I was in two minds about whether to take the phone from her. Eventually I did and he calmly said: "Everything alright for tomorrow? We're meeting at the ground at 11 and travelling by train to Ipswich."

"I'm not going if he's playing," I said, playing as hard to get as

I possibly could. There was a very lengthy silence before Dave came back at me in that softly-spoken way of his: "You know how much I think of you and how important you are to the team so I'll see you in the morning. Goodnight." With that, he hung up the phone.

How could I turn him down after that? Much to the amusement of the other players, Stan and I refused to acknowledge each other the following day. We kept as far apart as we possibly could but once we got in the dressing room at Portman Road, and were changing close to each other, things inevitably came to a head. Frank McLintock stepped in at that point and said: "Enough of this - shake hands and let's get on with it." We then went out and ripped star-studded Ipswich to pieces ... and lived together happily ever after.

My whole life was transformed in the early Eighties when Margaret and both of my parents died in the space of little more than three years. I surely don't need to explain what a devastating effect that had on me - and my children Neil and Jayne. When something like that happens it forces you to take a very close look at yourself.

My dad - he was called John but everyone always knew him as Jock - died in November 1982. He'd always been a heavy smoker but it still came as a massive shock when he died of a heart attack. He was only 60 years old. I dashed up to Middlesbrough to be with my mum and it hit me really hard. I just wish I'd had chance to say a proper goodbye. Some 18 months later, while Margaret and I were in Tenerife completing a deal to buy a couple of apartments as an investment, my mum, Barbara, was taken ill. She'd been looking after Neil and Jayne while we were away and bearing in mind that there were no mobiles in use at that time, we were shocked when we got back a couple of days later to discover she was in the Nottingham City Hospital. The doctors advised us that we could take her home but said she had lung cancer and only a few weeks to live.

We rapidly made changes to the house so we could create a downstairs bedroom and I have lovely memories of one day we spent together, a week before she died. She was a huge tennis fan and it really meant a lot to her when Margaret and I managed to take her to Wimbledon for the day in a wheelchair.

It was in the period immediately following mum's death that I became a Christian. The funeral director had said I would need a vicar to conduct the service and although it simply didn't rank on my list of priorities, because we were Scottish he put me in touch with Hamish Bailey at the local United Reform Church. Hamish came to our house the day before the funeral in Nottingham and although he'd never met my mum, he talked about her before and during the service as if he had known her all his life.

I cannot start to explain the impact that overall experience had on me. Nor would I want to try because it's far too personal. People talk about 'seeing the light' - and I believe that I did. Initially it frightened me more than anything ever had throughout my entire life but it felt as if a great weight had been lifted off me. The overwhelming feeling I had then, and still have to this day, is that I was so grateful to be given a second chance. I'd been gifted the opportunity to make amends, to try to make up for all those selfish and awful things I'd done over the years, and I was determined that I would.

Although Margaret was a church-goer, religion had never figured in my life in any shape or form but we started going together to the United Reform Church in a very low-profile way. I occasionally gave talks but never preached to people. It's a private thing as far as I'm concerned but if anyone asks me about how my life was turned around, I'm happy to tell them.

It was in April 1986 that Margaret died, just as I was trying to take my career in a new direction after 18 years as a professional footballer. What nobody knew was that she had been born with a venous malformation in her brain. It could have killed her at any time and eventually led to the aneurysm that tragically took her from us when she was just 39-years-old.

We had not long returned with great sun-tans from a brilliant holiday in Tenerife when she started complaining of headaches. She took to her bed and when the doctor came to visit her, she was immediately rushed into hospital. The bottom fell out of my world when I heard those fateful words: "I'm ever so sorry. There's nothing we can do for her." The consultant was probably in his early 40s but looked younger. How many times, I wondered, must he have delivered the worst possible news yet somehow remained detached as they fell apart in front of him? Apparently his own mother had died of the same rare condition so he will have fully understood how we were feeling.

After a spell in intensive care and a fortnight on the ward, Margaret had been allowed home. Within a couple of days, she was back in intensive care, undergoing a brain operation. When we got to see her again, two days later, she was on a life-support machine. Neil and Jayne, who were teenagers, were with me when the consultant said: "You have to make a decision because she is more or less brain dead."

We were all in a state of total shock. Margaret still looked amazing and we just hadn't seen it coming. There hadn't been even the slightest hint of a problem. I said I couldn't make that decision without speaking first to her parents - Tom and Jesse - and they immediately set off from Middlesbrough to travel down. We knew what had to be done but it was important for us to all be together to say our final goodbyes.

I was devastated. My biggest regret is that I didn't have more time with Margaret but under the circumstances, knowing her condition, it was a miracle we had 20 marvellous years together. I can only thank God for that. But to lose her and both parents in such a short space of time left me questioning whether I wanted to go on. Of course I had to. I had two lovely children who needed me like never before. Somehow I would have to cope with the worst situation imaginable but I know deep down that without my new-found faith, I wouldn't have got through it.

I had a call some years later from David McVay, who had made an instant impact at Notts County when he joined us straight from school after we'd just won promotion to the old Second Division. He was in and around the first team for a few years but eventually decided he would rather write about the game than play it and took to journalism.

I was pleased to see him but it wasn't an easy visit from his point of view. He'd come to tell me that he'd kept a detailed diary during his early days at Meadow Lane and had the opportunity to publish it in book form. The problem was that his entries didn't show me in a very good light. There's a surprise! David was concerned about how I might react and was at pains to explain that he hadn't set out to 'get' me, it was just the way things had worked out. I told him I didn't have a problem with it because I'm never uncomfortable with people telling the truth. He wasn't saying anything that I, and the people close to me, didn't already know.

The book apparently did very well. It was eventually turned into a successful theatre production and people seemed surprised that I accepted my invitation to go to the first night at Nottingham Playhouse, and even went up on stage at the finish. Some thought what David had written about me was close to character assassination but it honestly didn't bother me. In fact, I sat immediately behind him in the theatre and as soon as the performance ended, I was the first to shake his hand.

I was safe in the knowledge that it was all about me in my former life. I wasn't like that any more.

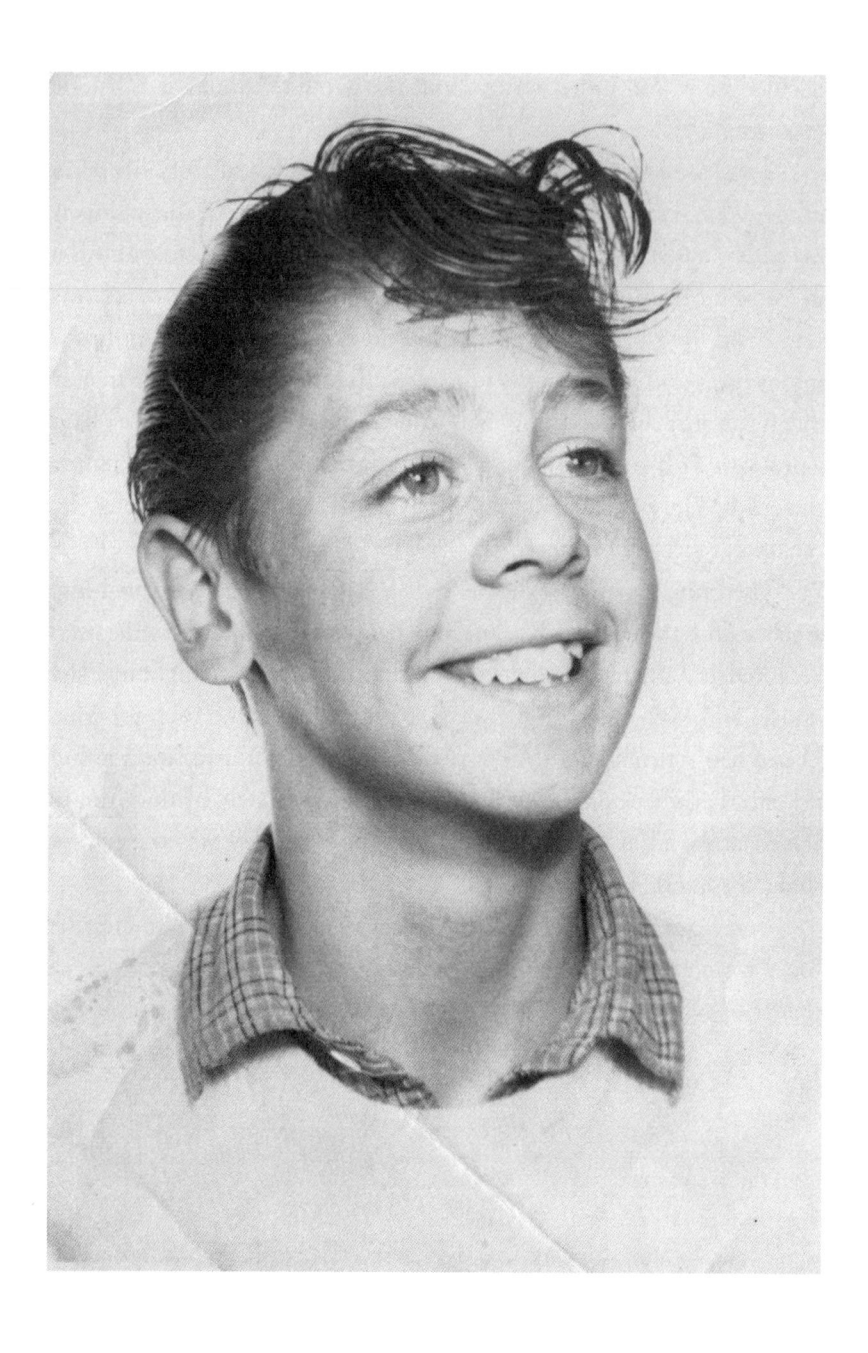

Is it Elvis Presley or maybe Bill Fury? Wrong!
It's me ... ready to make my way in the world.

Two
BORN IN A BOTHY – BUT WE WANTED FOR NOTHING
(1946-1958)

People look at me 'gone-out' when I tell them but it's the honest truth. I was born in a bothy, deep in the wilds of Aberdeenshire, and that's where I spent the first few years of my life. If you live on the south side of the border you tend to think of bothies as brick-built structures in isolated areas that offer some very welcome shelter to shepherds, or trekkers who might have lost their bearings. So they are. But for those of us living in the Scottish Highlands, bothy had a different meaning when I arrived in this world in August 1946.

Our bothy was little more than a wooden shack that sat on wheels – not that it was ever moved. It was an outbuilding to a farmhouse in Auchattie, a couple of miles outside of Banchory. Basic in every respect, it was home for my parents and me in the immediate post-war years and apart from the people living in the farmhouse, our nearest neighbours were several hundred yards away.

Banchory, the gateway to Royal Deeside, has expanded considerably in recent years. Surrounded by forests and agricultural land, the major town in the region now has a population of more than 8,000. Less than half that number lived there when I was growing up and there was certainly no shortage of space available for kicking a ball around. I was seven-years-old when my sister Joan was born. By then we had gone up-market. We'd moved into a nearby prefab and that was a big deal for my parents. They regarded it as real progress.

Dad, the shy and retiring type, lived for his family. He just wanted to do what was best for us. He was born with a hole-in-his-heart and that inevitably restricted his activities. It meant opportunities passed him by, but I think the simple life suited him. He certainly wasn't one for adventures so I was taken aback when he rang me, not long after I moved to Queens Park Rangers. For him to call me was unusual enough but it was completely out of character when he said he wanted to come down to a game. I was delighted, of course, and he got on a train and came down to London on his own. Because Margaret and I hadn't yet found a house in the south, I was temporarily living at the Kensington Hilton Hotel and dad joined me for dinner, and then stayed over. It was great to see him and I know he enjoyed his brief visit. Mind you, I'm not too sure what he made of Stan Bowles and Don Shanks when they turned up at the hotel as we were relaxing after dinner. They were great company, as always, but gave my dad a taste of a world he never knew existed!

I always think of my mum as a typical Scottish matriarch. She controlled everything in our house. At only 5ft 2in tall, she was full of energy and did everything at 100 miles an hour. Dad went to work and brought in the money but it was mum who decided how it would be used. As a family we didn't have anything - but we wanted for nothing. Our staple diet was Scotch Broth and traditional Neeps and Tatties. No one made those dishes better than my mum.

I have nothing but good memories of my early life and my parents never seemed happier than when they were playing whist. Mum was a bit of a fanatic and sitting around the makeshift card table on a Sunday afternoon became something of a family ritual. In fact, old habits die-hard and these days whenever we meet up with Joan, who now lives in Thornaby, just outside of Middlesbrough, it invariably leads to a game of whist.

The first person to notice I just might have some footballing talent was my mum and although she didn't take too much persuading as I recall, I used to coax her into playing football with me every day. Most of my primary school mates stayed for school dinners but I raced home as soon as the bell sounded for a quick sandwich and a kick-about with mum. People have often told me over the years that they weren't sure whether my natural kicking foot was my right or left. That's entirely down to her. From a very early age she made me use one foot as much as the other and it served me incredibly well in years to come.

I worked my way through Banchory Academy until the age of 12 and loved everything about it. Curiously, exams didn't figure in the Scottish education system in those days but I think I performed reasonably well. I certainly wanted to learn, made loads of good friends and don't ever recall being in trouble with teachers. Geography was my favourite subject, maybe influenced by the fact that the teacher also liked football. Years later, when I won my first cap for Scotland, I was really 'touched' that she sent a telegram to congratulate me. I'm sad to say I cannot remember her name but that kind gesture really meant a lot to me.

By the time I was 10, I was captain of the school's under-12 side and also played for the county at that level. Although Banchory is now in Aberdeenshire, it was part of Kincardinshire when I was growing up and I was proud to represent them. One of the things that experience taught me was how to be a bad loser. I remember scoring a hat-trick against Perthshire at St Johnstone's ground but it counted for nothing in my eyes. We lost 5-3 ... and I cried all the way home. Trips of that kind were great adventures for lads of our age and for me, they even turned into family affairs because dad used to drive the team bus and mum came too. Even she couldn't console me the day we lost at St Johnstone!

Things were looking up on the family front. We upgraded to a council house, around half a mile from where we'd been living, and dad got himself a new job with better pay. He used to work as a delivery man for the local bakery but progressed to driving a lorry that delivered diesel to the farming community in the area. He often used to take me with him and if those lunchtime kick-arounds were quality time spent with my mum, the diesel delivery trips were the equivalent with dad.

He was the eldest of four children. He had two brothers - Robbie and George - and a sister Margaret, and that extended family opened up yet more opportunities for me to enjoy new experiences. Margaret's husband Charlie was a gamekeeper, working the area of hills and forests north of Banchory. The next fall of snow was never far away in winter but even so it was a wonderful part of the world for inquisitive youngsters to grow up in. We were free to explore the great outdoors.

Banchory was on the train route heading north from London and we had an annual trip to the railway station during my school days when the Royals were en-route to their summer break at Balmoral. We had to line up along the platform with a Union Jack in our hands and wave it like mad as the Queen's train went past. I never understood it on two counts. First of all, why did the Scots have to make such a fuss over an English person and anyway, the train was going so fast that she couldn't possibly have noticed us.

I have eight cousins and I've got very fond memories of the times some of us spent together, often tagging along behind Uncle Charlie. He was a hero to me. A ruddy-faced man, big and powerful, he always looked the part dressed in his plus-fours, and seemed to know so much. He taught us how to do the 'beating' - chasing the birds out of the undergrowth when shooting parties had been organised - and how he culled the deer when their numbers grew out of control. He also tried to teach me how to drink whisky and I'm pleased to say that he failed miserably where that was concerned. He took a wee-dram on a very regular basis but it wasn't your everyday stuff that fortified him. Charlie's brother-in-law George worked in one of the distilleries that are so plentiful in that part of Scotland, and that entitled him to have easy access to 'the white stuff' as a way of topping up his wages. You couldn't buy that in the shops. It was whisky in its original form - pretty much pure alcohol before it matured - and it could be lethal.

Charlie liked to take a dram or two for breakfast, plus a fair few later at night, and on one occasion insisted I should try some. I was violently sick and have never touched whisky from that day to this. It won't surprise you to learn that he died at a comparatively young age. I'm sure the gut-rot whisky must have had a big influence.

Our house was situated on the one main street that ran through the town and at the rear was an area of grass that stretched all the way down to the River Dee. That's where I spent every spare minute, usually with my best mate Raymond Lovie and the Smith brothers. Raymond, who was a year older than me, was our goalkeeper in the school team. It's an odd fact that over the years, I always seemed to be particularly friendly with goalkeepers. Raddy Avramovic was one of my best mates at Notts County and so was Phil Parkes at QPR. Maybe it was because I always knew how important the last line of defence was to a team.

Even though we never had a ha'penny to spare, I still think of my early childhood as idyllic. We never tired of putting our jackets down as goalposts and pretending we were Scotland's finest, and we were full of good ideas for making our own entertainment. For example, we often used to float down the river on the inner tubes of tyres. A bit dangerous? I suppose it was but we never gave that a thought at the time. It was brilliant fun.

Most of the summer holidays in my early years were spent with my mum's uncle and auntie. They lived at a place called Rhynie, some 30 miles north of us, and I started to see life from a different angle when we visited them. I certainly enjoyed playing on a proper full-size football pitch for the first time while I was there and although I was small for my age and very shy, that never seemed to matter once an impromptu game of football got underway. I did spend a fair bit of time on my own in Rhynie but that was never a problem to me. I'd create my own adventures and one of my favourites was to climb a hill called Tap o'North. The views over rural Aberdeenshire when you reach the summit are spectacular and if I say so myself, it was some achievement for someone of my size and age to do that.

Football was the underlying theme across all my activities growing up but because of the isolated area in which we lived, I didn't have anything like the same opportunities as others. The lads I played alongside in later years all seemed to have stories to tell about their early links with the local League club and successes at schoolboy level. I struggled to compete with those.

Banchory FC were my local club. They played at a decent amateur level and because my dad was involved with them, I invariably went to see most of their games. He used to mark the pitch out on Saturday mornings, in his own incredibly meticulous way, and also regularly acted as a linesman. I enjoyed it but it didn't satisfy my urge for a taste of professional football.

The real treats for me came two or three times a season when dad took me to watch Aberdeen play. They were magical experiences for a lad of my age. I already knew that I desperately wanted to become a professional footballer but every time I went to Pittodrie, my determination to achieve that ambition was racked up by another notch. It took around 45 minutes by bus to make the 18-mile trip to Aberdeen and I loved the overwhelming feeling of anticipation as we pulled into Union Street and made our way down to the ground. All the hustle and bustle on the pavements ... impressionable youngsters needed eyes in the back of their heads to take it all in. There was so much going on around us, and the noise when we finally reached the front of the queue to the turnstiles and entered the stadium was so far removed from the life we lived at Banchory. I was totally hooked and vowed that one day, this would be my world.

What made those trips to Pittodrie extra special was that I'd actually met two of the Aberdeen stars. One was Graham Leggat, a brilliant right-winger who later played very successfully for Fulham, and the other was striker Paddy Buckley. Both were Scotland internationals, both played key roles in winning the Dons the Scottish League title in 1955 and it filled me with pride that I was able to tell people I'd met them personally, when they came to run a couple of coaching sessions for Banchory FC.

Aberdeen's result is still the first I look for every week and I always think it's a bit ironic that I never actually got to play at Pittodrie. Having played in all four divisions of the English League, I reckon there's a very good chance that I made an appearance at every one of the 92 grounds that were the established venues in those days. It would have been such a big thrill for me to play at Pittodrie - just once - and I'm very envious when I meet up with people who tell me they've done it.

Even though we only went occasionally, those trips to see Aberdeen play undoubtedly helped to shape my future. They certainly gave me a focus. I was very clear about what I wanted to do when I left school. My way forward was nicely mapped out ... or was it? What I certainly hadn't bargained for was to come down for breakfast one morning and be told by my mum that dad had gone to live in Middlesbrough.

With dad and his diesel lorry. I loved riding 'shotgun' for him.
It was brilliant fun with dad and my sister Joan, sailing down the
River Dee in an old inner tube. Joan and I have so many happy
memories of growing up in Banchory.

Three
WHOLE NEW WORLD... WHERE DO I SIGN?
(1958-1963)

It could just as easily have been Australia. As far as I was concerned, we'd moved to a foreign country - and I hated it. At the age of 12, I'd been lifted out of an environment in which I felt extremely comfortable and dumped in the middle of Middlesbrough. It could hardly have been more different to what I'd left behind. Full of people and cars, it was noisy and smelly, and I didn't know anyone. In short, I just didn't want to be there.

Dad was following his dream. He'd always wanted to be a bus driver and when the opportunity presented itself in Middlesbrough, he packed his bags and headed south. Apparently he had earlier tried to get a bus driving position in Aberdeen but because of issues relating to his hole-in-the-heart condition, he didn't pass the medical. How he got around that in Middlesbrough I have no idea. Maybe the medical was less stringent, maybe dad was less than truthful about his state of health. Either way, he landed the job he'd always wanted and that had huge consequences for the rest of the family.

Aberdeen was far and away the biggest place in our region and although we did occasionally go there, in so many respects when we landed in Teesside it was like a different world to me. To start with, I really struggled to understand what people were saying because of their 'strange' way of speaking and I guess it was the same in reverse.

Why was this happening? We didn't belong there.

Dad had rented a terraced house in Severn Street, with a lounge that you entered straight off the street, a scullery and an outside toilet. Once a week the tin bath would appear in the scullery and it took ages to fill. There were also two bedrooms and although that was good in theory, it was only half the story because we had three lodgers living with us!

They all had familiar stories to tell. Two of them had come down from Scotland to take up jobs as bus drivers - Campbell from Stonehaven and Sandy from Aberdeen - and the other was a 'clippie'. In those days the drivers sat up front in an enclosed cab and it was the conductor, otherwise known as a 'clippie' who controlled the bus. He, or she, patrolled the gangways, upstairs and down, shouting: "Any more fares please". And once they'd taken your money, the strange contraption they wore around their neck would spew out a ticket. The inside of the bus was their domain. It never moved until they'd rung the bell to signal to the driver that it was safe to do so. Big Norman, or 'Normie' as we knew him, had come from Huntly to become a conductor and he completed our line-up of lodgers. Needless to say a house that would have been ideal for two adults and two children became incredibly cramped and the sleeping arrangements were especially interesting. Mum and Joan shared one of the bedrooms, dad and I shared the other with one of the lodgers, and the other two lodgers slept in the downstairs back room.

Just as an aside, many years later when Queens Park Rangers were playing Spurs at White Hart Lane, I was getting off the team coach outside the ground when I heard a very distinctive voice. "Donald ... Donald," he was shouting. And although I hadn't seen big 'Normie' for many years, I knew straight away it was him.

I couldn't see him at first because there were so many people milling around behind the barriers but I only had to look along the row of heads. At 6ft 4in tall, he towered above the rest and it was lovely to see him again, with his young sons. I fixed them up with tickets, including some for the Players' Bar, and we had a good chat afterwards.

Fast-forward again many years to when I was back in Nottingham, and I got a call out of the blue from one of his sons. Apparently he had been researching his dad's history and it turned out that we were distant relations. It was news to me. I'm sure my mum and dad had never mentioned it but arrangements were made for 'Normie' to make a surprise birthday visit to us. We all had a brilliant day.

Things happen in life that have a massive impact but sometimes it can take years to understand the full implications. Our 'overnight flit' from Banchory to Middlesbrough hit me that way. It's only in recent times that I've come to see very clearly that it was a major factor in completely changing my personality. I'd always had a natural tendency to be a shy loner but was a nice, happy kid, rising to all the challenges that school-life offers the average 12-year-old, and sewing the seeds for a bright future.

That changed instantly when I arrived in Middlesbrough. All of a sudden I was a moaner, hating everything and everyone, and that especially applied at school. I'd missed out on taking the 11-Plus exam so I went straight into Marton Road Secondary Modern, which was close to where we were living, and really struggled to settle in. Chip on my shoulder or what? Absolutely I had one. I was never in trouble with teachers at Banchory yet I regularly was at Middlesbrough. It would be wrong to say that I was bullied because although I was small for my age, I could look after myself. But I never really felt welcome there. I was an intruder, a misfit that talked in a strange way, and although I was hungry for knowledge at school in Scotland, I turned off in Middlesbrough. Football was my one saving grace. I quickly showed that I had more talent than most and that gave me some status in the classroom.

Within a year of arriving in Middlesbrough, we moved into a semi-detached at Albert Terrace, just across the road from Albert Park, where a statue of Brian Clough now stands in recognition of his phenomenal scoring record of 197 goals in 213 appearances at Ayresome

Park. 'Cloughie', or Mr Clough as I always called him, transferred to Sunderland shortly before I signed for Middlesbrough so I never had chance to clean his boots. But I did feel 10ft tall many years later when our paths almost crossed at the City Ground. It was way after I'd finished playing but I'd been to a Forest match and as I was leaving the ground, I was conscious of the fact that he was walking down the corridor behind me. I overheard him say to the bloke he was with: "That's Don Masson. He could play." That's a compliment to treasure.

Middlesbrough as a football club were ahead of their time in some ways. They were among the first to reserve a special area of the ground for youngsters. Called 'The Pen', it was part of the terracing, up behind a goal, and I loved being there to watch Clough score three or four goals every time they played. We had an amazing forward line of Billy Day, Bill Harris, Clough, Alan Peacock and Eddie Holliday. They were all internationals and scored goals for fun. It was just a shame that the defenders couldn't match them for ability. I remember there was a lovely quote attributed to 'Cloughie' after one game had been drawn 6-6. He apparently asked: "How many goals do I have to score for us to win a game?"

Albert Terrace was a far better place to live. The lodgers had moved out by then and it was sheer luxury compared to what we'd had at Severn Street ... three bedrooms and a bathroom, and a nice big kitchen. Mum got a job in a local dairy while dad was as happy as 'Larry' on the buses. Maybe as a family we could make this work after all.

For some reason - presumably financial but I'm not quite sure - we moved again not too long afterwards. Mum became caretaker of the Methodist Church at The Avenue and there was a bonus involved because a tithe house went with that position. Even then we had another house move to do and again, it was tied in with mum getting a new job. We moved in above the doctors' surgery in Thornaby Road and as she was responsible for answering out-of-hours calls to the practice from 6pm until 6am, it severely restricted her activities.

The best example of that came many years later on the night when I was playing for Scotland against Wales at Anfield. Victory would take us to the World Cup Finals in Argentina and it was arguably the biggest game I ever played. All my family were there to support me … all except one. It wasn't mum's fault. I understood that but I was disappointed all the same.

From my point of view, the big plus about being in Middlesbrough was that it was much easier to get noticed and launch my career in football. Although just about everything in my life had been turned upside down, the one constant was that my heart was totally set on earning my living from the game. I soon managed to win a place in the school team at Marton Road Secondary and went on to represent Middlesbrough Schools at Under-14 and Under-15 levels. Then, right out of the blue, my games master pulled me aside one day. "Harold Shepherdson wants to talk to you about joining Middlesbrough," he explained. "I need to fix up for you and your parents to meet him."

Although Raich Carter was the manager at Ayresome Park, he was something of a mystery figure. He was seldom seen - certainly not at training. That was very much Harold's area and so was signing up the young talent. I liked Harold. He immediately came across as something of a father figure, someone you could trust, and it always seemed to me in the years that followed that he was the one who did most of the work behind the scenes. The War had cost him his playing career. He made just 17 appearances for Middlesbrough but fate helped balance the books in later years. He found fame through another route as Alf Ramsey's long-term assistant, playing a significant part in England's World Cup triumph, but that was still a few years away.

Harold had more important matters to attend to before that - like getting me onto the first rung of the ladder as a pro footballer. In those days clubs were not allowed to take youngsters onto their groundstaff until they were 16 but Middlesbrough found a way around it a year early by getting me a job as an apprentice painter and decorator. It was an interesting period of my life and I must admit that I often tested the patience of the chap who was tasked with teaching me how to hang wallpaper. On one occasion, when we were working on a particularly high ceiling, he was up the ladder and the idea was that I would fold the paper, concertina fashion, apply the paste and then feed it up to him. All of a sudden, the long stretch of paper landed on my head and nearly strangled me. I hadn't pasted it well enough for his liking so he threw it down at me and shouted: "Now do it again properly". There were highs as well as lows during my decorating career. I learned skills that served me well in later life but as a 15-year-old, all I wanted to do was play football.

Two days a week I left work early to go training at Ayresome Park in the evening and on Saturdays, I turned out for the youth team. I was probably the youngest player on the field initially because it was an under-18 league, but I don't ever remember feeling out of place. I joined the groundstaff as soon as I was 16 and was in my element. At last I was truly on my way - and I was getting paid for it. Not a lot admittedly, but that didn't matter. I got £2 a week, gave £1 to mum towards my board and lodgings, and the rest was all mine.

George Hardwick, who had played for Middlesbrough and England, was our boss. A dapper man with a well-groomed moustache he was the youth coach and a big part of his role involved making sure that our chores were carried out to a high standard. Despite the fact that I hated heights, I was regularly sent up ladders to clear out the gutters and although we were given all sorts of jobs to do, we also had regular responsibilities. Mine included cleaning the massive plunge bath every day, once the senior lads had used it, and also the four single baths. Three of us also had to clean the boots after training and one way or another, Middlesbrough certainly got their pound of flesh out of us.

I didn't mind. I had no doubts that it was a means to an end and found a couple of good mates to share the adventure with. Geoff Butler was a full back who went on to enjoy a good career with Chelsea, Norwich and Bournemouth, and Des 'Ginge' McPartland was a promising young goalkeeper. We often used to make the 15-minute drive to the seaside town of Redcar in Geoff's Ford Prefect, complete with three-speed gear-box. We had brilliant fun together. We worked hard and played hard. Nothing took priority over football but we were young lads with energy to burn and were determined to make the most of every opportunity that presented itself.

Lunch times were always a highlight. We were allowed an hour off from our duties and as Middlesborough had a games room with a full-size snooker table, plus table tennis and badminton facilities, we headed straight for them. My particular favourite was a snooker game called 'golf'. All the groundstaff lads chipped in a tanner (the old-fashioned sixpence) to play - so did our groundsman Wilf Atkinson - and I regularly used to clean up. In fact, without exaggerating, I often made more money from that in the course of a week than I did in my wage packet. Incidentally, the top table tennis player in the country at that time was Dennis Neale, who came from Middlesbrough. He used us to help hone his skills. I quite fancied myself at table tennis but even though he gave us a 19-point start, and the first to 21 points won, I don't ever remember beating him.

It was during that period that I discovered love for the first time. Every close season as a family we drove north to stay at the Dhualt, my grandad's cottage five-miles outside of Banchory, which we used as a base to visit relatives. One year, Geoff Butler came with us but probably wished he hadn't because I had other things on my mind. I've racked my brains to try and remember her name but I can't. What I do recall though was that it was very much love at first sight. I'd never experienced feelings like that before. I was totally besotted with her. I saw her as often as I could over the period we were there and when it was time to return to Middlesbrough, I couldn't tear myself away. The car was all loaded up when I announced that I wouldn't be going back with the rest of the family. Geoff was sitting in the back, looking a bit sheepish, and I remember my mum screaming: "Donald. Get in the car." I wouldn't be budged. Eventually they drove off without me. I'll always remember the expression on mum's face when I walked back through the door in Middlesbrough a week later. I'd been jilted ... she'd found someone else. So much for romance.

On the football front I felt very comfortable. I knew I was making good progress. Right-half, left-half, inside-right, inside-left ... I played in all of those old-fashioned positions and very regularly got on the score-sheet for the youth team and reserves. It seemed to come natural to me that I could kick the ball hard and get good distance. It was all down to timing and even though I was never involved with the free kicks in those days, I got loads of goals from outside the area.

What I needed to do was catch the eye of the manager but that was easier said than done. We hardly ever saw Raich Carter. As a player he'd been a huge star at Sunderland and Derby. He'd also had a long career in management before taking charge at Middlesbrough but that was in an era when managers sat behind a desk all day in collar and tie. In fact, he was dressed that way the only time I can ever recall seeing him on the training ground. It didn't do his smart suede shoes a lot of good as he pinged an inch-perfect pass across the field and then said to me: "Just remember ... that thing will only go where you put it."

Maybe he had noticed me after all because as soon as I reached my 17th birthday, he summoned me to his office to sign professional forms. It took all of 10 seconds to sort out the terms. I just wanted to know where I had to sign and my weekly wage instantly rose from £2 to a life-changing level. I cannot recall exactly how much but as I was still living at home, it meant I could make a real contribution to the family finances. Dad and I invested in a Ford Consul. Wow! I used to drive it down Linthorpe Road with my elbow hanging out the window, thinking I'd really made it. No one took any notice, of course, but in my mind, I'd arrived.

That's my mum - perched on the car that dad and I bought jointly when I signed professional for Middlesbrough.

Four

A DOUBLE-CELEBRATION YET THE FUTURE LOOKS GRIM
(1964-1968)

You could never claim Ayresome Park in the Sixties was glamorous. Just the opposite in fact but I've always thought it truly reflected the town where I spent many of my formative years. It was a place where straightforward, hard-working people came together on a Saturday afternoon to let off some steam. I loved the atmosphere and the general feel of the place. I loved turning up for work there every morning and I was proud to represent Middlesbrough. I just wish I'd been given more opportunities to represent them during the five years I spent on Teesside as a professional.

It all started promisingly enough because I was only a month past my 18th birthday when I made my debut in September 1964. Unlike today, when line-ups are seldom revealed until the last possible moment, Raich Carter told the local evening paper a day in advance that I'd be replacing the injured Ian Gibson in a League Cup tie at Charlton. A photographer turned up at the ground to get a picture of me sipping a cup of tea, and that was plastered over the back page on the big day.

Of course I enjoyed that moment in the limelight. I was young and impressionable, desperate to get myself on the radar, and it was brilliant to be involved with the first-team - even if it wasn't the most memorable of debuts. Gibson was a classy Scot who dominated our midfield. They were big boots for me to try and fill and although I don't think I let anyone down, we lost the game 2-1. One memory I do have of that night was the eerie atmosphere at The Valley. In those days there was a huge open terrace at Charlton that ran the full-length of the pitch and the crowd of 8,625 somehow got lost. It wasn't at all what I was expecting.

We had some really good players at that time. Even though we were in the old Second Division, our skipper Gordon Jones was one of the finest left-backs in the land and really ought to have played for England. He did at Under-23 level but never got chance to step up. As for Mel Nurse, a colossus of a Welsh international centre-half, I had so much respect for him. Margaret and I used to baby-sit for Mel and his wife in our teenage days and he repaid me when I hit the first-team scene by taking me under his wing.

I was particularly grateful to him after a match when I turned right as I drove out of the famous wrought-iron gates at the front of Ayresome Park and collided with a motorcyclist. I just didn't see him in the dim light. Fortunately it was only a glancing blow. The chap wasn't seriously hurt but I was so relieved that Mel arrived on the scene at that moment. "Leave it to me Boyo," he said. "You get off." I never heard another thing about it and I'll always be indebted to him.

Many years later, long after we'd finished playing, we went down to Swansea and stayed with Mel at the hotel he owned on the Mumbles. I knew that he was commonly known as 'Mr Swansea' and had been handed the Freedom of the City for the selfless part he played in keeping his debt-ridden local club alive when they were right on the brink of going under. Yet I had no idea how much the people loved him. Words cannot really describe the reaction when we walked into a packed pub. The bar was right across the other side of the room. No chance of getting a drink here, I thought but what followed was astonishing. It was like Moses and the Red Sea as the waves just parted and big Mel strolled through the middle.

We had a good laugh together just as we were about to set off for home from that visit. "I owe you a massive apology and I need to get it off my chest," he said. I had no idea what he was talking about. "The thing is," he explained. "Soon after you joined Middlesbrough as a kid I was talking to your parents and they asked me if I thought you had a chance of making a living from the game. I told them 'not as long as he has a hole in his arse'. I need to apologise for that ... I got it wrong." Every now and again you come across special characters in football, and life in general. He was one of them.

Gibson was back on duty the following Saturday, after that League Cup defeat, but I didn't have to wait long for my League debut. I played my part in a 2-0 win against Norwich, then got my first goal as we beat Swansea and was on the score-sheet twice in a 4-1 win against Swindon. By the time we got to Christmas I was really starting to feel I belonged and despite losing 2-0, the North East derby atmosphere on Boxing Day was incredible when we played Newcastle United at Ayresome Park in front of 38,194.

In those days, it was standard procedure to play your local derby opponents home and away over the holiday period so we went to St James' Park for the return on December 28. The crowd for that one was even bigger - 54,750 - and I was so disappointed that after a run of nine straight games I got left out. Maybe Carter thought the occasion would be a bit much for me. Whatever the reason, it proved to be a turning point in my season. I was in and out of the team over the next few months as we steadily slipped down the table. With two games left, there was a real danger that we would drop into the Third Division for the first time in the club's history.

I was recalled for the home clash with Leyton Orient and as it happened that proved decisive. We won the game 2-0 and although we finished just two points clear of relegation, we knew going into the final game that we were safe.

How did I feel about that first season? Well, I'd started 17 games and scored five goals. Not bad for a teenager feeling his way but building a platform was the easy bit. Hitting the 'take-off' button proved to be much more challenging.

I didn't figure at all in the first-team until October the following season and was substituted that day as we lost 2-0 at Bury. The stench of relegation hung over us from a very early stage and when Carter was sacked in the February and Stan Anderson took over as player-manager, he couldn't turn it around.

Stan was a good player. He'd given fantastic service to Newcastle and Sunderland before moving to Middlesbrough and one of the main reasons why I couldn't get a game was because he was filling my role. The other was Eric McMordie.

Eric found fame in an odd sort of way because he and George Best were a couple of Belfast lads who signed for Manchester United at the same time. They didn't stay long because they were both so homesick. Thankfully for all of us, Best returned to Old Trafford soon afterwards to give English football another try but three years went by before Eric turned up at Middlesbrough. He was a first-team regular for eight seasons and served the club well.

Ayresome Park wasn't a nice place to be as we slipped into the Third Division and I found it particularly frustrating, having to live with the embarrassment when things were totally out of my control. I couldn't get a look in. England won the World Cup that summer. Everyone wanted to talk football - not least because our ground was hosting the likes of Italy, Russia and North Korea in the North East group matches - but I was more worried about where my career was heading. What I really needed was a heart-to-heart with the manager, a chance to make my feelings known and establish what he thought I needed to do to turn things around. Incredible as it sounds, that just didn't happen in those days. It was virtually unheard of for a disgruntled player to go banging on the manager's door. We were like pieces of meat to be bought and sold, treated just as the club fancied. You had no say in what went on. You just had to get on with it - especially when you were stuck in the reserves because the player-manager had taken your position!

Having said that, life wasn't all bad. Arthur Horsfield fixed me up with a 'blind' date around that time with a mate of his girlfriend. Her name was Margaret, the daughter of a policeman who I later discovered was a good friend of Harold Shepherdson. I was instantly attracted to this tall, dark-haired girl with an infectious laugh and lovely personality. Shame she didn't feel the same way about me. It took weeks of hard work to win her round - but I got there eventually.

Apart from the football, I had no problem being in Middlesbrough. I'd grown to really like the place after the shock of arriving overnight from Banchory. My social life was good and I have very fond memories of some great nights out. It was a regular thing on Sunday evenings for Derrick Downing and I to go to the legendary Kirklevington Country Club, in the village of Yarm. It was a little bit out in the wilderness but well worth the effort to get there. We saw some brilliant acts, many of whom went on to become super-stars. They included the likes of Long John Baldry and the Moody Blues. I remember The Small Faces also playing there and Rod Stewart joining them for a couple of numbers.

Margaret, who was a very good clarinet player, shared my liking for jazz and we were thrilled to watch many of the big names like Kenny Ball and Acker Bilk in action at a club in Redcar. I've always had a fascination for watching people plying their trade when they're at the top of their game. Tommy Cooper and Jimmy Tarbuck definitely came into that category and Margaret and I saw them at the Fiesta Club in Stockton. In fact, I teamed up with Stan Anderson and Gordon Jones to play golf with Jimmy in a charity event, and then he fixed us up with tickets to watch him perform in the evening. That was one of the great days of my life. He's a very funny man who loves his football and golf.

Back on the football front, opportunity knocked when Anderson announced that he'd decided to retire from playing. That put the onus firmly on me to get myself into the team and stay there. I played in the opening game of the 1966-67 season, a 3-2 win at Colchester, but we struggled to build from there. If anyone thought that life would be easier down in the Third Division, they had got it all wrong. But Anderson's decision to replace many of the 'old guard' with younger players like Geoff Butler, Bill Gates, Downing, Horsfield and me, did eventually pay dividends.

Slowly but surely we worked our way into a position from which Middlesbrough could leap straight back into Division Two at the first attempt. Two things in particular had a big influence. The first was that we signed John O'Rourke from Luton Town and his strike-partnership with John Hickton and Horsfield produced an incredible 70 goals. The second was the Ayresome Angels.

Who were they? Well, they began as a group of fans who used to congregate at The Holgate End and although our relegation the previous year must have really tested their patience, they were totally loyal. Whatever the result, they would stick with us - home and away - and for them, having fun was key to the whole experience. Noisy and colourful, they often dressed up in an outrageous fashion and once the prospect of a promotion push started to emerge, more and more people wanted to be involved. Very few clubs ran supporters coaches in those days. We had a fleet following us to away games and the support they gave us was tremendous. Dozens became hundreds, even thousands at some games and they were a real inspiration. It was something new to English football. No one had ever seen anything quite like this before. It only lasted for about three years but was brilliant while it did.

I made my first visit to Loftus Road that season and remember it well. I was expecting something special when we arrived in West London to face Queens Park Rangers but the place was a dump. The difference was incredible when I went back to sign for them later in life. There was nothing wrong with their football team though, because they smashed us 4-0 and come the end of the season, they finished as runaway champions. In fact, they finished 12 points clear at the top and that was also the year when Rodney Marsh & Co came from 2-0 down at half time to beat West Brom 3-2 in the League Cup Final at Wembley.

I paid a heavy price for that result against Rangers in mid-September. I was immediately dropped and only figured once more until the closing stages of February. It was easier to slot in by that stage because the players were oozing confidence and having helped us to beat Watford 3-0, I was back to stay. The next couple of months turned into one of the most enjoyable periods of my long career. We had numerous spectacular victories in front of huge crowds and it was an absolute pleasure to be involved. Part of that, I'm sure, stemmed from the team spirit that developed on the back of our regular trips to Scarborough during the second half of the season. It was the perfect routine before home games. We stayed at the Grand Hotel, trained on the beach for a couple of days, enjoyed ourselves in the evenings ... then travelled back on the Saturday morning to do the business.

Instead of McMordie and I competing for the one place, we operated alongside each other in the final push for promotion and developed an excellent understanding. With Downing on the left and Dave Chadwick on the right flank, we were really effective in delivering the ammunition for our formidable front three. Chadwick must have hated me. I knew it amused the others that I used to 'play games' with him. The more they laughed, the more I did it. He had a tendency to jump out of the way in 50/50 situations and I often deliberately timed my passes so that they were 60/40 in favour of the defender. I can still see him now, jumping up and down with rage and saying he was going to tell the manager about me. I need to balance that off by saying that 'Chaddy' was a fine player - and I loved him really! He played for a long list of clubs before moving to the States and I was fascinated to learn that he'd been inducted years later into the Georgia State Soccer Association's 'Hall of Fame' in recognition for his efforts as a coach.

Promotion hinged on the outcome of our final two matches. We couldn't catch QPR for top spot but if we could beat Peterborough and Oxford, we'd be straight back into the Second Division. I guess it was a tense time but I don't remember it that way. Like I've said, we were oozing confidence and it was one of the great days of my life when we beat Oxford 4-1 to send 39,683 people home feeling ecstatic. The day could easily have turned sour, though, because I fell down the stairs of a nightclub later that evening. I thought at first that I'd seriously damaged my elbow but it turned out to be a false alarm.

I was ecstatic as well when I landed a £1,000 bonus for helping to win promotion because it enabled Margaret and I to put down a decent deposit on a brand new house in Acklam, a suburb of Middlesbrough. She was doing a three-year course at teachers' training college at Ripon when we met and I used to travel across on a Wednesday - our normal day-off - and drive back on Thursday for training. But we knew we wanted to be together and it wasn't too long before she gave up the teaching and moved back to Middlesbrough, where she got a job with the local Social Services.

Jubilant Middlesbrough players celebrating promotion left to right are: Don Masson, John Hickton, Gordon Jones and Geoff Butler. In the front kneeling: Derek Downing, John O'Rourke and Eric McMordie. (Larkin.

I still find it incredible to think that we fixed our wedding day for four months later - August 19. That was the first day of the new season! No one batted an eye-lid when I announced my plans. It was a totally different era. We already knew that we would be playing at home to Ipswich that day but so what? Why could I not get married in the morning and go off to play afterwards? That's what I did. Derrick Downing was my best man, Geoff Butler and Arthur Horsfield were among the guests and the four of us shot off after the briefest of receptions to play in the match. Maybe you won't be too surprised to discover that we lost 2-0.

That didn't work out as planned and nor did our short-term honeymoon. We had booked into The Grand at Scarborough but I picked up an injury during the game. I felt so sorry for Margaret as I told her I would have to be in at the ground at 10am the following morning for treatment. Welcome to life as a footballer's wife.

Anyway, we loved our new house. Hickton and Horsfield lived close by, so I had regular travelling companions to training and on the back of the promotion success, life was treating me well. Sadly, it didn't stay that way for long.

Although that opening-day injury caused me to miss the midweek League Cup tie against Barnsley, I was back for the next game and played regularly up until Christmas. But I still couldn't convince Anderson that I ought to be a key part of his plans. It just seemed that every time we lost a game, I was the easy scapegoat. The experienced Johnny Crossan had been brought in during the summer to play in midfield so basically I was back to a situation where McMordie and I were competing for the same place. In the last few months of that season, I didn't figure at all and the frustration I was feeling brought out the worst in me. It was hardly surprising that the senior players turned against me.

It wasn't until many years later that I got the chance to sit down with Anderson and ask him what he had against me at that time. He was 'big' enough to admit that not having faith in me was the worst mistake he made in his managerial career. Maybe he was just saying that... I don't know. But football has always been a game of opinions - always will be - and at that stage of my career it was very evident that he just didn't rate me.

Nothing changed. I was totally out of the picture as we built up to the 1968-69 season and although I actually enjoyed playing in a very good reserve team, there was no future in that. I was desperate for someone to come in for me. I didn't care who it was. I just had to get away and make a fresh start. I'd had such high hopes about what I might do for Middlesbrough when I joined the groundstaff as a 16-year-old. It had all turned sour. I knew there was no way back.

Poised to climb aboard for my first-ever flight - a pre-season trip to Holland - with Middlesbrough Gazette reporter Cliff Mitchell.

Margaret and I on our wedding day and (below) with Middlesbrough team-mates Derrick Downing, Arthur Horsfield and Geoff Butler.

CLEVELAND OFFICE EQUIPMENT LTD.

52-60 Fletcher Street : Middlesbrough

OFFICE FURNITURE – WOOD AND STEEL – COMMERCIAL AND EXECUTIVE

PORTABLE & STANDARD TYPEWRITERS
PHOTO-COPYING MACHINES
RECORDING MACHINES
ADDING MACHINES
VENETIAN BLINDS
OFFICE STATIONERY

OLYMPIA & ADLER
SKYCOPY & VECTOPRINT
GRUNDIG & PHILLIPS
BURROUGHS & OLIVETTI
VENTOLITE & VENTOLUX
EVERYTHING FOR THE OFFICE

For Efficient Service, Ring Middlesbrough 44043/4

DON MASSON — A PLAYER OF THE FUTURE

Our inside-forward trio in the last two games has been composed entirely of Scots.

Ian Gibson and Jim Irvine are well known to you. Don Masson is not, but we confidently forecast that he soon will be.

Masson has improved in leaps and bounds in the past month or two. It was the pre-season prediction of manager Raich Carter that he would be in the first team by Christmas. Well, he has already played in the Football League Cup and appeared in two Second Division games.

It was natural for Don to be nervous in his League debut at Ayresome Park. But those supporters who travelled to Rotherham will vouch for his confident play and spirit. He was a vital link in the team when Ian Gibson was injured.

Don was born at Banchory, a village outside of Aberdeen. He moved to Teesside with his parents and joined our ground staff after starring in local schoolboy football.

Masson is equally at home at wing-half or inside-forward. When he gains in experience he will prove another "discovery".

It is rare for our manager, Raich Carter, to sing the praises of a player. But

---

Tim Brown Garages Ltd.

CALIFORNIA : GREAT AYTON

YORKSHIRE

Telephone: GREAT AYTON 696

●

CAR HIRE

MORRIS DEALER   All Classes of Motor Repairs

Five

A FRESH START – THINGS CAN ONLY GET BETTER
(1968-1969)

I thought it was going to be Bradford Park Avenue. The message had been relayed that someone wanted to sign me and because I'd played particularly well for the reserves against them the previous evening, it all seemed to add up. I was really excited about the prospect. They were still in the League at that time and although it might not seem like it now, they were a good club with some good players - the likes of Kevin Hector and Bobby Ham. An added attraction for a move to Bradford was that it wouldn't involve a massive family upheaval. However, the overriding thing was that my life was poised to move in a different direction. I cannot tell you how much I needed that.

I'd got it all wrong. Harold Shepherdson gave nothing away when he banged on my front door and said that I must get myself to the ground at 3pm for transfer talks. I'd built myself up to shake hands with Jack Rowley but when I arrived, it wasn't him. Waiting to meet me was Billy Gray, the manager of Notts County, and his assistant Stuart Imlach.

I've never been a great one for studying League tables. Even so, I still don't quite understand how I found myself agreeing to join County without realising they were second from bottom of the entire Football League. How could I allow that to happen? It just shows how desperate I was to get away from the dead-end situation I was in at

Middlesbrough. By then, in September 1968, the Round Robin letter to get me out of the club had been delivered - completely unbeknown to me - and I hadn't had a sniff of a first-team chance in the early weeks of that season.

I already knew of Gray by reputation. He'd been a fine player, especially with Nottingham Forest where he figured in their FA Cup triumph in 1959. As a manager, he'd led Millwall to two promotions in successive seasons. What I hadn't realised as I sat in Stan Anderson's office with the neatly typed transfer forms in front of me was that I was to be part of a deal that was Gray's last throw of the dice at County. He'd agreed to pay a combined £7,000 for me, and our left-back Bob Worthington, and unless the two of us could inspire a rapid upturn in County's fortunes, he would be looking for a new job. Within six weeks, he'd gone from Meadow Lane.

Ironically, many years later, I renewed my relationship with Billy. He was working as a groundsman by then, and running a local greengrocer's shop. We regularly got together to play tennis and he never missed the chance to blame me for getting him the sack!

Moving to Nottingham was a real adventure for Bob and me. I was glad we were able to do it together. We hadn't been particularly close friends at Ayresome Park but suddenly we were on a mission. Neither of us needed telling that unless we could make this work, there was very little chance of having a lasting career as professional footballers. Although he never reached the dizzy heights of his big brother Frank, a gifted centre-forward with Huddersfield, Leicester and England, Bob was a great man to have on your side. He was a real 100-per-center, a strong character with a trusty left peg and a great sense of humour. For the next six years he was an important cog on County's journey up the leagues.

Of course I wondered if I was doing the right thing, dropping down two divisions to join a struggling outfit who had failed to win any of their first seven games of the season. I'd never even been to Nottingham and was only aware of two things about the city. A definite plus was that I knew from watching Test Match coverage on the television from Trent Bridge that the famous old cricket ground and the two football grounds were only a stone's throw away from each other. The other was that Nottingham had a ratio of five women to every man. Derrick Downing told me that staggering fact. He often travelled down for a night out and says he never went home disappointed!

Anyway, talking terms didn't take long. I took an immediate liking to Gray and it was like music to my ears when he said I'd be a regular in his team. It was clear that he genuinely wanted me on board. I'd waited years for someone to utter those words. Hearing him say that meant far more to me than when he told me my basic wage would be significantly higher than I was getting at Middlesbrough.

I borrowed my dad's car the following Saturday to drive down with Margaret and Bob. Although we'd signed on the Thursday, for some reason we were not picked to make our debuts in the home game against Newport County. Instead, having been to the ground, the three of us walked into Nottingham. We had lunch at The Cricketers, near the Ice Stadium, and then joined the crowds for a stroll back along London Road to Meadow Lane.

Maybe it was just our presence that inspired County to record their first win of the season! Clearly not but more importantly, Bob and I were very impressed with a couple of strapping young lads. The performances of David Needham at the back and Les Bradd up front gave us a real boost. We felt we'd be able to work with them to form the nucleus of a decent team. Bob and I stayed for a few weeks at a hotel in West Bridgford, along with our part-time goalkeeper Graham Smith. We shared an attic room and had a great time. I immediately took to Nottingham and was convinced moving there would prove to be a good decision. I just had to make it work on the field.

Ironically, my first League appearance was at Darlington, just down the road from Middlesbrough, so all my family and friends were out in force that day. I managed to mark my debut with a goal but we lost 3-2. We only won two of my first 14 games. Turning things around was clearly going to be a tough ask but I was delighted to be given the added responsibility for making that happen. Jack Wheeler had taken over as caretaker-manager after Gray was sacked and it still staggers me to think that he continued in that role for the next 14-months. He was an amazing man. In fact, I've never met anyone quite like him. He was obsessed every day with doing things the best he possibly could and he didn't have an enemy in the world.

Jack had been a top-flight goalkeeper with Birmingham and Huddersfield. For 26 years after arriving at Meadow Lane as Tommy Lawton's assistant he was the old-fashioned trainer, complete with 'magic' sponge. He filled that role with County from 1957 until an arthritic hip forced him to retire in 1983. Over the course of that period, he racked up 1,152 consecutive first-team games. Jack was devoted to his lovely wife Olga but that aside, his whole life revolved around Notts County. He was there seven days a week, totally committed to the cause.

One of his greatest strengths was that he was a superb listener. Players get very 'down' when they're injured. It can really knock their confidence. They get filled with doubts about what the future might hold for them and I'm absolutely certain Jack's ability to act as a sounding board and treat minds as well as bodies was key to our rise through to the top flight. He always had time for the players. Nothing was more satisfying to him than passing on the benefits of his experience within football and life in general.

As caretaker-manager during that 1968-69 period, he trained the players, treated injuries, organised match-days, trekked up and down the country on scouting missions and even turned his hand to decorating the dressing rooms during the close-season. I don't know if the chairman, Jack Dunnett, ever broached the subject of Jack becoming the 'permanent' manager but he wouldn't have taken it anyway. He knew his limitations, much preferred to be in the background and fortunately for me, he reckoned I could help to fill in the gaps.

Looking very much at home in a Notts County shirt and so proud to be made captain of the World's Oldest League Club at the age of 22.

Although Gray was given the credit for signing me, I've always believed Jack had a big hand in getting me to Meadow Lane. He did much of the scouting in those days, was well connected in the game, and I was led to believe he spotted me in the first place and recommended County should sign me. I don't know that for certain but I do know that he was quick to spot my leadership qualities after I arrived.

By then, I'd launched my self-imposed regime for doing extra training. I was utterly determined to make a success of the opportunity I'd been given to make a fresh start. Not much got past Jack. I knew he'd taken note and it soon prompted him to call me into his office. He wanted me to captain the team. I was only 22 so it was a great honour. I was absolutely delighted and that decision had a huge influence on my life. It really brought out the best in me - and was an incredibly shrewd move on Jack's part.

He knew changes would have to be made. It was inevitable. We couldn't carry on the way we were. We had an ageing team and several players were just seeing out their time. But easing people out and bringing in others can sometimes lead to confrontation. Jack definitely didn't do confrontation but I think he could see that it didn't bother me in the slightest. All I was interested in was playing my part in creating a team that won matches. I was more than ready to lead from the front.

It had been made clear during our chat that I would have no part to play in selecting the team. That was totally down to Jack but once we got out on the field, he left it up to me to organise things. I wasn't slow in making my feelings known if people came up short. That didn't go down well with some but I really didn't care.

Bob and I were right about Needham and Bradd. Both had the potential to go right to the top and from my point of view, the great thing about them was that they shared my desire and hunger to make the most of their talents. Les had been a bit of a late starter in the professional game and was striving to make up for lost time. His big hero was Roy of the Rovers, the cartoon comic character. It was easy to see why because if they'd turned that into a film, he'd have been perfect for the part. A strapping six-footer, blond and handsome, he had all the attributes you look for in a centre-forward. He was brave, brilliant in the air, always made himself available for balls played forward and had a good first touch. Add to that a powerful shot and good all-round finishing ability and he had the lot. All except one thing. He was too nice. How can you criticise him for that? You can't, of course, and Les had an outstanding career that includes the fact that he will - almost certainly - be Notts County's all-time record goal-scorer forever. I've always felt, though that he just lacked the little bit of 'devil' that the really top players must have.

In today's world, Les would have been snapped up by a bigger club within months of winning a regular place after his £1,000 move from Rotherham. The same applies with Needham, who had been a regular in the heart of County's defence since he was 16-years-old. Both of them served County with distinction for more than 10 years - and they were real winners.

It took a lot longer than I'd hoped for things to take shape and at the end of that season we were 19th in the table. We were only three points clear of having to apply for re-election but I could see genuine signs of progress. We consistently struggled to score goals - I finished top scorer with 13 - but the most telling statistic was that we kept clean-sheets in nine of our last 14 games. Build from the back, as they say.

Off the field, Margaret and I were loving life in the East Midlands. We used my £350 signing-on fee as the deposit for a semi-detached house in Keyworth, a village on the outskirts of Nottingham, and planned to expand our family. Neil was a year old at the time and we were delighted when Jayne arrived to keep him company. However, that delight was so close to becoming despair a few months later. Margaret turned her back on Jayne for a few moments while she attended to Neil and by the time she went back to the cot, our baby girl was turning blue. When she screamed for help, our next-door neighbour Wendy Cumberpatch came to the rescue. Jayne made a full recovery after spending the next few days in hospital and we were in no doubt that without the timely intervention of Wendy, she would have died. Many years later we met up again at a function. There was so much I wanted to say to her, but how do you put your thoughts into words in that situation. I just hope she fully understood how eternally grateful I was.

I wasn't there when that incident happened because I'd got myself a summer job, working with a fruit wholesaler at Sneinton Market in the centre of Nottingham. In those days it was written into your contact that you took a drop in wages during the summer period so players were expected to find themselves short-term employment. Getting up at 4am every day wasn't ideal, especially with a young family, but at least I knew it would only be for a few weeks. It was, though, a really sharp reminder of how incredibly lucky we were to be professional footballers.

With very limited resources Jack had made some decent signings, adding the likes of Mick Jones, Richie Barker and Barry Butlin to the squad. He also introduced another youngster who was to have a massive impact at Meadow Lane. Big Brian Stubbs was as raw as they come. Lean and lanky, he was a natural defender. His body language alone was enough to make attackers think twice about trying to get past him. He would climb over his grandmother to win the ball in the air. Once he started to understand the game he quickly became established as a key man alongside Needham. He was clearly going to be a major asset to County.

I was hugely impressed at the way he and Needham sorted things out between them. It's essential that your two central defenders operate as a partnership if they're going to be effective. It becomes total chaos if they both try and do the same thing. Dave, in his early days, wanted to attack every ball played into our box and was brutal in the way he dealt with opposition front-men. But they were big Brian's greatest strengths. Somehow they had to find a way around it and despite their lack of experience, they did just that. 'Stubbsy' used to frighten the life out of opponents. No one wanted to tangle with him and Dave let him get on with building his 'hard man' reputation, while he changed his game to accommodate him. He could certainly dish it out when necessary but always had a touch of class about him. He turned himself into a cultured defender, reading situations brilliantly, and became the perfect foil for Brian. It was a change of approach that would eventually take him to the top as many years later he joined me at Queens Park Rangers, then returned to Nottingham to play his part in Forest's League Championship and European Cup triumphs.

I played with some top central defensive partnerships over the course of my career... Gordon McQueen and Martin Buchan for Scotland, David Webb and Frank McLintock for QPR and Roy McFarland and Colin Todd at Derby County. As a pair, Needham and Stubbs were every bit as good. They were certainly just as effective and I'm sure they would have been very comfortable together in the top flight.

I'm only aware of one attempt to lure them away from Meadow Lane but I'm certain there would have been many more. Wolverhampton Wanderers had a joint £125,000 offer turned down when Bill McGarry was their manager and that was a small fortune in the mid-Seventies. All credit to County chairman Jack Dunnett for not just grabbing the cash. Quite simply, we would not have achieved what we did without Needham and Stubbs.

Incidentally, big 'Stubbsy' was a Keyworth lad and while we were living there, he helped us out three times with some baby-sitting duties. I often have a laugh with him about the fact that he had a different girl with him each time he came and he got engaged to all of them! If he hadn't eventually found Jean he would probably have qualified for an entry in the Guinness Book of Records.

As a footnote to this chapter, it was just as well Bradford Park Avenue were not the club trying to sign me when I left Middlesbrough. Come the end of that 1968-69 season, they were cast adrift at the foot of the Fourth Division. I wonder what path my career might have taken had I joined them instead.

Six

JIMMY'S BEST ADVICE
(1969-1972)

I knew my life was about to change massively when a bag full of footballs appeared the first time Jimmy Sirrel took charge of a training session. Incredible as it might seem, it was unheard of in those days. All we ever did to get ourselves fit and prepare for the following Saturday afternoon was pound our way around the perimeter track. To actually practice with a football set us apart from the vast majority of clubs. Very soon, it started to set us apart through our results and performances as well.

People often ask me how I felt about Jimmy becoming our new manager. It's the absolute truth to say I'd never even heard of him. I certainly didn't know what he looked like. Our chairman Jack Dunnett came into the dressing room, after we'd lost at Wrexham in November 1969, to tell us we had a new manager. The lads just looked at each other when he gave us the name and asked: "Who?"

My immediate concern was for Jack Wheeler. I knew more than anyone how much time and commitment he'd put into his role as caretaker-manager over the previous 14 months. He'd built some solid foundations. I didn't need to worry. He was to revert to his previous role as trainer/physio and that was the way he wanted it.

As for Jimmy, it would have been easy to treat him as a figure of fun. Unfortunately for him, his distinctive features left him wide open to that and although he always insisted on calling me 'little fella', he was a fair bit smaller than me. But you could never, ever underestimate

Jimmy. Maybe he wasn't the brightest button in some respects but he was as street-wise as they come. He'd honed his survival instincts in the toughest of environments, growing up around the shipyards of Glasgow. That's where he learned to scrap and fight for everything he got in life and he adopted exactly the same approach to football. He wasn't going to allow a lack of inches to stand in the way of him achieving his ambitions.

He hadn't been at Meadow Lane for long before we began showing those same characteristics within our dressing room. Jimmy thrived on being the underdog. It acted as inspiration to him if ever people wrote us off - as they frequently did - and that passion for proving people wrong was right at the heart of Notts County's incredible climb from the Fourth Division to the First.

In truth, we did laugh at Jimmy. We laughed a lot, in fact, because although most of the time he wasn't trying to be funny, he just naturally was. Stories about him, not just in Nottingham but across the football community in general, are legendary. He had some really strange mannerisms and talked a language all of his own. What he also had was a vicious streak that simmered away, never far beneath the surface. You crossed him at your peril. Many a media person can vouch for that.

Lots of books have been written and television programmes made about the impact of Scottish managers within the British game. Something within the make-up of Sir Matt Busby, Jock Stein, Bill Shankly and Sir Alex Ferguson carried them to a different level in the management game. I genuinely believe you have to include Jimmy on that list. As Sir Alex said when he spoke so movingly at Jimmy's funeral, he was a football pioneer - always looking to stretch the boundaries - and was hugely respected within the game.

 His achievements as a player were modest. He managed only 111 appearances in total for Celtic, Bradford Park Avenue, Brighton and Aldershot. As he regularly told us, if he hadn't suffered a lot from injuries he would have been the best! That might have been the end of it for some people but rather than dampen his enthusiasm for the game, those setbacks made him even more determined to succeed in management.

Was it luck or was it skill that brought Jimmy to Meadow Lane? I'll never know for sure the truth of that but of the many key decisions Jack Dunnett made in his eventful life, inside and out of football, surely none can top the move to appoint Sirrel as manager of Notts County. As I've already stated, Dunnett was the shrewdest man I've ever met. Somehow, he always managed to see the bigger picture more clearly than most and although often accused of being too cautious in the way he ran the football club, he wasn't afraid to take calculated risks.

Dunnett had been chairman of Brentford before putting down his marker in Nottingham, where he served as an MP for 19 years. He'd introduced Sirrel to management during his time at Griffin Park and although they didn't work together for very long, he'd seen enough. Low profile or not, he was convinced Jimmy was his man.

From my point of view, it was very much a case of right place, right time. I'd established myself in the County midfield and was thoroughly enjoying the responsibilities of captaincy. Now I wanted to channel my energies into helping to build a successful club. Jimmy gave me the platform to do that.

Looking back, many of the methods he introduced were so obvious for a manger wanting to create a successful team. Of course you needed to work with a football if you wanted to improve your skills. Of course that was the best way to develop teamwork and patterns of play. Back in the day though, those training routines were anything but obvious. It's astonishing to think that football brains couldn't get past the fact that pounding the track was what you did. Not all the players locked into Jimmy's ideas initially. I wasn't one of those. On the contrary, I thought from the outset that the way he wanted us to operate in training was fantastic.

Most days we would have 11 v 11 matches. They weren't practice matches as such because they were very stop-start affairs. Jimmy would constantly call a halt while he explained to individual players what he wanted them to do with the ball in a given situation, or what position he wanted them to take up without it. He simplified everything. He'd often run alongside you, chirping away, and forcing you to think about every move you made. Two hours of that on a chilly February morning was guaranteed to upset some lads but none of us could argue with what he was trying to achieve. What he did was to make every player accountable. Come 3pm on a Saturday afternoon we knew exactly what was expected of us as individuals. And by practicing it every day, we also had a thorough understanding of how to carry that forward into the heat of the battle. We all had a role to play and Jimmy's way meant none of us had any scope for excuses.

Thanks to Jack Wheeler I was already a fairly influential figure in the dressing room. Jimmy was not only keen for me to continue in that role, he wanted me to step up a notch. The message he delivered in that familiar drawl of his when I was summoned to his cramped little office beneath the old main stand was that he wanted me to take his thoughts onto the pitch. Almost overnight I became 20 per cent more effective as a player. I had a very clear view of what he wanted from me and stopped thinking just about myself. From then on, it was all about what was best for the team.

The absolute ideal for a new manager with fresh ideas, looking to convince players you really are the man for the job, is to get off to a winning start. Jimmy won his first three games in charge - away to Workington and at home against Scunthorpe and Chester - and I played a full part by scoring five goals during that period. Come the end of the season I'd scored 23 League goals in 43 appearances and as Jack Dunnett had told me when I signed that I'd get a bonus for every goal I scored, I was delighted. I wonder why he cancelled that particular clause in my contract the following year!

Anyway, it won over most of the doubters when Jimmy really hit the ground running. Although we lacked consistency there was clear evidence that we were taking shape. A run of six straight wins during March got us into a position where there was a realistic prospect of promotion. Sadly, we fell away badly in the closing weeks. Even so, we finished in a respectable seventh place. The seeds had been sown.

People might not have realised it at the time but it was hugely significant that Charlie Crickmore and Jon Nixon had arrived on the scene during the second half of that season. If we were to adopt the system Jimmy wanted to use, we needed two direct wingers with genuine pace who could go past defenders and deliver quality crosses. Those two fitted the bill perfectly and as the gaffer explained, my No. 1 responsibility was to keep them supplied. We're back to the business of playing matches in training every day. We worked and worked on me dropping diagonal balls in behind the full backs for 'Nicco' and Charlie to run onto. It became second nature to do that during matches. Having said that, things didn't always go according to plan and me being me, I wasn't slow to make my feelings known if one of them mis-controlled the ball or failed to deliver the right cross. 'Nicco', a really bright lad with a brilliant sense of humour, used to just let it bounce off him if I fired insults in his direction. Not so with Charlie. He always took it to heart and we regularly had to kiss and make up after training or matches. He wanted to hit me, I recall, during a game at Aldershot early the next season. I told him to wait until after the game but because we'd won, it was soon forgotten.

Our flying wingmen were right at the heart of things during the 1970-71 campaign, which surely must rank as one of the most enjoyable in Notts County's long history. We won the Fourth Division Championship with plenty to spare but it wasn't just the results that were impressive. We ran teams ragged.

It was a massive statement of intent in the November when Tony Hateley was signed from Birmingham City. He was a big player in every sense. He oozed confidence and apart from being a major physical presence and an incredibly loud and brash personality, he was an out-and-out winner. He'd started his career at Meadow Lane, averaging better than a goal every other game, and the fact that Aston Villa, Liverpool and Chelsea had paid small fortunes to sign him said plenty about his capabilities. His best days were behind him by the time Jimmy added him to our squad but he was still a brilliant trainer who had never lost his hunger for goals. It was such a shrewd move to sign him. The 'Big Fella' was just what was needed at Meadow Lane at that time.

You could sense the change of atmosphere in our dressing room when Hateley arrived. I think people were looking at me, wondering if I would see him as a threat to my situation. No chance. He was a man after my own heart with the way he demanded full commitment from the players. I was delighted to have him on board.

Incidentally, just in case there was an issue with him getting above himself, Jimmy soon cleared the air by pulling Hateley off against Lincoln, in only the second game he played. Tony responded by ripping off his shirt and tossing it towards the bench as he left the field. That played straight into Jimmy's hands. Seeing those two facing off immediately after the game could hardly have been a bigger mismatch but Jimmy backed down for no one. He made it abundantly clear that he was the man in charge and he'd do whatever he felt was best for the team. He never had cause to repeat himself.

Right-back Bill Brindley had joined us from Forest shortly before the start of the season. He brought with him his own very special brand of humour and dogged determination. It was noticeable that our dressing room had become full of really strong characters. Every day there was a lot of laughter but I always felt it spoke volumes for the group that the mood changed completely when it was time to work. We developed an incredible bond and, because I was surrounded by good players, who knew their jobs inside out, the game became so much easier. Jimmy has to take immense credit for that. On the back of all the drills we did in training, which were designed to make us become 'thinking' footballers as well as practical ones, we felt we couldn't fail. The sky was the limit as far as I was concerned and a throw-away comment from Hateley when he first arrived really helped to spur me on. He told us he had just bought a house in Nottingham and had paid cash for it. "You lucky bastard," was my first impression. But then I thought: "If you can do that by working hard to make the most of your talents, why can't I?"

It was part of our regular routine in training that I'd spend hours standing out wide on the halfway line, whacking balls to the edge of the area. The idea, in part, was that it enabled Needham and Stubbs to work on attacking the ball in defensive situations. Practice certainly made perfect. They got to the stage where they could head it far further than most players could kick it. In the same way, I would set time aside to hang balls up for Hateley, Bradd and Barker to climb in and head for goal. With that lot to contend with whenever we got a corner or free kick, it was no wonder we frightened the life out of opponents. And we did. We could see it in their eyes that they really didn't want to be out there competing against us - especially at Meadow Lane when the crowd were in full voice. We truly were a formidable unit. I've always said that if we'd transferred that team straight into the First Division, we would have coped. I remain firmly convinced of that.

A goalless draw at York was all we could manage in the opening fixture. But then we won seven of the next eight League games and our stall had been firmly set out. Once we hit the top, no one was going to shift us and the goals kept flying in from all angles - especially when Hateley came on board. He finished with 22 goals in just 29 games. That tells everything about the impact he had. We were soon pulling in five-figure crowds on a regular basis and when Exeter City came to Meadow Lane for the final fixture, the attendance was 18,002. We only managed a 1-1 draw but the title had already been clinched a couple of weeks earlier. It was a day for celebrating and we certainly did that. So did our success-starved fans and it was fantastic to see the pleasure we'd given them.

Jimmy was desperate to get across the message that it was only the start. He was right about that, of course. By the time he - and I - had finished, Notts County would have won two more promotions and be playing in the top flight. But that was all for the future.

I've often wondered how my life and career might have turned out had Jimmy not stepped into it when he did. Maybe I would still have gone on to reach international status, maybe not. Either way, I owe him so much. He became like a father figure to me, certainly in the footballing sense. It would be wrong to say that we were 'bosom buddies' but we did have a brilliant working relationship. It used to embarrass me when he told people that I was his "jewel" but it's hard to imagine being paid a bigger compliment. That was pure Jimmy. He just had a way of saying or doing little things that lifted players. It certainly worked with me, knowing that he thought that highly of me. I was determined not to let him down.

For several years we lived in the same road in a new housing estate in Burton Joyce and his daughter Audrey baby-sat for Margaret and me. But we never used to socialise. It was only many years later, long after he'd retired from football, that we struck up a real friendship. I used to go and visit him and it was great to reminisce about the good old days.

I was at a stage of my career in the early Seventies where I was hungry for all knowledge. Jimmy recognised that and was keen to pass on the benefits of his vast experience. On numerous occasions after we'd finished training he would be looking out for me as I made my way down the back of the stand, past his office. "Hey, Little Fella, what are you doing for the rest of the day," he'd ask. If the answer was "nothing special", he would often take me with him on scouting missions. I couldn't fail to enhance my football education, just by spending time with him.

Mind you, I wish I'd got past his office a bit smarter on one occasion. He never used to tell me where we were going. He just said he'd pick me up from home at a certain time. It wasn't until we were halfway to Torquay that I discovered where we were heading.

An important part of this story is to understand that Jimmy was

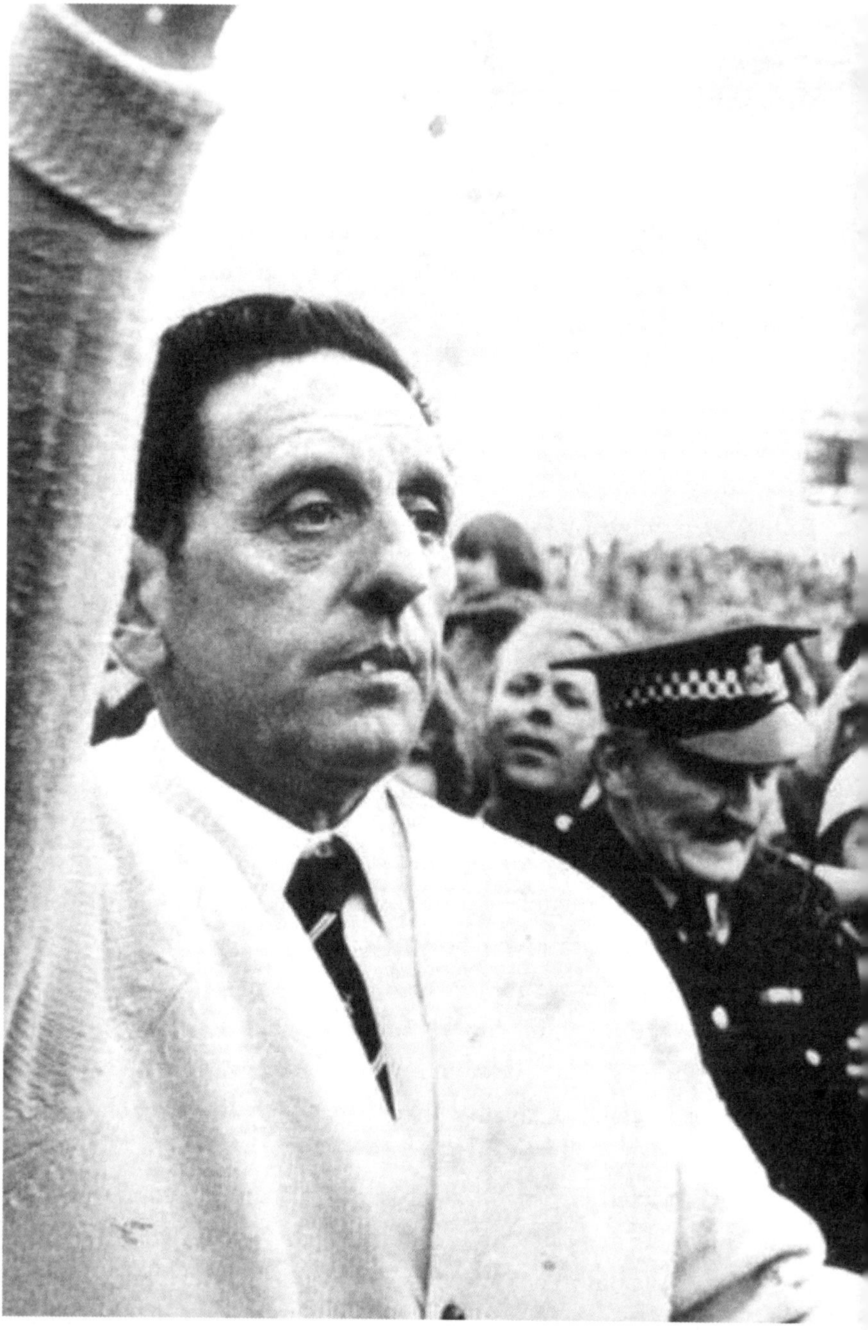

An iconic Notts County picture from 1971 ... with Jimmy Sirrel as he acknowledges the cheers from adoring fans after we'd clinched promotion.

the worst driver in the world. The way he operated the pedals, you'd have thought he had two left feet and he had an astonishing record for hitting things. Watching him trying to reverse into the manager's space at the ground was a sight to behold. You took your life in your hands by agreeing to go with him. I was past the point of no return. I could only buckle up for a 10-hour return trip and hope for the best. To make matters worse, we only watched the first 30 minutes of the game. I had no idea who he had gone to watch but he suddenly tapped me on the knee and said: "I've seen enough, let's go." On the way back he eventually told me that he had been tipped off about the right-winger and the analysis that followed was so revealing. All the things that player could do, all the things he couldn't. By the time Jimmy had finished, I realised I still had so much to learn about football.

That day-trip to Torquay was so thought provoking. Listening to Jimmy strip down the cans-and-can't of their little winger hammered home the message that professional football is not about having fun in matches and doing nice things with the ball. It's about thoroughly understanding your role within the team pattern and making sure you influence the game.

I think the best of many pieces of advice he gave me was to 'sell myself'. I guess it would have been easy after the way in which we'd stormed the Fourth Division to believe I'd made it as a player. Just in case I was thinking that way, he made certain that I raised my sights and dedicated myself to setting new standards. He insisted I must always assume a manager or scout had come to watch me and would be studying my every move. Consequently, my No. 1 aim every time I set foot on the field, must be to impress them. Be sure to catch their eye ... don't let them give up on me after watching the first 30 minutes.

It wasn't that he wanted to encourage other clubs to make offers for me - far from it. The sole aim of focusing my thoughts on trying to sell myself was to get me to perform to the peak of my ability every week. In Jimmy's opinion, the best way for me to achieve that would be to get totally immersed in the game. He wanted to see me getting on the ball at every opportunity, and that included taking all the corners, free kicks and penalties - even the throw-ins. I didn't need to be told twice. I was always comfortable getting on the ball anyway, and to be given license to do it at every opportunity was just the ultimate.

I knew there would be consequences attached. I was putting myself into a situation whereby if I didn't perform properly, regularly giving the ball away or delivering sloppy free kicks and corners, the whole team would suffer. That didn't bother me. It was just the opposite in fact. I was in my element when I had to accept responsibility and lead from the front.

That little piece of advice from Jimmy was simple but so effective. I immediately set to work in training on improving my delivery from set-pieces - including from free kicks around the edge of the area. Jimmy would get some of the apprentices to form a 'wall' in the afternoons and the poor lads would stand there shivering while I worked on bending the ball just over their heads.

A couple of years later, when Ray O'Brien joined us from Manchester United, he really perfected the art with his wand of a left-foot. By that time, Jimmy had got the club's maintenance man to build a wooden 'wall' and we staged regular afternoon sessions on the car park behind The Kop, Ray whipping balls in from one side and me from the other. That was the source of so many goals for us.

Life was good - very good - on and off the field. I couldn't wait to tackle the Third Division and I certainly didn't see us staying at that level for long. Also, I'd invested my promotion bonus on moving us up the housing ladder. We switched to Burton Joyce, on the other side of Nottingham, and Foxhill Road turned into a gathering of the football clans. Jimmy lived just down the road, Neil Martin - Forest's Scottish striker - was his next-door neighbour and the great Dave Mackay lived in the big house at the top of the hill. One of the highlights of the year for our little community was when everyone went round to Dave's on New Year's Eve. He was a fantastic footballer, a really nice man and an extremely generous host.

Our reward for winning the Fourth Division was an end-of-season trip to Rimini, on Italy's Adriatic Coast. I roomed with Alan Mansley, a left-winger we'd signed from Brentford and as bonding exercises go, it was right up there with the best. Mind you, it could have ended in tears for me - and for Jack Wheeler. For some reason, Jack was in charge because Jimmy joined us halfway through the trip and by the time he arrived, I'd done myself a mischief. I ripped a hole in my knee trying to learn how to jet-ski. It threw Jack into a complete panic. He was desperate for Jimmy not to find out but it was impossible to keep it from him. We had a couple of low-key games lined up to help finance the trip and there was no way that I was able to take part in those.

We hit the ground running in August 1971 with five wins in the first six matches. None of us was surprised. Stepping up to the Third Division held no fears for us. It was a high-class league with the likes of Aston Villa, Brighton and Bournemouth especially strong but we were doing fine until the start of March. Then Villa came to Meadow Lane and outclassed us before a massive crowd of more than 34,000. We started to lose our way. We were in third spot going into that game but our confidence had been dented. A burst of good results looked to have got us back on track but then back-to-back defeats in away games at Halifax and Barnsley killed off our promotion chances.

It certainly didn't break our spirits, though. We were convinced we would go up the following year. So we did and the irony was that when we eventually got promoted, we did it with five points less than we'd accumulated the previous year.

Notts County's Fourth Division champions. Back row (left to right):
Les Bradd, Bill Brindley, Brian Stubbs, Barry Watling, David Needham,
Bob Worthington, Mick Jones. Front row: Jimmy Sirrel, Jon Nixon,
Richie Barker, Tony Hateley, Don Masson, Charlie Crickmore, Jack Wheeler.

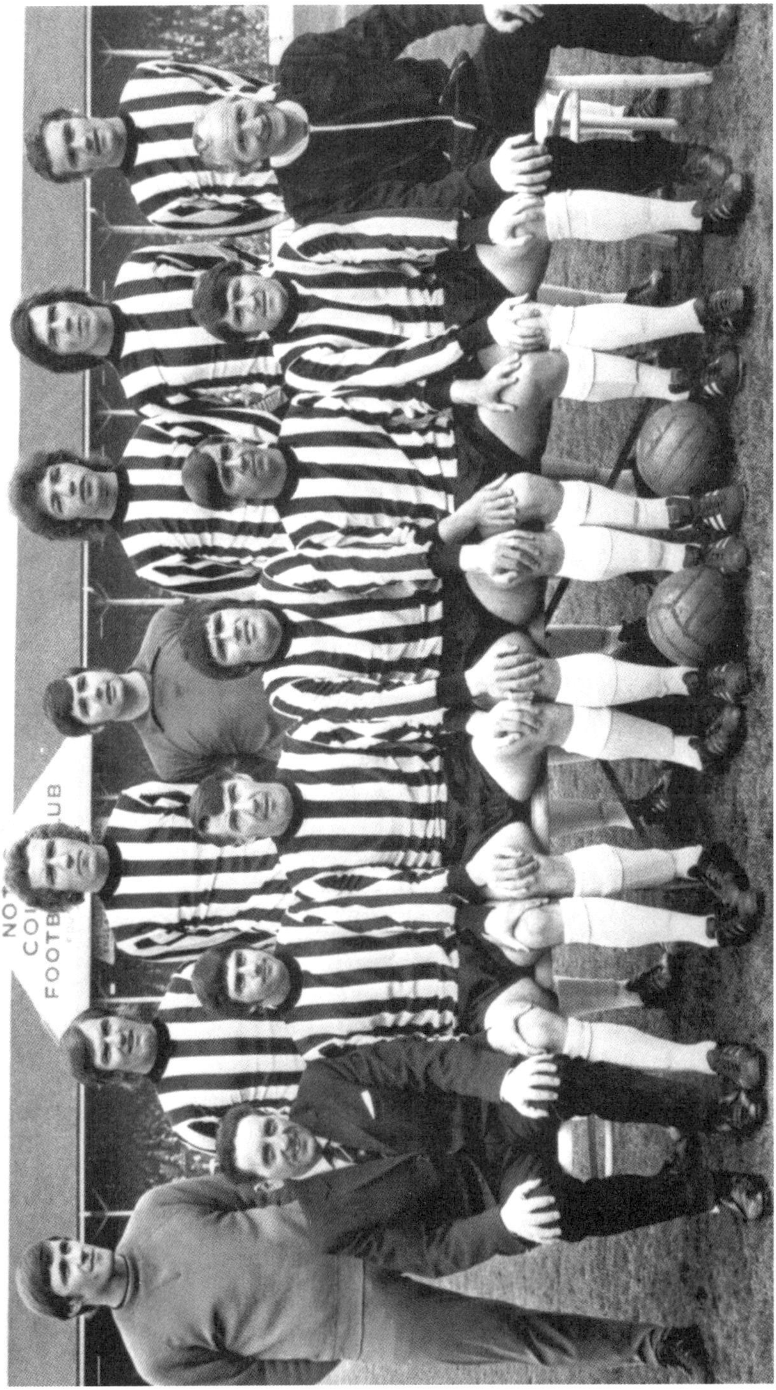

Looking smart outside the Old Bailey before one of the most daunting experiences of my life.

Seven
"CALLING DONALD SANDISON MASSON"
(1972-1973)

I'm sure there must be others - just a few - who can match my record of having played League football at 92-plus grounds across England. How many can claim they also made an appearance at the Old Bailey?

It still makes me shudder when I think back to that morning in July 1974 when I arrived at the most famous court in the land, ready to be called as a witness. Photographers started clicking away as I made my way to the imposing entrance. This was a whole new experience for me. Many of the biggest trials in history have taken place at those famous old courts, tucked away in the EC4 area of London, and this one was all about me. Not that I had any influence whatsoever over what happened. I was just a pawn, trapped between two football clubs whose squabbles two years earlier over how to secure my services had got ridiculously out of control.

An important part of this story is to understand that footballers in those days had absolutely no control over their own destiny. Slavery is a strong word to use but once you signed a piece of paper and became registered with a club, you were their property for as long as they wanted you. When the day arrived that they no longer did, they simply tossed you aside. They were the rules we lived by when we signed up as professional footballers. We all understood that and in the main, accepted it without complaint. You could put in a written transfer request if you really wanted to leave but it was entirely up to the club how they responded to that.

I'd done well in my time with Notts County. After two excellent seasons in which we won the Fourth Division and then narrowly failed to go straight through to the Second, maybe it was inevitable that the tom-toms started to bang. Sunday newspapers, especially the Sunday People and News of the World, boosted their circulations every week with the alleged scoops they produced, linking players with a move to one club or another. Every now and again my name cropped up and the one club consistently linked with me was Bournemouth.

They'd been our fiercest rivals for the past two years. They were runners-up to us in the Fourth Division and then, in 1971-72, we had two epic battles before they finished third with us in fourth spot. It's an understatement to say there was no love lost between the two camps. That especially applied where the two managers were concerned. Jimmy Sirrel despised everything that John Bond stood for and made no attempt to hide his feelings. Whenever we were due to play Bournemouth, it was as if someone had lit the blue touch-paper. He was desperate for us to get the better of them. In fact, it might have been more entertaining if the players had stayed in the dressing room and left the managers to sort it out on the bench!

Before taking charge of Bournemouth, Bond had played nearly 400 games during a 16-year stay with West Ham. He always preached the values of 'pure football' and was very vocal about the fact that he didn't approve of the way we played. I'm sure it was partly deliberate. He knew full well that it was bound to put him on a collision course with Jimmy and used it as a tactic to unsettle him. The gaffer had a real thing about what he described as 'Fancy Dans' - and Bond fitted completely into that category in Jimmy's eyes. He was a tall, imposing figure, always immaculately dressed without a hair out of place. And he never missed the chance to make a headline. He really got under Jimmy's skin and it can only have added fuel to the fire that he was able to regularly pay out big transfer fees.

I don't think there's any doubt that Bond made good use of his strong Fleet Street connections to put the word about that he fancied taking me to Dean Court and there was regular speculation in the newspapers long before things came to a head.

I did my best to ignore it and just get on with my job. I was more than happy with my life in Nottingham but as speculation increased, the whole thing became very difficult. Everywhere I turned people were asking me if I was staying or going and although it prompted a lot of light-hearted banter among the players, after a while that wore a bit thin. Eventually, in July 1971, a story broke that County had turned down offers from Bournemouth of £80,000 and then £100,000. Bond came out and said he was very concerned about how that information had leaked out and would launch an investigation. It was all part of the 'game'.

I was disappointed that Jimmy and Jack Dunnett made no attempt to put me in the picture. Like I've said, in those days you didn't go banging on doors, demanding to know what was happening. If a deal had been agreed you went. If it hadn't, you stayed. Simple as that.

Part of the difficulty was that I knew that most people - including my colleagues - automatically assumed that I'd been 'tapped' up by Bournemouth. That just wasn't true. I was as much in the dark about what was happening as everyone else. In fact, the first time I ever spoke more than two words to Bond was when I was at Derby County and went to Norwich to meet him for transfer talks.

The speculation really got to me. How could it not? It seriously affected my form and attitude and maybe that had an influence as the team struggled to maintain the high standards we'd set during the previous two years. We started well enough, picking up points in the first five games but then hit a rocky patch. It included a 6-1 defeat at

Charlton but in fairness, we actually played well that night. It was a freak result. Three straight wins put us back on track. Then we were at home to Bournemouth in mid-October. Guess what everyone was talking about?

I couldn't get away from it and my head was 'screwed' even more when I bumped into Ian Gibson at Meadow Lane during the build-up to the game. My old midfield partner at Middlesbrough, a fine player, had signed for Bournemouth a couple of weeks earlier and greeted me by saying: "I hear you're joining us next week." It was total news to me and definitely not what I wanted to hear as I prepared for another epic showdown with our arch-rivals.

That day I made what has to rank as the worst decision of my career. I should have turned my back and walked away when we were awarded a penalty midway through the first half, but logic said I had to take it. I was our designated penalty-taker, had scored from the spot the previous week to give us a 1-0 win at Halifax and by way of coincidence, had also converted a penalty against Bournemouth in the corresponding fixture the previous year. Anyway, I'd never been one to shirk responsibility. But logic should not have come into it. Common sense should have told me my reputation was at stake. I failed to convert that penalty - and I had to live with the consequences. The natural conclusion for some people was that I'd done it on purpose. That haunted me for years. I've told myself many millions of times that I ought to have walked away but you cannot turn the clock back. What's done is done. We eventually lost that game 2-0. Jimmy knew it had seriously affected me and left me out for the following week's game at Wrexham.

The move that 'Gibbo' seemed to think was a formality didn't materialise yet still the speculation went on. There were newspaper reports that I was set to join Bournemouth for £125,000, which would have been a record fee between two Third Division clubs, and the next episode was that the clubs were arguing over the method of payment. Finally, in mid-November, the air was cleared. Any proposed transfer was off because Bournemouth wanted to pay the fee in instalments and County insisted it must be paid in one lump sum. It came as such a relief to know that was the end of the matter. At last, I could get on with my life.

Actually, it wasn't quite the end of the matter because more than two years later I found myself sitting in the corridors of the Old Bailey, waiting to hear those dreaded words: "Calling Donald Sandison Masson." Being a professional footballer puts you into a lot of pressure situations. It goes with the territory and you learn to handle it but I was way outside my comfort zone as I made my way into the witness box. I wasn't there for long. From memory, the barrister only asked me one question: "Would you have been willing to move to Bournemouth." I told him that I would.

I'm sure at the time that will have come as a surprise to many County supporters but I had to be honest. Despite all that we'd achieved in the previous couple of seasons, Bournemouth struck me as a club who were really going places. They already had a lot of good players and were busy signing up more, with money appearing to be no object. I also have to admit that I was also very flattered that Bond seemed so determined to sign me.

One of their best players was Phil Boyer and our paths have crossed quite regularly since we both retired from playing. Nottingham-born, he returned to his roots at the end of a hugely successful career and we've often talked about what might have been. I really rated Phil. His strike-partner, Ted MacDougall got most of the headlines because he was the more prolific scorer and he moved to Manchester United for a big fee around the time Bournemouth were trying to sign me. But I always thought that Boyer, a clever and incredibly industrious player, had a lot more going for him and was massively important to making them tick.

Anyway, County, who were claiming £125,000 in damages for breach of contract, lost the case when it finally got to court. I cannot remember the ins and outs - not sure as I ever really knew or understood them - but the whole thing was a chapter in my history that I could have really done without.

I didn't need telling that I had to put it behind me as quickly as possible once any prospect of a deal was shut down in November 1972. We were in the middle of a very indifferent run - only two wins in nine games - and were way adrift of the promotion places. We were, though, still a very capable team. We proved that by reaching the 5th round of the League Cup with a run that included a win at Southampton before we knocked out holders Stoke City. Somehow we had to get back to consistently showing that form in League games and the captain had to play his part in making that happen.

By Notts County standards, we'd been quite bold in the transfer-market the previous summer, signing Kevin Randall from Chesterfield and Arthur Mann from Manchester City. Kevin was a brilliant signing. He'd been arguably the best striker in the lower divisions for some time, scoring 96 goals in six years at Saltergate. We needed someone to replace Tony Hateley, who had been struggling with injuries and had gone to Oldham to end his career in the closing stages of the previous season. Everything pointed to Kevin being an ideal choice. The only doubt was whether he could fit into a different environment and hit the ground running. In fact, it did take a while for him to find his true form and that had an influence on our indifferent start to the season. But once we started to click again, he emerged as a real asset.

We used to call him 'The Claw' because he had a knack of grabbing opponents when they were trying to challenge him and holding them off. It was a foul every time ... definitely. But I cannot recall him ever getting penalised and that little 'trick' used to buy him vital time and space that he was very adept at exploiting. Kevin told me years later that I "frightened him" - his words not mine - with the demands I used to put on him. He was the nervous type, who never seemed really confident of his own ability. Shame that because he would definitely have achieved even more had he managed to overcome it.

As for Arthur, he not only proved to be another shrewd signing but also became my best mate after joining us from Manchester City. He'd become the most expensive full back ever to head south from Scotland when he switched from Hearts to City and he figured in their 1970 League Cup Final victory over West Brom. Joe Mercer and Malcolm Allison had built the best team in the land at that time and Arthur seemed to have the world at his feet. But the problem for him was that he was petrified of flying. Later that year, when City went on to win the European Cup Winners' Cup, he wasn't there to share in the triumph. City did all they could to help him overcome the problem and even arranged for him to attend a series of sessions in the flight simulator at Manchester Airport, sitting in the cockpit alongside a trainee captain. He never did manage to overcome his fear and eventually, Mercer and Allison lost patience. They understandably didn't like the idea of changing the team every time an away game involved a flight. That meant he was no good to them.

City's loss was definitely County's gain but Arthur inevitably found that hard to take. He also found himself with another challenge that he hadn't bargained for when he landed at Meadow Lane. Jimmy's idea was that he would replace Bob Worthington in the left-back spot - but Bob was having none of it. He wasn't ready to surrender his place and although Arthur did have a brief run in the No. 3 shirt during September, it was only brief. Jimmy soon reverted to his tried and tested back-four - Brindley, Needham, Stubbs and Worthington - and decided to use Arthur further forward.

It proved to be a master-stroke. Arthur was a tremendous athlete, capable of running all day, and the change of role gave him license to play to his strengths. In those days there was no such thing as an overlapping full-back but he would have been the nearest to it. The crowd used to love it when he set off on one of his regular surges down the left touchline. The challenge for the rest of us was to get forward quickly enough to take advantage of the opportunities he created by switching from defence to attack so rapidly. A great enthusiast who would do anything for anyone, Arthur was just a top bloke and he quickly became a popular figure in our dressing room.

Although I'd never met him before he arrived at Meadow Lane, we clicked instantly and became great friends. I don't know whether it's still as pronounced today but in my era as a player, you were automatically attracted to people of the same nationality. Most clubs had a little clique of Scottish lads and there was a popular theory that you couldn't be successful without one. For example, you'd probably say that Arsenal, Leeds United and Liverpool were the cream of the crop in the late-Sixties and Seventies. Liverpool were built around Ron Yeats, Ian St John and Tommy Lawrence, Leeds had Billy Bremner, Eddie Gray and Peter Lorimer and Arsenal's Double-Winners of 1971 were significantly influenced by Frank McLintock, George Graham and Bob Wilson. That was the way it was in those days and just as McLintock took me under his wing when I joined Queens Park Rangers, I did the same for Arthur at County. Our wives - Sandra and Margaret - became great friends, so did our children and it was a regular routine on our Wednesday days-off that Arthur and I would play golf together. Also, quite often on Sunday evenings, we would link up with Neil Martin for a pint at the local to put the world to rights.

As with Randall, it took time for Arthur to show his true worth and I didn't do much to help in the early part of the 1972-73 season. We were sitting 17th in the table when we lost at Scunthorpe going into Christmas and promotion was simply not on the agenda. But the whole thing changed on the back of an own goal by Colin Franks, which gave us the points in a Boxing Day clash with Watford. We lost only one of the next 10 matches. At last, we were back in business. Slowly but surely we worked our way up the table and we timed our late run to perfection.

Randall and Jon Nixon were getting plenty of headlines as they went goal-happy and I'm not sure that the fans quite understood the contribution that Willie Carlin was making as the pressure started to mount. Jimmy was very clever when it came to signing players. Most of the time - not least because of the club's limited finances - he went for youngsters with potential that he could work to develop. But he was also very skilled at bringing in players in the closing stages of their careers to do a specific job. He did it to brilliant affect with Hateley and the same was true with Carlin.

By rights, wee Willie probably shouldn't have still been earning his living as a professional footballer when he joined us from Leicester City. He was plagued with problems from an arthritic hip but Jimmy believed that properly managed, he would be able to use his character and experience to have an influence on getting us into the Second Division. He couldn't run any more but that didn't change the fact that he knew what it took to win promotion, having helped Carlisle and Derby to success. Jimmy's judgement was spot on.

Willie was only 5ft 4in tall - but what a competitor! Brian Clough, his former boss at Derby, once called him "a belligerent, aggressive little Scouser". No one could argue with that. Many of the game's so-called hard-men backed away when Willie confronted them and he taught me a lot in terms of techniques for looking after myself. I loved playing alongside him. He was brilliant for me because he'd win the ball, then give it to me to use. I really admired the way he refused to bow down to his considerable injury problems. He was a fantastic professional who had a thorough understanding of the game.

I cannot remember who we were playing against during that run-in period but on one occasion at Meadow Lane we were in all sorts of trouble at half time. I was sure I knew what had to be done to put it right and Willie agreed when we discussed it as we left the field. Jimmy couldn't wait to get 'wired' into us when we reached the dressing room - quite rightly - but he saw things differently to Willie and me. He said his piece with an even bigger dose of expletives than usual and as per normal, he and Jack Wheeler then disappeared into the treatment room at the back. I knew there could be repercussions but looked across at Willie and then said to the players: "Forget what the Gaffer's just told you, this is how we're going to play it in the second half." We ran out comfortable winners after a vastly improved display and an excited Jimmy greeted us by saying: "What did I tell you?" The lads all looked in my direction, wondering if I might say something. I just looked at the floor.

I wasn't slow to make my feelings known a few weeks later, though, when we found ourselves in a ridiculous situation. We'd worked incredibly hard to get involved in the thick of the promotion race but it was asking a lot to think we could keep that going throughout March. Ahead of us was a demanding seven-game schedule and the very last thing we needed was to have another fixture squeezed in - especially as it involved a couple of flights to and from Gibraltar. I think the idea behind taking us away for a meaningless match was to give us chance to do some team-bonding before the final push. If so, it badly backfired. Jimmy and Jack Dunnett didn't get things wrong too often but I cannot imagine what got into their heads this time. We won the game against a Gibraltar XI 7-0, for what it was worth, and we finally got home to bed at 3.30 on the Friday morning. The following day, we were back on the road, heading north for a massive game against second-placed Oldham Athletic at Boundary Park. That poor planning could have ruined everything but somehow we emerged with a 1-1 draw. During the course of that season we hit some real high-spots but taking everything into consideration, that had to rank as our best performance and result.

An off-shoot to that story was that we somehow managed to persuade Arthur Mann to come with us to Gibraltar. It was such a brave decision on his part because I'm sure he thought no one would ever get him on board a plane. But he made it with the help of his guitar, a few double-brandies in the Departure Lounge, and Willie Carlin and I on either side of him. I know it's a story that has been told many times before but it's always worth repeating. It was a classic situation as he sat there strumming the Beatles song: 'She Loves You' while the plane gradually picked up speed down the runway. The faster it went, the faster Arthur sang. And he kept that going until well after we'd cleared the clouds. He achieved a lot during his football career but I cannot imagine he ever felt more proud of himself than he did that day.

Decisive wins over Grimsby and Plymouth meant the Second Division was almost within reach but only by producing a strong finish would we make it. If we could just pick up a point at Brentford on Good Friday, we'd be right in the driving seat for the runners-up spot. Okay, there was no way that we could catch Bolton, but we were set to finish the season with three successive home games and we were absolutely flying at Meadow Lane. We got a 1-1 draw at Brentford, which was ideal. But on the downside goalkeeper Roy Brown, who had been so steady and reliable and was rightly voted our 'Player of the Year', fractured his cheekbone. He was automatically ruled out of the remaining games and it put Eric McManus under immense pressure. The amiable Irishman had only played one senior game since joining us from Coventry the previous summer. What a time to have to make your home debut. I really felt for him. We all did but although we got that message across to him, there was nothing more we could do. It was all down to Eric. We couldn't catch the crosses and stop the shots for him.

He was right in at the deep end, just 24 hours after we'd left the field at Griffin Park, and there was a huge amount riding on the game against Blackburn. We were in 2nd place and Rovers 3rd. A draw wouldn't be disastrous for us but defeat would hand them the initiative. Eric came up trumps, keeping a clean-sheet as we secured a valuable goalless draw, and when he did it again as we beat Scunthorpe on Easter Monday, it was our 12th consecutive clean-sheet in home matches. That remarkable statistic spoke volumes for our defensive qualities. Brindley, Needham, Stubbs and Worthington ... take a bow!

So, having been right out of the picture at Christmas, our destiny was now in our own hands. We only needed a point against Tranmere Rovers at Meadow Lane in our final fixture and Notts County would be back in the old Second Division after an absence of 15 years. That hardly crossed our minds. We wanted to finish the campaign by winning in style and I didn't see any way we wouldn't because we were right back to our formidable best. An early goal from Nixon added to that feeling and the irony wasn't lost on me that Randall also converted two penalties in our 4-1 win. I'd handed over the job after all the pain and anguish caused by me missing from the spot against Bournemouth. Remember that? It all seemed such a long time ago as the celebrations got under way again. Two promotions in the space of three seasons really was an achievement to be proud of.

No longer did we have to think of ourselves as lower division journeymen and our new-found status meant we could look forward the following year to playing at places like Sunderland, West Brom and Aston Villa. There would also be a chance for me to go back to Middlesbrough, and our fans were really excited about the prospect of having local derbies against Nottingham Forest back on the agenda.

A photograph that's very dear to me. It's not in great condition but this shows me with my best pal Arthur Mann – preparing for our regular Wednesday game of golf.

Eight
JIMMY'S PLEDGE TO MAKE BLACK AND WHITE FASHIONABLE
(1973-1974)

Jimmy Sirrel used to love telling the tale about his early days in Nottingham when he stayed in a hotel on Wilford Lane, about a mile or so from Meadow Lane. I must have heard it at least 100 times - but I always let him finish. It brought a twinkle to his eye and particularly towards the end of his life, he'd become quite emotional as he told it. The story goes that as he sat looking out of the hotel window, he often saw people wearing red and white scarves as they wandered past. Only very rarely did he see one of the black and white variety and that prompted Notts County's new boss to make himself a promise. "I shall change that."

Four little words ... but talk about setting yourself a challenge! How on earth could he seriously believe that he could bring about a shift in the balance of football power within Nottingham when the gulf between the two clubs was so vast? At that stage, in November 1969, Forest held all the aces. They were still living to some extent on that fact that they'd won the FA Cup in 1959 because the knock-on effect was that it won over a generation of local youngsters. Forest were the classy First Division outfit, accustomed to entertaining the finest clubs in the land every other week and inevitably, pulling in big crowds. On the other side of Trent Bridge, the club that Jimmy joined was in the bottom half of the Fourth Division, far more interested in staying alive than competing for trophies. The gap between the two was simply immense.

Even allowing for the fact that Jimmy thought himself capable of achieving absolutely anything, he surely in his wildest dreams could never have seriously imagined it would take less than four years to reach parity. As the build-up to the 1973-74 season got underway, there was an added ingredient. The two Nottingham clubs were preparing to meet in a true local derby for the first time in 15 years. Perhaps even more significant, our active fan-base had grown to such an extent that it was now just as big as Forest's. Our final home attendance the previous season, when we'd clinched promotion by beating Tranmere, was 23,613. Forest, who by then had been relegated to the Second Division, had signed off their home programme a week earlier with a 1-0 win over Sunderland. The attendance was significantly smaller than ours.

Jimmy had kept his promise. He had "changed that". Black and white scarves were every bit as prominent around the city as the other lot. That became abundantly clear as the season went on, and we crossed swords with Forest in two blood and thunder derbies.

The nearest I'd come to playing in a local derby was for Middlesbrough in a Christmas fixture against Newcastle in front of a packed stadium. I'd never sampled the real thing so I didn't quite know what to expect but if I'm strictly truthful, it didn't turn me on as I'd expected when we clashed with Forest at Meadow Lane on Boxing Day 1973. It was a big game - of course it was - but I'd expected to find myself caught up in the fire and passion. That didn't happen. It made me realise that unless you were actually born and bred in Nottingham, brought up to love one club and despise the other, it couldn't possibly mean as much to you.

Footballers didn't come any more passionate than Brian Stubbs and Bill Brindley and it was blatantly obvious that the outcome of that game was a massive thing in their lives. For that reason alone, the rest of us were desperate to win. That aside, it was easy to understand that the overall derby thing was far more important to the fans than it was the players.

We lost that game 1-0 in front of an all-ticket crowd of 32,310. George Lyall scored the only goal of a game that was distinctly unmemorable and the same could be said of the return at the City Ground in March, which ended goalless in front of 29,962.

The most memorable thing on the second occasion was a decision Jimmy made which actually shocked me. He was always far more interested in what we did than worrying about the opposition so my mouth must have dropped open in astonishment when he announced that David McVay was to do a man-marking job on Duncan McKenzie. Very much the 'big-cheese' at the City Ground at that time, it was impossible to say whether McKenzie was a striker or midfield player because he popped up all over. He was as an off-the-cuff player. You never really knew what he was going to do next - not sure that he did either - but if he was in the mood, he could be brilliant. He was a real talent and certainly very entertaining to watch. It was a huge responsibility to give to McVay, a promising teenager with only a handful of League games behind him, and he did a brilliant job. His

Local derbies were back on the agenda and three players who served Notts County with great distinction - David Needham, Les Bradd and Brian Stubbs - are in the thick of the action at the City Ground.

performance in that rarified atmosphere was incredibly mature, and so disciplined that he hardly allowed McKenzie a kick all afternoon. He fully deserved all the praise that was heaped upon him. Another of the local lads who got an extra kick out of being involved in a derby-day clash, the situation certainly brought out the best in him. We got a lot of 'stick' afterwards from the Forest fans for being so negative but you could see what Jimmy was thinking. The No. 1 priority was to avoid defeat. He was desperate to deny Forest the chance to gloat about winning both derbies. It was all about keeping up the 'scarf percentage'.

McVay had also been the centre of attention on the day we launched ourselves onto the Second Division stage. Our opening fixture was away to Crystal Palace and on paper, we could hardly have had a more difficult start. Talking of big-cheeses, Malcolm Allison was as big as they came at that time. After an epic period as Joe Mercer's assistant at Manchester City he'd just taken charge at Selhurst Park and set out to make his mark in typically extrovert fashion. All sorts of gimmicks were introduced, including changing the traditional Palace kit and even giving the club a new nickname - and it was just what Jimmy wanted. There was an inescapable feeling when we arrived at the ground that we had come as lambs to the slaughter and Jimmy, the Patron Saint of Underdogs, was fired up to put one over on Allison. In Jimmy's eyes, he was another fully paid-up member of the 'Fancy Dan' brigade.

The problem was that we had turned up for the game without three of the players who had been so integral to hoisting us out of the Third Division. David Needham, Les Bradd and Willie Carlin were all missing because they were suspended. I think we were a bit taken aback when Jimmy announced that McVay would slot in alongside Stubbs in the centre of the defence. He was 18-years-old, had only left school some four weeks earlier, and it was a massive 'ask'. But just as he would a few months later against Forest, Dave responded superbly to play his part in a truly astonishing 4-1 win. Why did he not go on and achieve so much more in his playing career? Only he knows the answer to that.

I say 'truly astonishing' and I mean it. Of all the games I played in during the course of my career, I cannot think of any that produced a more unlikely result. Like it or not, without our suspended trio everything in advance did point to the fact that we would be lambs to the slaughter but although Palace took the lead, all of our trademark strengths bubbled to the surface. We equalised before half time when big 'Stubbsy' scored with a classic header from my free kick and then we picked them off with three superb breakaways in the second period as Kevin Randall (2) and substitute Mick Vinter found the target.

Travelling back up the M1 that night, I was really contented. Part of that, I'm sure, was on the back of the pre-season trip we'd had to the Highlands. We went back to God's own country to play Arbroath, Elgin and Inverness Caledonian Thistle and I bored the lads silly with stories about my adventures growing up in the area.

The burning question was, after two promotions in the space of three seasons, did we have enough about us to keep climbing? I'd already sampled life in the Second Division because I'd played around 30 games at that level for Middlesbrough. I knew the likes of Needham, Stubbs and Bradd would have no problems lifting their games but although plenty of the other lads would cope with moving up a grade, did we have another promotion challenge in us? Could we, as a group, go all the way from the Fourth to the First Division?

Talk about from one extreme to another. Based on what had happened at Crystal Palace, the answer to that question was definitely "yes". Two weeks later, you wouldn't want to put any money on it. Three days after the Selhurst Park triumph we had a painful reality check when Fourth Division Doncaster Rovers won 4-3 at Meadow Lane to knock us out of the League Cup. Then we lost 4-1 at home to Sunderland and the following Saturday, we went down 3-0 at Carlisle. Our defence, which had been virtually impregnable for much of the previous season, had shipped 11 goals in three games. Forget about promotion. We needed to think about how we were going to survive at this level.

Logic suggested there must have been some money available to spend on strengthening the squad after the belated push for promotion had attracted big crowds but for whatever reason, it didn't happen during the summer. Maybe Dunnett and Sirrel had such faith in the squad that they thought there was still more to come and we could charge on together. Maybe they just thought it was time to consolidate.

Either way, our only newcomer was Eric Probert, signed from Burnley to play alongside me in central midfield because Willie Carlin's time at Meadow Lane was up. Probert had built himself a huge reputation at an early age, making his League debut in the top flight as a 16-year-old at Turf Moor and helping to win the FA Youth Cup. Yet for some reason, his development had stalled. A switch to Notts County was seen as a much-needed fresh start, a chance to reignite his career and inspire him to fulfil his undoubted potential. It's hard to say whether he achieved that. He clearly had ability - good touch, good vision and not afraid to put his foot in - but he always seemed to leave you thinking that he could have given you more. Maybe I'm being a bit unkind but one way or another, our midfield unit needed to function better after that dreadful sequence of early results - so did our defence and attack.

Great credit to the boys because we did turn it around. On the back of successive home wins against Fulham and Preston in October, we found ourselves looking down from the dizzy height of second place in the table. The 2-1 win over Fulham was down to me converting two penalties and I really put the cat among the pigeons that day. Peter Mellor, the Fulham 'keeper, went loopy because I checked halfway through my run-up and then stroked the ball in when he committed himself too early. He was booked for whinging about it, so was Alan Mullery if I remember rightly. It created such a storm that when we were awarded the second penalty, late in the game, I couldn't resist using the same tactic. Mellor told the newspapers afterwards that he'd been on a coaching course where they'd said checking your run-up was not allowed. As far as I was concerned, the Brazilians had been doing it for years. If it was good enough for them, it was certainly good enough for me.

What was it about penalties and me? There always seemed to be some drama attached whenever I placed the ball 12 yards from goal - and there would be plenty more to follow later in my career. Just a few weeks earlier I'd got tangled up in yet more spot-kick nonsense when we were playing at Portsmouth. Kevin Randall's penalty was saved but because the goalkeeper had moved too early, a re-take was ordered. Kevin didn't fancy going again so I took over and although I hit the crossbar, again the referee said it must be re-taken because I'd struck it before he was ready. Enter big 'Stubbsy', with 'I'll sort this out' written all over his face. But the goalkeeper, John Milkins, saved that one as well to finally put an end to the fiasco. It was just as well we managed to come away from Fratton Park with a 2-1 win or we'd never have heard the last of it.

We were jogging along quite nicely, thinking that maybe we could, after all, mount another challenge. But a huge turning-point in our season came when 'Stubbsy' was injured in the home game against Middlesbrough. Jack Charlton's team were really flying at the time. They were well clear at the top of the table and we were relishing the challenge, thinking it would give us a good guide as to how we compared with the best. With that in mind, we were feeling very pleased with ourselves as we trooped off at half time. Les Bradd had given us the lead, I added a second and the 2-0 scoreline was no less than we deserved. But a reckless high challenge by Graeme Souness put Brian in hospital and opened the way for Boro to get a 2-2 draw.

I like Souness and have always got on well with him. He was a very fine player, hugely influential to Liverpool's era of European and domestic dominance during later years, and I'm almost embarrassed to say that at one stage he used to be my understudy. When I went to the World Cup with Scotland in 1976, our first-choice midfield as we boarded the plane was Bruce Rioch, me and Asa Hartford. Our understudies were Lou Macari, Souness and Archie Gemmill. What would the Scots give now to have that array of talent to pick from? For whatever reason, Souness always seemed to have a nasty challenge in him. He was such a good player that he didn't need to do it but there are plenty of old timers up and down the country who have tales to tell about how he left his mark on them. Stubbs certainly comes into that category.

The challenge caught him on the top of the knee and followed through, right up to the groin. With Jack Wheeler's help he somehow managed to get back to the dressing room, closely followed down the tunnel by Jimmy Sirrel, who said he wanted him back on the pitch as quickly as possible. "I think you need to take a look at this boss," said Jack. 'Stubbsy's' testicles were the size of cricket balls. As he made his way into an ambulance and was driven off to hospital, Jimmy headed up into the stand to find Brian's wife Jean. "Just letting you know, he said, "that I don't think Brian will be home tonight!"

Was it a deliberate act, intended to inflict damage on Brian or just a mistimed 50/50 challenge? Only Souness knows the answer to that one. Either way, that injury kept 'Stubbsy' out for a few weeks and in his comeback game, he was stretchered off again - this time with a cartilage injury. In total he was out for 11 matches and that three months spell underlined what we already knew. He, along with Dave Needham, his sidekick at the heart of our defence, was a massively important part of what we were all about. We failed to keep a single clean-sheet while he was missing. By the time he returned in mid-February, to help beat Portsmouth 4-0, we'd slipped to 9th place and were losing contact with the leaders.

A little highlight for me while he was away was when we went to Sunderland on New Year's Day, beat them 2-1 and I scored both goals. It was a bit of a ritual if we were staying in a hotel on New Year's Eve that the players would all come to my room just before midnight. Nothing outrageous, just one celebratory drink and a few quality minutes together before we went off to bed. Jimmy never said anything but not much got past him. I'm sure he knew what was going on.

Anyway, it certainly didn't do us any harm on this occasion because we really turned it on at Roker Park and silenced the big crowd. The pitch was frozen but that never worried me. I always wore rubber soles and while others were slithering around in those conditions, they just seemed to be made to measure for me. My folks had all come through from Middlesbrough for the game and it was a brilliant way to start the New Year.

Unusually for us, we went through a lengthy spell where we were doing really badly at home but picking up some excellent results on our travels. One of those came in February when we won 4-1 at Swindon. That was the day when an old 'wound' was re-opened.

The game had to kick off at 2pm at the County Ground because, with the 'Miners' Strike' in full swing, electricity restrictions meant the floodlights couldn't be used. That though, is incidental to this story. The thing was that John Bond, who had taken charge of First Division Norwich City three months earlier, was at the game and Terry Bowles, who reported on our activities for the Nottingham Evening Post at that time, did his job. He happened to know Bond because he'd previously reported on Gillingham for the Kent Evening Post when Bond was their coach. Having been asked the obvious question when they spoke, Bond admitted that he was at the game to watch me. The following day, Terry did what he was paid to do and the story was plastered over the back page of the Post. Jimmy Sirrel was absolutely furious. He immediately broke off diplomatic relations, refusing to speak to him for the next week, and it might well have stayed that way had Jack Dunnett not intervened. I found it all very amusing, as did the other players, and as far as the interest was concerned, nothing ever came of it. I did later find out that Basil Hayward, the Norwich chief scout, had followed me around for weeks but if an official approach was made, I never got to know about it.

The inconsistency was really haunting us and definitely standing in the way of progress. Heavy home defeats against Carlisle, Crystal Palace, Blackpool and Sheffield Wednesday turned the fans against us and caused attendances to plummet. But right through until the end of the season, we continued to perform creditably on our travels. The one exception to that was when we went to play Middlesbrough at Ayresome Park at the start of April.

Needless to say, it was special for me to be going back to where it had all begun. Not too much had changed. Lots of familiar faces, including some friendly ones. My old colleague and neighbour John Hickton was still banging in the goals and Boro were still in the Second Division ... but not for long. They'd actually clinched promotion the previous week so there was a proper party atmosphere when we arrived for the game. The last time Boro had won the promotion, I was out there wearing one of their red and white shirts. Now I was in the opposite corner and this time, we really were lambs to the slaughter. You wouldn't have thought so at half time because it was still goalless and we were every bit as impressive as Jack Charlton's very experienced side. Final score ... Middlesbrough 4, Notts County 0. They turned up the gas and blew us away.

One significant event that had happened in advance of that game was the arrival of left-back Ray O'Brien from Manchester United. It signalled the end of Bob Worthington's career at Meadow Lane and I was sad about that. We'd been through a lot since moving down together from Middlesbrough and I was sorry to see him eased out. Of course football is a cut-throat business. It's every man for himself at the end of the day. We all know what we're letting ourselves in for but we are still human beings. Being told you're no longer wanted in a very public way can leave deep scars and it's especially unfortunate when a really good bloke is involved. They don't come any better than Bob.

As for Ray, a fiercely competitive Irishman with a superb left foot, he hit the ground running. Jimmy had introduced him to us when he signed as one for the future but when he made his debut at Preston three days later, he excelled in a very impressive 2-0 win. I don't remember the incident but Ray insists that one of my first dealings with him was to deliver a sharp volley of abuse midway through the first half. Apparently when he played the ball forward and just stood where he was, I screamed across at him: "Are you going to move or what?" Yet another player I'd managed to upset with my vicious tongue who would carry the memory around with him but I can look back on that and see it was a means to an end. As Ray explained to me years later, he'd never really been taught how to play the game. Although Manchester United wanted to sign him as a youngster, his father had insisted he must complete his apprenticeship as a printer in Dublin before entering the precarious world of professional football. It meant that when United called again and he moved across to Old Trafford, he'd missed out on the football education most players have and he was left to play catch-up. He needed help to do that but Ray was a quick learner. He was very cute when it came to sizing up people and situations - on and off the field - and Jimmy and Andy Beattie, his trusty scout, deserved big pats on the back for getting him to Meadow Lane. He was definitely one you could look at and say: 'He'll be ready if and when we get to the First Division.'

We finally managed to find some consistency in the closing stages of the season. That trip to Middlesbrough was the only defeat we suffered in the last eight games. But that sequence was maintained at some cost from my point of view because I managed to make yet more enemies when we went to Leyton Orient for our final away game. It was massive from their point of view. Victory would put them in prime position to win promotion and the Match of the Day cameras were at Brisbane Road, hoping for something special. I would argue they got something special because they captured one of the best goals I ever scored - a crisp strike from the edge of the area. It came six minutes from time to give us a 1-1 draw and Orient missed out on promotion by one point. It was nothing personal, of course, but after that I was always assured of a special 'reception' whenever I played against them.

In the end, we finished 10th. Our first season in the Second Division could easily have been so much better but we'd learned a lot from the experience. We were capable of doing more than just surviving at that level and we were all agreed that it would be fascinating to see in which direction Dunnett and Sirrel chose to take us.

From a personal point of view, I was so chuffed to be selected in the Second Division 'Team of the Year'. Knowing that it was decided on votes cast by players of all clubs at that level, I was really flattered. The lads got up a table to go to the PFA Dinner in London, where the team was officially announced, and Jimmy came with us. We had a great night. Incidentally, how's this for an amazing coincidence? My midfield partners in that 'Team of the Year' were Bruce Rioch (then with Aston Villa) and Asa Hartford (then with West Brom) - the same combination that started out with Scotland when we went to the World Cup in 1978.

I also won the Notts County 'Player of the Year' award in 1974 but it was brought home to me very vividly on the night I picked up the trophy that you cannot please all of the people all of the time. Football is all about opinions. I'd had an issue with a supporter from my very early days at County. I don't know what I'd ever done to upset him but he really had it in for me. In those days, it was possible for spectators to move around the ground and many of them would switch at half time from one end to the other, depending on which end we were attacking. Maybe I'm exaggerating, but only slightly when I say that whenever I was taking a corner or throw, this bloke would be hanging over the railing, hurling abuse at me. He was constantly telling me I was no good and ought to get off the field and make way for the substitute. It bothered me a bit to start with but I eventually learned to ignore it. But then, he suddenly appeared at the function room on the night I was handed the 'Player of the Year' trophy. He was beside himself with rage, telling me that I didn't deserve it and it should have gone to Kevin Randall. The players around me couldn't believe what they were hearing and I had to restrain Arthur Mann because I was convinced he would hit him.

Many years later, long after I'd hung up my boots, I happened to spot this chap in a supermarket. I told my wife Brenda that it was 'him' and I was going to have a word. She was really worried that I'd cause a scene and did her best to talk me out of it. I couldn't pass up an opportunity like that. I just strolled up to him, asked how he was and whether he was still going to Notts County's games. I'm not sure as he actually said anything as he scuttled away. Like I said, you cannot please everyone.

Jack Dunnett and Jimmy Sirrel share a pre-match meal with the chairman's wife Pamela.

Nine
LONDON BOUND – BUT WHERE WOULD I END UP?
(1974)

I never wanted to leave Notts County. Since joining from Middlesbrough, when we were next to bottom of the entire Football League, I'd made it my mission in life to help us reach the top flight. I firmly believed it was possible to achieve that but the years were slipping by. I knew I was approaching the stage where a massive decision had to be made. Nothing had changed in many respects. I still desperately wanted to finish the job I'd started, but somehow I had to try and strip away the emotion.

I believed that not only was I capable of making an impression in the top flight, I was also good enough to play for Scotland. I kept telling myself: "Keep doing what you're doing. Given time, these things will take care of themselves. Eventually you will go on and achieve both ambitions."

All of a sudden though, I looked into the mirror and reality kicked in. I was 28-years-old. If something didn't happen quickly, those twin-targets would pass me by. You only get one playing career.

I've mentioned before that we were in an era when heart-to-heart conversations with managers and chairmen just didn't happen but Jack Dunnett was very fair with me. I didn't need to explain what my situation was, or what I was thinking. He 'got' it. Eventually he did pull me aside. He admitted there had been lots of interest in me from other clubs and explained that if we didn't make a good start to the 1974-75 season and look capable of mounting a genuine push for promotion, he'd let me go.

Even though we'd finished a respectable 10th the previous year, attendances had gone down and he wasn't inclined to gamble. Rather than throw money at it, he and Jimmy Sirrel opted to pin their hopes on the emerging young talent - of which there was plenty. The likes of Ian Scanlon, Steve Carter, Ian Bolton, David McVay, Mick Vinter and Pedro Richards looked as if they had a real chance of making the grade. It was, though going to take time for them to turn into potential match-winners - and I didn't have time. It was all part of the quandary. One option was to continue as I was and dedicate myself to helping develop that rich vein of talent. But what if they didn't emerge as expected? What if I suddenly suffered an injury that ended my career? Would I be able to live with the fact that I'd not pushed myself forward to show I could compete with the best?

Let's be honest, I also needed to consider the fact that I could be passing up the opportunity to massively improve my financial situation. Although I've always liked money as much as the next person I never allowed it to dominate my thinking. My philosophy was that if I was doing well, money would come to me. That outlook has served me well over the years. However, I had a wife and family to support in 1974 and I couldn't just turn my back on the chance of a taste of international stardom, no matter how slim that might be.

We loved living in Burton Joyce. Margaret, who was much more sociable than me, had developed a big circle of friends and Neil and Jayne were nicely settled in the village school. We'd grown particularly friendly with John and Daphne Mounteney, who lived at the other end of the village. When I first met John he was a central figure in the Notts County Centenary Club. It was made up of staunch fans who had their own room beneath the old main stand at Meadow Lane. Most players frequented it after matches and the atmosphere was always great. I was delighted when Dunnett invited John to become a director of the football club. Another shrewd move by the chairman.

John was a very successful businessman who understood the ways of the world. He also put his heart and soul into County and over many years, no one contributed more to the cause than him.

We used to go on family holidays with the Mounteneys and there was an amusing incident when we stayed at Paradise Bay in Malta - although John didn't find it so funny. The kids covered him in sand, all except for his head and feet, and he fell asleep. His feet were red raw when he woke up and he spent the rest of the holiday hobbling around.

It was standard procedure on Saturday nights after home games that we would meet up with John and Daphne, together with Pete and Jill Hallam, at the World's End pub in the nearby village of Lowdham. Arthur and Sandra Mann often joined us and we had such good times. Mind you, only very seldom would you have found me there if we'd lost in the afternoon. The pub was always full of County fans and I couldn't face them. I'd be at home, hiding behind a pillow.

I was itching for a chance to sample the First Division and although the ultimate would be to do it with County, it soon became clear that wasn't going to happen. The chairman's decision not to invest in players during the close season was reflected in results - and attendances. We'd only won three of the first 15 League matches before we smashed Hull City 5-0 at Meadow Lane, but there were promising signs.

It was clear to see that in signing Scanlon and Carter, Jimmy had done some great business. They'd both arrived the previous season, Scanlon from East Stirling for £10,000 and Carter from Manchester City for £15,000, and were a couple of wingers with plenty of pace and trickery, plus an inclination to be very frustrating, which is so often part of a winger's make-up. Jimmy kept them tucked away in the reserves for a year or so while they learned their trade, but it was only a matter of time.

They both had that rare ability to lift the fans off their seats and Scanlon underlined that in a game against Sheffield Wednesday when he scored a hat trick in just 165 seconds. It was something like the third fastest of all-time - an astonishing feat and I'm going to claim that I played a key part in it. He'd already scored with a shot and a header when he was brought down inside the penalty area. How could I deny him his big moment? He'd never taken a spot-kick before but when I waved him forward, he duly obliged. That gave us a 3-1 lead and although Wednesday hit back to get a 3-3 draw, the day belonged to Scanlon. In today's world, film of that remarkable feat would have been shown over and over again on a global basis. He would have dined out on it for the rest of his life. Sadly, back in the day, there wasn't a TV camera in sight to capture the action.

'Scanny' was an old-fashioned dribbler and a lot of what he did was instinctive. He was so good at gliding past defenders and delivering teasing crosses - not to mention scoring goals for himself - that he ought to have gone on to become a really top player. In later years he went to Aberdeen and helped them win the Scottish League Championship but no way did he fulfil his true potential. He and little Stevie were as thick as thieves. You hardly ever saw them apart. People used to talk about the Goalkeepers' Union - those two could have formed a Wingers' Union. Neither had much to say for themselves but they were nice lads who fitted in brilliantly in our dressing room. Carter had already played a few games for Manchester City, even scoring twice in a Manchester derby before switching to Nottingham. Like 'Scanny', he never seemed to quite grasp just how good he was and what he could become. It's so essential in the professional game to have self-belief as part of your make-up.

I don't want to sound too arrogant but looking back, I'm sure I could have helped to bring out the best in them if we had worked together for a bit longer. It brought back memories of the brilliant understanding I developed with Charlie Crickmore and Jon Nixon in the early part of our rise up the leagues. But less than a month after Scanlon's miracle hat-trick against Wednesday, I was on my way out of the door.

It sounds a laughable situation when I tell it now but it's absolutely true ... I refused to have a telephone installed in our house at Burton Joyce because if we'd done that, people would ring the number and want to talk to me! That was all well and good but what about when someone needed me urgently? On this occasion, Jimmy Sirrel did and he had to call his wife Cathy and get her to come round and bang on our door. The whole thing was a bit cloak and dagger. You couldn't make it up. Her instructions were to tell me that I must meet Jimmy at Nottingham station at 2pm. "No discussion," was Jimmy's message - "just do it." Terms had been agreed for a move. That was all the information I had and weirdly, I didn't have much more to work with as we boarded a train to London.

No one in the world kept secrets better than Jimmy. He would have made a brilliant spy. Jack Dunnett had told him to tell me nothing and trying to get him to lower his guard would be a total waste of time. There was nothing certain about the fact that I was en-route to a London club, of course. All I knew for sure was that I was heading south but inevitably I spent much of the journey weighing up the possibilities. Maybe Arsenal needed a central midfielder or was it Tottenham? I knew that Cyril Knowles, who was a good friend of mine from our days together at Middlesbrough, had recommended me to Bill Nicholson. It wouldn't be Fulham because they were in the Second Division at the time but what about Chelsea? I also remembered seeing a Sunday newspaper story a few weeks earlier saying that West Ham were keeping 'tabs' on me. After weighing up all the possibilities as we sped through the countryside, my money was on Tottenham.

It really set the juices flowing and when we finally eased our way into St Pancras, Jimmy could keep his secret no longer. He had to give the cab driver a destination and I heard him say: "Take us to Queens Park Rangers Football Club please." Was I disappointed? Absolutely not. They were much less fashionable than most of the other clubs in the capital, no argument about that, but I knew they had loads of good, experienced players. The only thing that truly mattered to me was that they were in the First Division. They were in a position to give me the platform I desperately wanted. It would be entirely up to me to show that I belonged in that company.

Jimmy had been very subdued throughout the journey down. He couldn't disguise the fact that he was bitterly disappointed about losing me and it was sad that we would be parting company without completing the job we'd set out to do together. Yet he knew as well as I did that it was a case of 'needs must'. He also knew that it was right for Notts County. I was eight months short of my 29th birthday and Dunnett will have weighed that up very carefully. He realised that it was now or never if he was to cash in on me.

Jimmy pulled me aside as we arrived at Loftus Road and said: "Little fella, whatever you do, don't sign anything until you have talked to me again." I told him I wouldn't but needless to say, I got swept up in all that followed once I went through the doors. I was so desperate to launch the new chapter in my life that it was almost a case of saying: "Where's the form? Give me a pen!" Dunnett was already there when I arrived, chatting with the Rangers chairman Jim Gregory. I didn't spend long with them. They introduced me to Rangers boss Dave Sexton and the two of us went through to his office.

Sometimes you just know the chemistry is right. I would have said 'yes' to Rangers even if it wasn't but I was so grateful that it was Sexton who wanted to sign me. I'd never met him before and he really wasn't the man I'd expected. I knew he'd had seven years in charge of Chelsea, where he'd tasted success with a group of extremely talented players who were not so much professional footballers as showbiz personalities. I fully expected some of that would have rubbed off on him. I couldn't have been more wrong. He was a delightful man and in all the time I worked with him, I don't think I ever heard him swear or raise his voice. He was always immaculate, normally in a sports jacket with collar and tie - just as he was that afternoon.

More important than that, he was a superb coach, an innovator who was years ahead of his time, and it probably took him all of five minutes to convince me that I wanted to work with him. He'd only been at Loftus Road for two months and I was flattered that he wanted to make me his first significant signing. In real terms, that counted for nothing. What did matter was how he saw me figuring. Terry Venables had been Rangers' midfield organiser as they worked their way up to the top flight and when he moved to Crystal Palace, it left a big hole. Dave wanted me to fill it. "All I want you to do," he explained, "is exactly what you've been doing at Notts County for years. Get the ball off the back-four and control the game. We've got good players all over the park and I want you to link them all together." Absolutely brilliant. If he'd turned it around and asked me how I'd like to play it, I would have said exactly that.

I must have been a really soft touch where the money was concerned. The figure Dave mentioned was substantially more than I was getting at County but bearing in mind that I would have to move my family to in or around London, I would need every penny of that. Anyway, I just said yes to his offer without even trying to negotiate. The club doctor's surgery was just around the corner from the ground. I was whisked away for a medical, which didn't take long, and went back to the ground to sign.

The gaffer shook his head with disappointment when I told him the deal was done. "Little fella, what did I tell you?" he said. That's when he revealed that a number of clubs wanted to talk to me - including Manchester United, Leeds United and Southampton. I cannot imagine that any of them had offered more than the £100,000 Rangers had agreed to pay for me, otherwise Dunnett would have been pushing me in their direction. I did, though, get the strong impression that Jimmy thought I was joining the wrong club.

I didn't care. I'd waited my whole life for this opportunity to come along. The last thing I was going to have when it finally arrived was regrets.

Dave, thoughtful as ever, knew that the whole thing had been thrust upon me and wanted to give me chance to sort out my life before getting down to work. The first thing I had to do was get back to Nottingham to tell Margaret she was moving. She was a Northern lass, through and through, but I couldn't wait to tell her what was happening. The reaction was just as I'd expected. She was really excited about having chance to sample the bright lights of London. It wasn't all about that, though. I was very aware that it was going to be a big culture shock to us - and it was. To start with, I'd be living in a hotel for the foreseeable future, so as not to disrupt the children's schooling, and travelling up and down as often as possible. It was going to be a huge upheaval in every respect.

Dave told me that he wasn't going to include me for the following Saturday's trip to Burnley but I should get my head straight in readiness for making my debut at home to Sheffield United. It couldn't come quickly enough. I'd be ready.

Getting a feel for Loftus Road with QPR boss Dave Sexton and my son Neil.

QPR's new No.9 ... really 'up' for the challenge.

10
MAYBE I WAS THE LONE RANGER... BUT I LOVED IT
(1974-1975)

It's a curious thing within football that no matter which club you go to, you always seem to find a link to your past or a friend of a friend who is happy to show you the ropes and help make you feel at home. That didn't apply for me when I walked into the QPR dressing room for the first time. I knew absolutely no one.

There were lots of very familiar faces, people like Frank McLintock, David Webb, Gerry Francis and Stan Bowles, but I didn't actually know any of them. And while I had the advantage of having regularly watched them on television or read about them in newspapers or magazines, they hadn't a clue who I was.

It would have been very easy to be intimidated but I couldn't afford to be. One of the good things about Dave Sexton giving me a week off after I'd completed my transfer was that I'd had time to get my head around the whole situation. I soon came to the conclusion that even if he thought I might need a settling-in period, I didn't have time for that. Right at the top of my 'to do' list was to prove to my new colleagues that if they were thinking I was a lower-division player with ideas above my station, they should think again. I was desperate to show them I could improve their team.

There was a slight problem because I reported for duty on the Thursday before our home game against Sheffield United and as Thursdays was the players' regular day-off at Rangers, Dave had a decision to make. Under normal circumstances, Friday would be a fairly light session - maybe a bit of running and a gentle five-a-side. On this occasion he told the players to get stripped and ready for a full-scale practice match.

That didn't go down too well with a few of them but they didn't need to be too alarmed. Some 15-minutes after we'd kicked off, Dave blew his whistle and told us to go and get changed. He'd already seen enough. As he told me years later, he didn't think it would be right for me, or the other players, to be tossed straight in on the Saturday afternoon. But in his words, I'd "taken control within 15 minutes". He knew everything would be fine. More to the point, the other players no longer needed convincing.

I got off to a winning start - thanks to a goal by Don Rogers - but not only that, we also won our next three games. Two of them were London derbies so it really cranked up the excitement level for supporters. One of my favourite memories from that debut against Sheffield United was that for the first time in my life I wore the No. 9 shirt. Wow! I loved that - but it really didn't seem right. Only the likes of Brian Clough, Tony Hateley and Les Bradd got to do that in my experience. But that number stayed with me throughout my time at Loftus Road and it gave me a special thrill every time I pulled the shirt over my head.

Rangers had been having a tough time before I arrived. They'd finished eighth the previous season, which was a good effort in their first year back in the top flight, but then Gordon Jago left to join Millwall and after Stan Anderson and Frank Sibley had a spell in caretaker charge, Sexton moved in. He struggled to turn it around initially and they'd lost 3-0 at Burnley while I was back in Nottingham, weighing up my new challenge.

It only takes a result or two to totally change the mood, however, and when we followed up that Sheffield United success with a 2-1 win at Tottenham, the smiles were back on faces. Cyril Knowles played for Spurs that day. Maybe Bill Nicholson should have listened to him after all!

We returned to Loftus Road to beat Leicester City, coming from behind on Boxing Day to win a brilliant match 4-2, and that put us in a great frame of mind for a trip to Chelsea. Only three and a half miles separate Loftus Road from Stamford Bridge and I soon picked up the vibes. This game was huge. All of a sudden the memories came flooding back and it dawned on me for the first time that I was back in a situation I knew so well in Nottingham. Without realising it when I joined Rangers, I was signing up yet again to become a serious underdog. That wasn't just for the trip down the road to Chelsea - it was for the vast majority of games we played in the First Division. We were always seen as a soft touch, an easy way for the 'big boys' to boost their points tally, but over the next few years, I took great delight in the way we forced them to treat us with respect. That outlook was a huge source of motivation in my time at County, and so it was at Rangers.

Chelsea, especially along the Kings Road with its fashionable shops, clubs and restaurants, was always regarded as the area that defined the Swinging Sixties. Inevitably it rubbed off on the football club. If ever you went to Stamford Bridge you couldn't turn round without bumping into a famous person or spotting a face you recognised. It was choc-a-block with beautiful people, actors, pop stars, Page 3 models - most of them claiming to be Chelsea fans. In fairness, the club did give them plenty of encouragement during the late Sixties and early Seventies, winning the League Cup, FA Cup and UEFA Cup.

The team played with a flamboyance that fitted perfectly with the club's showbiz image of that time and I certainly admired them from afar. Crowd pleasers like Peter Osgood, Alan Hudson and Charlie Cooke strutted their stuff on a regular basis, and the crowds flocked to watch them. David Webb was also part of that scene for 200-plus games, so too was Dave Sexton as their manager. Now those two earned their wages working for QPR and that was a key part of making that trip to Chelsea such a special occasion. A natural-born winner like 'Webby' badly wanted to put one over his old mates in his first return to Stamford Bridge and it was easy to see that Dave was still smarting about being sacked three months earlier.

What else do I remember about that game? Well, it was certainly feisty but we went toe-to-toe with them in the first half and eventually ran out comfortable 3-0 winners with goals from Don Givens (2) and Gerry Francis. I also remember that it was the first time I met up with Ray Wilkins at close-quarters. I had to give myself a sharp talking to. My first reaction was to wonder if I was worthy of being on the same pitch as him but it was no time for self-doubts. There were 38,917 people at Stamford Bridge that day and although our fans were heavily outnumbered, they certainly made themselves heard. For years afterwards people used to come up to me and say how much that result meant to them.

Although Chelsea and Rangers were practically neighbours, the areas in which they were located had very little in common. That was one of the first things that struck me when I moved to London and took up temporary residence in the Kensington Hilton Hotel. I was amazed at how quickly you could move from one district to another and within minutes things could be so totally different. I'm sure people living in the south don't give it a second thought. It's a natural way of life for them but I found it very strange. The contrast between the areas in which Stamford Bridge and Loftus Road were located was a good example. There was very little of the swish and swanky Chelsea scene to be found at Shepherd's Bush.

The most obvious claim to fame for Shepherd's Bush was that it was home to the BBC Television Centre and I soon took advantage of that. Margaret and the kids had come down to spend the weekend with me and as it was just before Christmas, the BBC 'Sports Personality of the Year' event was taking place. Many of the stars were staying at Kensington Hilton and I was totally in awe of them. Neil had taken his autograph book to London, hoping to collect the signatures of the QPR players, and I borrowed it. Rubbing shoulders, as we were, with the likes of Mary Peters, Jackie Stewart and that year's winner, Brendan Foster, it would have been silly not to ask for their autographs! I have to admit that when it came to the crunch I couldn't resist it ... I asked them to sign "To Don".

That was the world I now lived in - and it was to be my world for the next five months. I agreed with Margaret that we didn't want to disrupt Neil and Jayne's education any more than we had to, so we took our time finding a house we could move into during the summer. It was hard for Margaret and demanding for me in the sense that I spent many hours every week sitting on the M1, driving back and forth to Nottingham, though I have to say that Rangers were very generous in covering my petrol money.

I had a reserved car parking space during my time at the Hilton. It was pure gold dust in that part of the world - and more than I ever managed at Loftus Road. Parking your car could be a nightmare there and on match days the club had to call on the goodwill of neighbours. Our normal routine for home games was that we would meet at White's Restaurant in Bayswater Road for our pre-match meal and then drive to the ground. It wasn't far in terms of distance but the journey could often take more than half an hour. When we got there we parked on the streets, in a specially cordoned off area in front of the houses, and joined with supporters walking to the ground.

Terraced houses and tall blocks of flats hem in the stadium at Loftus Road. The chairman Jim Gregory - 'Slippery Jim' as the players called him - did a brilliant job in his term of office, overseeing the building of new stands on all four sides, but you cannot create space where there is none. Consequently it's a really tight little ground. Compact, I think, is the word commonly used but I loved the fact that the crowd was right on top of you during games. Give them something to shout about and the Rangers fans generated a terrific atmosphere. Unfortunately, over the years, they've seldom had anything to shout about. They won the League Cup while they were still in the Third Division, were FA Cup finalists in 1982 and have spent a fair few years in the top flight. But I had the feeling in my early days there that it wasn't all about winning for the fans. Rangers are their club. They're heartwarmingly proud to support them come thick or thin, and if and when a period of relative success came along, as it did during my time with them, they appreciated it so much more than fans of those clubs that are always winning things. It's a true 'community' club. That's an often over-used description, I think, but certainly in my time at Rangers it was a happy place to be, full of good people who enjoyed their jobs and genuinely cared about the club.

The whole experience for me was a great adventure and even though I was living alone, I had absolutely no difficulty filling my time each day. I did need to make a quick adjustment to my body clock when I discovered that our normal start time for training was 11am - far later than I'd been used to at Notts County. The reason for that, quite simply, was that people struggled to get there any earlier. Dave Sexton, for example, lived in Brighton and it took him two hours to get to Loftus Road. Several of the lads lived in Essex, which could often be a nightmare journey, so a later start just made sense. You couldn't have a situation where only half the group were training together.

Our training ground was in Ruislip, half an hour's drive from Loftus Road. Because I didn't have my bearings, I'd arranged first day that I would go to the ground and travel up on the mini-bus that transported the youth team lads. Gerry Francis' dad Roy, who was our kit man, used to drive it. I stuck with that same arrangement afterwards because it worked - and one of the senior players who lived in Essex would normally drop me close to my hotel on their way home. Sometimes there was a detour involved, especially if David Webb was my chauffeur. He knew everyone worth knowing in the King's Road area and I thoroughly enjoyed the guided tour of Chelsea that he gave me over a period of time. It was an incredible scene, packed with interesting characters - a totally different world to anything I'd ever encountered before.

I've often wondered what might have happened had I been say 22-years-old. It would have been so easy to get distracted in London but fortunately I was that little bit older and wiser. Checking out the scene was a key part of my great adventure. I loved it, but I never lost sight of the fact that I was there to prove myself as a First Division player and set up the chance to play for Scotland.

Despite the fact that I knew none of them when I arrived, the players made me really welcome. It helped, I suppose, that we won the first four games I played and most went out of their way to be friendly and helpful. That was especially true of Frank McLintock - we Scots must stick together - and I soon became good friends with Dave Thomas and Don Givens. Frank owned a couple of bars in the Islington area, where he was still viewed as a god after leading Arsenal to a League & Cup 'Double', and he sometimes took me with him when he went across to count his money! I remember one occasion when he pointed out a bloke who he insisted was a 'professional' pickpocket. Apparently that man also specialised in pinching stuff to order. I thought Frank was joking at first but he wasn't. I resisted when the chap asked me if there was anything I needed. It was a sharp reminder of how easy it was to fall into bad company.

Our training facilities at Ruislip were nothing special. I was disappointed to be honest. I thought they'd be at least a couple of notches up on what I'd been used to but there was nothing glamorous about the set-up. The playing surfaces were poor but interestingly, you heard very few moans. I thought that spoke volumes for the group. They were there to work and just made the best of what was available.

My first week was a real eye-opener - not least at my first Monday training session. We were handed over to work with Ron Jones, the former Olympic sprinter, and the weekly sessions were hard but extremely rewarding. We all donned our spiked running shoes and were put through a series of challenges against the stopwatch. I was never any good at the sprints. I left those to the likes of Givens and Micky Leach, but I got real benefit from improving my technique and times over the longer distances. I prided myself on my ability to run for 90 minutes anyway, but I'm sure that work helped to improve my stamina.

That whole business was so typical of Sexton. He was far ahead of his time with his thinking and planning, and it was very much the same off the field. Attention to detail was his 'thing'. For example, Rangers became the first club in the country to serve the players with hot meals on the way back from away games. Our executive team coach was especially designed to cater for it and a steward did the cooking and served the meals. We even had bottles of wine to go with it. Normally it was Liebfraumilch or Blue Nun. You cannot have everything in life - but we appreciated the thought.

I was incredibly lucky to get to work with Dave at that stage of my career. Just as Jimmy Sirrel had come into my life at precisely the right time, so the same was true of Dave. He was a real innovator as a coach. For example, I thought at first it was really strange that our goalkeeper Phil Parkes used to train most of the time away from the rest of us. I'd never come across that before but you didn't need to think about it for long to realise how sensible it was for him to concentrate on the things that mattered to him. Nowadays of course, every club employs a goalkeeping coach. They all owe a debt of gratitude to Dave for getting them employment.

Dave was a disciple of Rinus Michels, the Dutch coach who was credited with introducing 'Total Football' in the Seventies. I was told he often used to pay his own way to travel across to meet up with Michels and watch him work with the likes of Johan Cruyff when Holland were a real force in the world game. He brought those ideas back to Ruislip and passed them on to us. How lucky was I?

Training was a treat. I loved every session we did and nothing was done without having a purpose. It always had to be a means to an end.

I've already talked about our constructive Monday running sessions and we regularly did circuit training, supervised by Dave, to help ensure our fitness levels were where they should be. Unlike what went on at many clubs in those days, everything else was done with a football. At least twice a week we played small-sided games in a confined area, normally six-a-side, and they were really intense. You were allowed two touches but had to either control and pass or control and shoot. Defenders would be tight up behind you all the time, with orders not to hold back with their tackling. It meant your first touch had to be perfect every time. Come Saturday afternoon, matches were so much easier on the back of the work we did.

'Piggy in the Middle' was another game we regularly played that was well ahead of its time. Players in a circle would pass the ball around among themselves and the one in the middle had to get it off them. If he did, the person who had touched it last went in the middle. It was a fun exercise but reputations were at stake. Players took it as a personal insult to go into the middle. It was a slight on their skills and we did our utmost to make sure we weren't next. I don't think Gerry Francis, Stan Bowles or I ever found ourselves in the middle.

Just an aside to that, I used to play a little game with McLintock during our keep-ball sessions. I'd bide my time and when the opportunity arose, deliver the perfect 'nutmeg' (play it through his legs). The rule was that it didn't count unless you nominated it before doing it. Frank knew it was coming but still didn't manage to prevent it happening. As he's told me many times over the years, it drove him to distraction!

Frank was great. I was wondering when I signed for Rangers what I would find with him because he was 35-years-old with a bucket-full of caps and medals to show for an outstanding career in the game. No one would have been the least bit surprised if he was just seeing out his time - but how wrong would they be? Although Gerry was our captain, and also captain of England at that time, I hope he won't take offence if I say that in many ways, it was Frank who was our leader.

Gerry, a local lad from Chiswick, was Rangers through-and-through. He contributed a vast amount to the club during two spells as a player and one as manager and everyone had the utmost respect for him. I certainly did and it was a privilege to say that he was one of my midfield partners throughout my time in West London. But in my opinion, it was Frank who set the bar. Every day mattered just as much to him as it had 10 years earlier. He instilled that attitude throughout the dressing room. He tackled just as hard in training as he did in matches and if any of us allowed our standards to slip because we didn't quite feel in the mood on any particular day, he was on us like a ton of bricks. It was so noticeable when I first arrived that the attitude of the players as a group was exceptional. They gave 100 per cent every day. In my opinion, a lot of that was down to Frank.

Training tended to consist of short, sharp sessions, very intense, and Dave - he never allowed us to call him boss - was in his element. Coaching was definitely his forte. He was never happier than when he was working on the training ground, and he was bloody good at what he did.

Most days I had a lot of spare time after training and I used it well. I would go back to the hotel, collect my car and set off to explore London. There was no satnav in those days of course. You just relied on old-fashioned sense of direction but it never phased me, even when I got hopelessly lost. I cannot tell you how much pleasure I got from just driving around, seeking out places that I'd only ever read about or seen on television. These included football grounds. I never ventured south of the river but targeted most of the other London clubs and sought them out. I could walk comfortably from my hotel to Stamford Bridge and Craven Cottage and would drive to the others, park up and do a tour around the outside. I let my imagination take over and would try to sense the atmosphere - with me out in the middle lapping it up.

Sometimes I'd just hop on a tube, get off at places like Oxford Street, Westminster or Buckingham Palace and act like a tourist. I had no problem at all filling my days and rather than being nervous about driving around London, I thrived on it. I must admit though that taking on Hyde Park Corner for the first time was an experience

I'll never forget. I had no idea what I was heading into as I drove up Park Lane but all of a sudden, I was confronted with about 10 lanes of traffic, ducking and diving in all directions. The golden rule, of course, is that you must not stop. You just keep going and somehow, all the vehicles manage to miss each other. Amazing.

When my dad came down to visit me while I was living in the hotel, he couldn't believe his eyes. He was a bus driver in Middlesbrough, used to negotiating his way through traffic every day, but he'd never seen anything like this. He spent most of his time complaining about the standard of driving in London but finally got the message that if you don't push yourself out at a junction, you'll sit there all day.

Back to the football and I just didn't believe it when I was told who we'd been drawn against in the fourth round of the FA Cup. I shrugged it off as a joke at first but it was true ... we would be up against Notts County at Loftus Road. Little more than a month after waving goodbye we'd be meeting up again. I'd shared so many good times with those lads and sadly, upset quite a few at various times. This would be their chance to extract some revenge and I was fully expecting to collect a few 'souvenirs' when we played. It was an obvious storyline for the newspapers to follow and Monty Fresco, the legendary Daily Mirror photographer, pictured me in a café near Loftus Road. It appeared on the morning of the match in a preview feature.

I wasn't aware of it at the time but something very revealing happened on the day of that game. Regardless of the opposition while I was with County, Jimmy Sirrel always had complete faith in his players. He feared no one and our preparation for every match was geared towards what we would do. Inexplicably, for the first time that I could ever recall, he allowed his guard to slip for this Cup tie.

It was played on a Friday evening because Chelsea and Fulham were also drawn at home and the Police were concerned that they wouldn't cope with three Saturday games at the same time. Consequently, County followed their normal night-match routine. They travelled to London in the morning, had lunch at a hotel and the players then went to their rooms to rest or sleep for a couple of hours. Terry Bowles, who reported on County at that time for the Nottingham Post, always travelled with the team and that day Jimmy apparently pulled him aside before lunch and asked him to do a little job while the players were resting.

Jimmy borrowed a typewriter from hotel reception and Terry did the typing while the boss dictated an individual analysis on each of the QPR players - plus an insight into how we played. Jimmy then handed it to Jack Wheeler and instructed him to make sure that every player read it before they came down for their pre-match tea and toast.

Putting words on paper was not exactly Jimmy's strength and although it was very much best of intentions, that little departure from the norm rebounded on him badly. The idea had clearly been to make the Notts lads feel a lot easier about the prospect of taking on in-form First Division opposition. Instead of that, they just found it hilarious when they read through the analysis and as he told me after the game, Bill Brindley was particularly taken with the description of McLintock. Jimmy's verdict was that he "couldn't tackle, couldn't run and couldn't head the ball". In conclusion … "he was as soft as shit".

What on earth was Jimmy thinking about? I believe he lost a little bit of respect from the players that day. It was so out of character but I'm sure it reflected the fact that he was very concerned about how things might turn out. As it happened, he had every reason to be.

Frank played as if he knew what was being said about him. He and 'Webby' were right at the top of their game and as a team, we were brilliant. We won 3-0 and it could easily have been 10. To be honest, if it hadn't been for some wayward finishing and a brilliant display by Eric McManus, who even saved an early penalty from Stan Bowles, it probably would have been. We were 3-0 up after little more than half an hour and were so dominant that it was amazing that we didn't add to that tally. We had good players all over the pitch. In those days there was none of this nonsense about fielding weakened teams for Cup ties. We put out our strongest available side and the one consolation for County was that we would have beaten any team in the country that night. I thoroughly enjoyed having a drink with the County lads afterwards. It was great to see them again and I didn't need to explain why I'd left them to join Rangers.

It crossed our minds that if we could keep playing like that, we would have a real chance of winning the FA Cup. Best laid plans and all that - we fell at the next hurdle, beaten 2-1 by West Ham at Upton Park.

We'd actually travelled across London to play the Hammers a couple of weeks earlier and it was a special day for me because I scored my first top-flight goal. I drilled the ball into the top corner when Stan touched a short free kick to me on the left-edge of the area. We drew 2-2 and I was told when I got back to the dressing room that the great Brian Moore wanted to talk to me on the TV gantry. He'd been commentating on the game, which got top billing on the following day's 'Big Match' programme, followed by me talking about my goal and about generally living the dream.

A crushing win over Derby County and a draw at Coventry was followed by a long haul to Carlisle United, who were appearing in the top flight for the first time in their history. We showed a lot of character that day, coming from behind to win 2-1 with two goals from Don Givens, but I had to come off in the second half after taking a whack on the ankle. We were due to play at home to Middlesbrough three days later. Naturally I wanted to play in that game but by the time we got back to London, I could hardly walk. I went straight to see the club doctor the following morning and he gave me a cortisone injection. That certainly helped and I agreed with Dave Sexton that I'd have another one before the match. He wasn't convinced that was a good idea but I insisted I wanted to play. I hated missing matches at any time and I certainly didn't want to drop out of the team when things were going so well. We could only draw 0-0 with Middlesbrough but I completed the 90 minutes and the ankle never troubled me. Players these days are very hesitant about having injections and I can understand that because the theory is they could cause problems in later life. I can only say that they worked for me.

I was getting more than my share of media coverage and my profile had risen through the roof. Surely someone involved in picking the Scotland team would have taken note yet to be strictly honest, I didn't feel I was doing myself justice. I knew there was more to come and with so many good players to work with, I was confident that it was only a matter of time.

I'm not trying to claim more than my fair share of credit but we lost only one of my first 11 League games for Rangers - 1-0 at home to Burnley - and there was a really good feel around the club. The attendance when I made my debut against Sheffield United was just 13,244. Within a couple of months we were pulling in 20,000-plus every time we played at home. Could this be the start of something big? The fans were certainly beginning to believe and when a goal from Dave Thomas proved to be enough for us to complete a League 'double' over Chelsea, they saw that as a sign. It all fell a bit flat when we won only one of our last seven games and finished in 11th place. There was, though, a collective feeling that we were better than that. I knew what had to change in my life to help prove that point. Top of the priority list was to buy a house, get the family nicely settled during the summer and be 100 per cent ready to tackle one of the biggest seasons of my career.

I'd done a fair bit of research during my time driving around the area, trying to find a nice place to live at a price we could afford, and I'd sounded out the other players. Some lived in Essex but I didn't fancy the journey they made every day, while central London properties were way out of our price range. We decided in the end to head west into Berkshire and set up home in the lovely village of Crowthorne.

Don Givens, Dave Clement and Don Rogers all lived there and a number of others were close by. Dave Thomas and Phil Parkes were in Workingham, Ian Gillard in Sandhurst and Gerry Francis in Bagshot.

They already had a 'car club' going and were happy for me to join them. It took about an hour to drive to Loftus Road, 40 minutes on a good day to the training ground at Ruislip and we used to pile into two cars, taking turns to drive.

Much as I enjoyed my time exploring the delights of London, it was great to be back in a proper family environment again and we thoroughly enjoyed sharing a new adventure. Margaret loved exploring London for herself whenever she got the chance and Neil and Jayne soon settled in school. As for me, I discovered something at Crowthorne that was to have a huge impact on my life. Bob Reynolds, who lived across the road from us, introduced me to tennis. I can't say I'd ever played the game before, certainly not seriously, but I instantly took to it. Even now, well into my Seventies, I still play to a reasonable standard two or three times a week. I owe a big debt of gratitude to Bob for that, and also for the fact that his house backed onto Royal Berkshire Golf Club. Don't tell anyone but I often used to hop over his fence late in the evening with a couple of golf clubs and wander round a few holes when there was no one around.

During my time at QPR I enjoyed passing on some tips to local schoolboys near my home in Crowthorne. Life was really hectic and this was a nice release.

STILL SAYING SORRY

Gerry Francis ... his Goal of the Season summed up what QPR were all about. Arguably the best team that *didn't* win the Championship.

11
'GERRY'S GEM' LAUNCHES A SPECIAL SEASON
(1975-76)

It didn't take long to produce evidence that Queens Park Rangers meant business in 1975-76. Our very first goal of that memorable campaign was so good that BBC Match of the Day viewers voted it 'Goal of the Season'. The fact that it came against Liverpool, somehow made it extra satisfying.

Forgive me, please, if I take this opportunity to talk you through it in some detail. Our goalkeeper Phil Parkes rolled the ball out to Frank McLintock and as was the way of things, I collected it from him. Stan Bowles had his back to goal inside the centre-circle but even though Emlyn Hughes was marking him tightly, I always had faith in him to find a way. This time, even Stan excelled himself when I knocked the ball up to him. He instinctively flicked it through his own legs, straight into the path of Gerry Francis. I can still sense the gasp of astonishment and delight from the crowd when he did that. Gerry, in full gallop, set up Don Givens for the perfect 1-2, ran on to collect an inch-perfect return and nonchalantly stroked it into the net.

It was sheer perfection. The stuff that coaches dream about all the time - then wake up and tell themselves not to be so stupid.

Less than an hour into the new season and we'd scored a goal of such quality that no team would better it during the course of the entire campaign. That triumph, in the space of 10 seconds or so, perfectly summed up what we were all about. The first thing to stress is that it highlighted the level of ability we had running throughout our team. You don't score a goal like that, especially against opposition of Liverpool's pedigree, unless you have people who can 'play'.

The other major point, which I see as incredibly revealing, was that it was a true collective effort. We were Dave Sexton's brainchild and right at the heart of his masterplan to introduce 'Total Football' to this country was teamwork. I'd watched it taking shape after joining Rangers during the second half of the previous season and a few months down the line we were busy smoothing the rough edges. We'd all locked in to what Dave wanted to achieve and after weeks of hard work during pre-season, we felt we were ready. There was no better way to deliver our statement of intent than 'Gerry's Gem'.

Over the course of the next nine months we were a breath of fresh air for the English game. People loved our expansive style of play and I don't just mean fans of the blue & white hoops. We became everyone's second-favourite team and although we eventually had to concede the title to Liverpool, even to this day I get told we were the best team never to win the Championship.

Nottingham Forest, a few years later, came from no-where under Brian Clough to lift the crown in their first season back in the top flight and more recently, Leicester City proved all the doubters wrong by hitting the top and staying there. Just as we did back in '75-76 those clubs made it fashionable to be unfashionable. The only difference in our case was that we finished one solitary point short of the target we needed.

It was heartbreaking in a football sense to get so close and then miss out but once I got over the immediate disappointment, I've only ever seen that season as a positive experience. I'll be forever grateful that I was part of a special scene at Loftus Road, surrounded by great players and fantastic team-mates. What we achieved, and especially the manner in which we achieved it, fills me with pride.

From a personal point of view I relished the challenge that Dave was setting us as we approached that season. He wasn't prepared to just settle for more of the same. He wanted to take us to a new level, adopt a style of play that required us to 'think outside the box'. All credit to him for weighing up our strengths and weaknesses and coming up with a way that suited us.

Strictly speaking we had a 4-3-3 formation and we all had a set role within the team framework. But then again, we didn't. The best way to describe it is to say it was off the cuff, with discipline. Most of us had been round the block in football terms and he trusted us to use our experience to work together to make good things happen. The key ingredient was flexibility. The midfielders and front players had license to roam into areas where we thought we could do most damage and when we combined that with the slick passing style Dave had instilled into us, the opposition couldn't handle it. 'Goal of the Season' against Liverpool was the ultimate but that was just one example. We were irresistible, not just sometimes but on a fairly regular basis, and it was a joy to be a part of it. As I often say to people, we played five-a-side on a big pitch.

No way could Dave's masterplan have worked without us having a top goalkeeper and a back-four that was both well-drilled and utterly reliable. We had both. I've mentioned before that for some reason I always seemed to develop a bond with goalkeepers and Phil Parkes became a good friend. I really rated him. He had a fabulous career, playing 743 senior games, and it was a travesty that he only won one England cap. I guess that was a reflection of how many outstanding goalkeepers England had to call on in that era. Anyway, with Phil as our last line of defence, we always had a chance of collecting at least a point.

I've already sung the praises of McLintock and Webb and on either side of them, Dave Clement and Ian Gillard gave 7/10 or better performances every week in the full back positions. Between them, they made close on 900 appearances for Rangers and a succession of managers filled in their names on the team-sheet without giving it a second thought. Both were Londoners who came up through the youth ranks and remembered QPR as the club used to be. Dave was fresh on the scene when they stormed to the Third Division Championship and won the League Cup the same year - and he spent 14 years at Loftus Road. Everyone liked Dave. He was a fitness fanatic and a great competitor who read the game well. He was a massive asset to Rangers. It was such a tragedy when he committed suicide at the ridiculously young age of 34 after suffering a bout of depression.

As for Ian, he also devoted 14 years of his career to Rangers, playing more than 400 senior games, and it would be interesting to know how many 'nightmare' performances he and Dave produced between them. I bet you wouldn't need the fingers of both hands to count them. They were terrific pros and for obvious reasons, what we achieved that season meant more to them than most of us. I thought it was fantastic that on the back of our 'success', they both won England caps that year.

That was another big deal for Rangers, which underlined the fact that we were not just making up the numbers in the First Division any more. When I arrived at QPR about half of the players were internationals. By the end of the 1975-76 season all of the regular team - including me - had caps that they could put on the table. All except one.

The only one to miss out was David Webb. I guess if you got him in one of his quieter moments he would say he had big regrets about that - but it didn't stop everyone from loving him. He became a bit of a folk hero in his time at Chelsea and certainly knew how to work 'the' crowd at Loftus Road. He hated sitting around in the dressing room before matches so his normal routine was to get changed as late as possible. On one occasion, he cut it even finer than usual. So much so that we took the field without him! In those days, there was none of this business of going out side by side with the opposition and then going through the handshaking rigmarole. You took to the pitch for the first time about four minutes before kick off, just in time for the captains to toss a coin. When the referee pressed the buzzer in our dressing room to signal that we should take the field, 'Webby' still wasn't ready. We had no option but to go out without him and when he finally appeared from the tunnel, the crowd went wild. He jogged out to the middle waving to all four sides of the ground, did one gentle lap of the centre-circle as a warm-up and then took his position alongside Frank. Priceless!

Anyway, I digress. It was absolutely fundamental if we were to achieve what Dave Sexton wanted that we had a goalkeeper and back-four that he could rely on. He had that - and just for some extra insurance he went back to Stamford Bridge in September and signed John Hollins. Nobody knew 'Holly' better than Dave. He'd been his captain at Chelsea and like so many of the players we already had, he was a vastly experienced 'pro', renowned for his consistency, and he knew what it took to win things. My son Neil, who would have been eight at the time, immediately adopted 'Holly' as his favourite player and he also got on well with his son Chris when they used to meet up on matchdays at Loftus Road. That's the same Chris Hollins who went on to become a top television presenter and Strictly Come Dancing winner.

We used to joke that the only reason 'Holly' joined us was so that he'd be reunited with Dave Webb and they could perfect the ventriloquists act they'd developed at Stamford Bridge. It was absolutely fantastic - especially when we'd had a few drinks on the coach coming back from an away game. 'Holly' would sit on Dave's knee and they had us in stitches as they went through their 'Gottle of Geer' routine. As with Frank, 'Holly' trained like a 17-year-old every day and his enthusiasm was infectious. He was tailor-made for us and Dave already had a job earmarked for him. He took on the anchor-role in midfield, giving extra protection to the back-four, and that allowed Gerry Francis and me to operate with complete freedom in front of him.

I've often said to people that I found it so easy playing at Rangers, and it really was. Providing you could control the ball and pass it, you couldn't fail. I just used to feed it to Gerry, Stan, Don Givens and Dave Thomas - then stand back and admire the terrific ability they all had. Dave Sexton always encouraged us to attack and as the very essence of his 'Total Football' plan was that none of the front five would be pigeon-holed, life became one big adventure, full of exciting twists and turns.

Gerry says that he and Stan were telepathic. He reckons they could have played together blindfolded. I'm not sure about that but I know what he means. They were brilliant at making themselves available in a little bit of space and were different class when it came to beating someone and delivering a cross. All I had to do was give them the ball and let them get on with it.

The way we operated created havoc for opponents trying to mark us. We were never where they thought we were supposed to be and at that time, no one had ever come across that before in the English game. You see Manchester City do it now but in those days it was unheard of. One of the things Dave did that gave us some structure was to urge Stan to seek out the ball down the right and then cut inside and shoot with his left-foot. Dave Thomas did the same in reverse on the left and between them, they scored no end of spectacular goals using that tactic.

I thought Dave was a brilliant player who should have won many more than his eight caps for England. He was so brave and positive in the way in which he attacked defenders and he always put himself at risk because of his insistence of playing with his socks around his ankles. You're not allowed to do that these days - and rightly so. Another thing he did - or should I say we - was that he and I always played in 'rubbers', (moulded sole boots) whatever the conditions. Most players would switch between long or short studs, especially with pitches in the state they were in the Seventies, but Dave and I always stuck to the 'rubbers'. As we used to say, you can get away with that when you have superior balance. That always went down well in the dressing room!

Just as an aside, Dave had this weird obsession for cutting grass and creating the perfect stripes. He was part of the Berkshire 'car club' we had going, which took a group of us each day to training and matches, and more often than not when we arrived to pick him up, he'd just be giving his lawn a quick trim. Good bloke Dave - I like him a lot and we always kept in touch in later life.

I would bracket Don Givens alongside Dave in that he never seemed to get the recognition he truly deserved. An Irish international from Limerick, he arrived at Loftus Road via Manchester United and Luton and was another who gave Rangers great service, playing more than 250 games in a six-year stay. Maybe he wasn't a prolific scorer but he was perfect for what we wanted up top in our system. Intelligent movement, an excellent first touch and when chances came his way, he was a really good finisher. What more can you want from your centre-forward? Had he decided to take his career in a different direction, I'm sure Don could have made a decent living as a professional golfer. We often used to pair up together in Pro-Celebrity charity events and also represented Rangers in the annual competition between London's football clubs. I was off single-figures in those days, Don would have been close to scratch and we had some great days out. I remember on one occasion we played with Manuel Pinero, the Spaniard who won nine titles on the European Tour, and his face was an absolute picture on the first tee when Don smashed a drive 40 yards past his!

I guess the only one of that '75-76 team that I haven't really talked about is Stan Bowles. I'm going to be gushing about his ability, of course I am, but I might also explode a few myths about him. I can only speak as I find and although it suited the media to label him as this wayward genius whose life was out of control because of his gambling habits, that's not how I like to remember him.

I'd heard a lot about Stan before I arrived at Loftus Road. His reputation went before him, on and off the field, and I was keen to see for myself. What I found didn't match that reputation at all. He was a really pleasant lad, quiet most of the time and if anything, he seemed a bit introvert. There had to be a bit more to it than met the eye. Only a strong character with great belief in their own ability could achieve what he did in taking over the No. 10 shirt previously filled by Rangers' legend Rodney Marsh. He didn't just fit that shirt - he arguably performed over time even better than Marsh.

Stanley, as I always preferred to call him, had flitted around from Manchester City, Bury, Crewe and Carlisle and somewhere down the line, he needed to settle down and make use of his rare talent. You wouldn't really have backed him to do that in London, with all the easy distractions, but he found a spiritual home at Loftus Road. I got to know Stan well because during the five-months period when I lived in the Kensington Hilton, while Margaret and the children were still back in Nottingham, he and Don Shanks used to join me for dinner at least once a week. He was brilliant company. He liked a laugh and was always up for a bit of mischief but there was never anything malicious about him. Although some like to say his life revolved around gambling, that wasn't the case in my experience. There was at lot more to him than that. Maybe that was being naïve on my part but having established early on that I wasn't the slightest bit interested in gambling, the subject very seldom cropped up in our conversations.

Clearly his 'habit' did get him into more than a few scrapes and they were the source of a lot of amusement for the players. I'm told he mixed with some very dodgy characters, particularly around the White City dog scene, and although he was partial to a game of cards it was the dogs that cost him most of his hard-earned cash. There always seemed to be someone chasing him for money and as I understand it, before I arrived the club came up with a scheme to try and protect him from himself. Stan had a wife and daughter back in Manchester and apparently a percentage of his wages every week was paid directly to them. The rest used to be handed out to Stan in dribs and drabs, as what the players called his "pocket-money".

He was friendly with a jeweller in the West End who was a big Rangers fan and always gave the lads a generous discount if we needed anything. One day, as I arrived for a match, the chap was standing outside the Players' Entrance and when I passed the time of day he said he was waiting for Stan because he owed him money. Just at that moment Stan appeared and reacted to the polite approach from the jeweller by pointing towards a group of others and saying: "I owe that lot money as well - you'd better join the queue!"

Frank Clark, the former Nottingham Forest player and manager, told me a great story about when he and Ken Knighton took charge at Leyton Orient and Stan was there as a player, edging towards the end of his career. One morning they had a really hard running session around the perimeter track and Stan, as always, was fully committed to it. When the players went off to get changed afterwards, Frank and Ken were sitting on the wall alongside the tunnel, chewing the cud, when Stan re-appeared. Still in his training kit and carrying his clothes, he raced straight across the pitch, clambered up the fence on the far side and disappeared. They looked at each other, totally bewildered, then went to the dressing rooms to investigate. "Don't worry about that," they were told. "There are two 'heavies' waiting in reception to collect a gambling debt and he wasn't keen to speak to them!"

Incidents like this were not an everyday occurrence by any means and I guess the art of good management was to balance that off against what Stan could give us on the football front. From what I could see, Dave Sexton handled it brilliantly - and so too did Jim Gregory. The chairman loved Stan and it was not difficult to see why. The main thing was that his crowd-pleasing antics kept people coming back for more and if 'Slippery Jim' had to bail him out from time to time when debts were getting out of control, it was worth it. We strongly suspected what was going on but none of us minded.

The only question that really needed to be asked was: How is Stan's habit affecting the dressing room and the performances of the team? I can tell you without hesitation that it didn't affect us at all. In fact, that's not strictly true. There was one occasion I remember it getting in the way. We had a landline telephone in the dressing room and

Stan was already on it as we filed in at half time during a game. He was desperate to find out how his punt in the 3.15 at Kempton Park, or wherever, had performed. I can still picture the scene now. We were all sitting in our places, relaxing with a cup of tea, and Dave waited very patiently for Stan to finish his call before starting his team-talk!

Joe Mercer came up with a fantastic quote when he picked Stan to play for England. "He could thread a needle with his left foot," he said, and I wouldn't argue with that. He was the most skilful player I ever played with. His natural ability was second to none and it annoys me when people go on about him not fulfilling his potential because while I worked with him, he was a very committed professional footballer. He was a brilliant trainer and come Saturday, you could never accuse him of not performing. He played the game professionally for 17 years and scored 97 goals in his seven years at Loftus Road. It was a privilege to play alongside him.

Once he got out on the football pitch, he came alive. I reckon his brain was 'wired-up' differently to most of us and I mean that as a compliment. He understood he had a special gift that enabled him to do things out of the ordinary yet he never performed his tricks at the expense of the team. He worked as hard as anyone on the pitch. Winning always mattered to him and if he could do that and have a laugh along the way, that was perfection in his eyes. Stan's mischievous streak often came through and I'm sure most of you will have seen the iconic picture of him and 'Shanksy', standing by the near-post reading a copy of the match programme as we're about to take a corner. That was so typical. You never quite knew what was coming next.

Our matches against Chelsea were always a bit feisty and on one occasion, it had all 'kicked off'. I can't remember what had caused it but virtually every player had piled in and punches were being thrown. Not Stan, though. He stayed well out of it. I burst out laughing when I turned round and saw him sitting on the ball, patiently waiting for it all to die down.

His poise and balance was superb and no matter how little space

The irrepressible Stan Bowles ...
the most skillful player I ever played alongside.

he had to work in, he'd find a way. It appealed to his sense of fun to target one of the opposition and set out to create 1-v-1 situations as often as possible, so that he could make a mug of them. Big Micky Droy at Chelsea was one who came into that category. Stan made his life a misery whenever we played against them - and he certainly wasn't the only one.

People said he was 'all left foot' and that was understandable. But there was so much more to Stan. He loved it when defenders used to set themselves to cover his left foot. He'd just suddenly switch to his right - and do some damage. On more than one occasion that 'damage' was to fire the ball into the net with his weaker foot.

Incidentally, going back to Stan joining me at the hotel for dinner, I thought at one point that he'd landed me in trouble. 'Shanksy' was often with him and sometimes they were also joined by a chap who was known as Jim 'The One'. I've no idea what his background was but Jim liked people to think he had upper-class breeding and from the way he spoke and the way he dressed, maybe he did have. He always introduced himself as "the personal manager of Stanley Bowles, the famous England footballer". He wasn't, but Stan happily went along with it and Jim used that as his passport to gain entry to just about anywhere he fancied. Anyway, once we had finished our meal at the hotel, I would sign the chitty to cover everyone and the cost was added to my bill, which then went through to the football club. One day, I got a message that Ron Phillips, the Rangers' club secretary, wanted to see me. "I need to talk to you about your expenses," he explained. "They are, shall we say, a bit excessive." I told him that Stan often joined me to eat and he said: "Ah! If Stan's involved, that's different." He could get away with murder at that time.

He could be pretty much unplayable on occasions and he certainly was on the second Saturday of the 1975-76 season when we went to Derby County to take on the reigning champions. We'd followed up that impressive 2-0 win against Liverpool on the opening day with a 1-1 draw at Aston Villa but the trip to the Baseball Ground would be a real test for us. It had to be because we were without our injured central defenders, McLintock and Webb. A couple of youngsters, Ron Abbott and Tony Tagg, were drafted in as replacements but if we were going to get anything out of that game, someone would have to step up. The stage was set for Stanley. We won 5-1, he scored a hat-trick and his performance was world-class. Incidentally, a little 'small world' story ... Dave Mackay was Derby's manager at that time. Little did we know that a few years down the line, it would become an annual event to see in the New Year at his house, just across the road from where I lived in Burton Joyce!

We'd hardly got to the end of August and the 'secret' was out. Rangers had adopted a brilliant new brand of attractive, attacking football and unless opponents could quickly discover a way to counter it, we were going to be a real force in the First Division. We were undefeated in our first 11 matches and although that run ended at the start of October - 2-1 against Leeds at Elland Road - we bounced straight back by thrashing Everton 5-0.

Throughout much of that period we were sitting proudly on top of the First Division. It was completely foreign territory. QPR had never experienced such dizzy heights in their entire history and although the quality of our football was winning us praise from all parts, it was inevitable, I suppose, that the cynics were saying: "Yes, but ..." We only had a squad of 16 players and if any of those picked up long-term injuries, Rangers didn't have the resources to bring in quality replacements. Add in the fact that none of us, apart from McLintock and Webb, really understood what was involved in chasing top honours in the English game and it was easy to argue a case that it wouldn't last.

We handed the cynics a load of ammunition over the New Year period when we lost four times in six matches - against Liverpool, Arsenal, Manchester United and West Ham - but rather than fade away, we came back so strongly that I think we surprised even ourselves.

A 2-0 win at Aston Villa on the final day of January, when we played particularly well, proved to be a turning-point. It sparked off a run of five straight League wins and it was also the start of an astonishing run that took us right through to the end of the season. From the trip to Villa Park onwards, we won 13 of our last 15 games. And it wasn't just results that were impressive, it was the sparkling way in which we achieved them. Over the years I played in a number of very capable teams who oozed confidence but nothing to compare with that three-months spell. It was something else. It was the ultimate situation for a professional footballer. We had total faith in each other and the next game couldn't come around quickly enough.

We managed to keep our key men fit - that was crucial - and come the end of January we had nothing to distract us. Our interest in the cup competitions was at an end and although I was disappointed because I fancied our chances of lifting one of the trophies, it was probably a blessing in the circumstances.

I was among the scorers when we launched our League Cup campaign with a 4-1 win at Shrewsbury and I had an interesting re-union that night. Richie Barker was assistant to Shrewsbury boss Alan Durban - the same Richie Barker who had tried so hard to hit me during a Notts County training session when I refused to pass to him because I said he "couldn't play". Fortunately, time is a great healer and if he carried a grudge he didn't let it show. I was delighted that he made the effort to come and find me after the game and we had a good laugh about it.

I was also on target in the second round as we won a replay 3-0 against Charlton at the Valley. I couldn't escape the feeling that life had turned full circle. Away to Charlton in the League Cup was the fixture when I made my senior debut for Middlesbrough as a naïve 17-year-old. Our League Cup hopes ended when we went down 3-1 against Newcastle United at the next hurdle - the only time we lost at home all season - and by way of coincidence, it was also Newcastle that knocked us out of the FA Cup. They held us to a goalless draw at Loftus Road and although I scored in the replay, we ended up losing 2-1.

Talking about coincidences, you couldn't make it up. The only two matches that Rangers failed to win during our 15-game surge towards the title were against the teams managed by Jimmy Sirrel and John Bond! Jimmy had taken on mission impossible four months before we went to play Sheffield United. They were so far adrift at the bottom when he took over that there was already very little chance of turning things around but they had enough about them in February to frustrate us and earn a goalless draw. That was a blow - but surely to drop one point would not be the end of the world? Far more costly was the 3-2 defeat we suffered against Bond's Norwich City, three games before the end of the season.

From what I can remember, we played to our usual high standards that day but we didn't get the breaks. We were much the better side and scored a couple of good goals but a controversial header from Phil Boyer was decisive. I'm not a great fan of VAR but if the system had been in use that day, I have no doubt that Phil's 'goal' would have been ruled out. I looked it up on YouTube to double-check that my memory was not playing tricks and the reaction of David Coleman, who was doing the commentary, summed it up. "No. Offside," he instinctively said as the ball hit the net, followed by: "Well, he's given it ... I thought he had given offside." Absolutely right, he was offside. It wasn't even a tight call and I can't believe how readily we accepted the decision. Given the same situation today, with so much riding on it, all hell would have been let loose but we just shook our heads and got on with it.

Again, we showed great character in bouncing straight back from that damaging defeat. It was a special moment for McLintock when he scored one of the goals that gave us a 2-1 win over Arsenal and that meant we went into the final game knowing a win at home to Leeds would, at the very least, ask questions of Liverpool. It would put us a point clear at the top but as they had a slightly superior goal-average, a draw from their last game would give them the title. We still had hope but our destiny was not in our own hands. All we could do was beat Leeds - then wait for 10 days to see whether we had done enough.

It was an incredible situation. No way would that be allowed in the modern game and it was a complete nonsense. Liverpool's fixture away to Wolves was postponed because they had players on international duty for Wales. It meant that by the time the game was played, they knew exactly what they needed to do and had loads of time to prepare for it. The pressure wouldn't be off them completely but it would certainly be toned down a long way.

There was a record attendance at Loftus Road for that final game - 35,353 - and the expectation levels were so high you needed to be made of ice not to feel the tension. That especially applied when we began the second half still goalless and Leeds, with Bremner, Hunter, Madeley & Co., were masters at shutting up shop. I'd begun to wonder if we were ever going to find a goal when Dave Thomas scored with a brave header. Then, having sweated for 15 minutes or so as Leeds put us under real pressure, Stanley's exquisite left-peg eased the nerves by making it 2-0. It had a lovely ring to it when the crowd started chanting: "Champions" in the closing stages.

We all knew it was far too early to start celebrating on that scale but whatever happened in 10 days time, no one could take away from us the fact that we would finish the season in the highest position that Rangers had ever achieved - and we'd qualified for Europe. It would be such an honour if we went forward as England's representatives in the European Cup. Regardless, we were already assured of a place in the UEFA Cup.

There's no happy ending to this story from our point of view. We became very aware that neutral football fans all over the country were firmly rooting for us but it wasn't to be. Wolves had all to play for because they needed to beat Liverpool to avoid relegation. They toyed with our emotions by taking the lead but Liverpool scored three times in the final 14 minutes and the title headed off to Anfield.

So near and yet so far and that became a bit of a theme from a personal point of view because it's on my CV that I was a runner-up three times in a very short space of time. The Rangers' 'Player of the Year' function at Hammersmith Odeon was a fantastic night and although Phil Parkes took the award, I was really chuffed about 'pipping' Stan for second place. He was incredibly popular with the fans so for me to pick up more votes than him really meant something.

It had certainly meant something a few weeks earlier when notification came through that I was one of three players nominated for the prestigious PFA 'Player of the Year' Award. I didn't dare tell myself that I had a realistic chance of winning it. We had a QPR table at the plush dinner at The Dorchester, all dressed up in our 'dickie' bows, and I was blown away by all the nice comments I got from people that night. I didn't win. The award went to Pat Jennings and no one would argue with that. In my opinion, the big man from Northern Ireland was the finest goalkeeper of his generation - and there were so many good ones around at that time. Mind you, when you saw the size of his hands it was no surprise that he was so good at catching the ball. His party-trick was to come out and catch crosses one-handed. Amazing!

Was I disappointed to miss out? Of course … but I was absolutely delighted about making the short-list and anyway, I had the considerable compensation of being named that night as QPR's only representative in the PFA First Division 'Team of the Year'. Wow! Can it get any better than to be recognised in that way by your peers? Every First Division club in the country had an outstanding central midfield player and when the votes were cast, they reckoned I'd performed better than any of them that season. Just two years earlier, I'd been selected in the Second Division 'Team of the Year'. I'd come a long way.

For reference, the First Division team came out - in a 4-3-3 formation - like this:

Jennings was in goal and the back four was Paul Madeley (Leeds), Roy McFarland and Colin Todd (Derby County) and Kevin Beattie (Ipswich). Kevin Keegan and Alan Hudson were my midfield partners and up front were Duncan McKenzie, John Toshack and Dennis Tueart.

As soon as our League season was over, the club treated us to a five-day trip to Tel Aviv. I don't remember it as a 'boozy' affair - we didn't have anything to celebrate with the Liverpool result still pending - but it was a memorable experience, which included fascinating visits to Jerusalem and Bethlehem. Just before we were due to return home, Dave Sexton suddenly called all the players together and said: "I have an announcement to make. Don Masson has been named in the Scotland squad for the Home Internationals against England, Wales and Northern Ireland."

I don't think of myself as a particularly emotional person but I had to make a sharp exit to the toilet. I struggled to hold it together. I'd never given up hope that one day I'd get the call and when it finally arrived, three months short of my 30th birthday, it was the ultimate. Frank McLintock, bless him, followed me into the toilet because he could see what the news had done to me. He just wanted to check I was alright and offer his congratulations. I really appreciated it. He knew exactly how I felt.

I'd really 'put my lot in' for Rangers that season. I'd played in all 42 League games, plus our six cup games, and could have done with a rest before taking on our European challenge. But there was still work to be done before I could think about a summer break and I was so excited at the prospect.

Dave Sexton didn't say much but his words were well chosen. He thanked me for all I had done for him in the 18-months since I'd arrived from Notts County and said that the Scotland call was my just desserts. That was typical Dave. He'd tipped me off before the Leeds game that Scotland boss Willie Ormond was coming to watch me - and the Leeds winger Eddie Gray - and my instant reaction was to think: "Not before time!"

I'm saying that because back in 1973, when I was doing well with Notts County, Jimmy Sirrel told me he'd recommended me to Ormond with a view to me being included in the 1974 World Cup squad. Apparently he'd instantly rejected the idea, saying that he didn't pick Second Division players. To the best of my knowledge, he didn't even send anyone to look at me. That was unfortunate. I've always argued that I never played any better for QPR than I did for Notts County. Now I had the chance to prove a point and although there were no guarantees that I'd get picked to play in the internationals, I was determined to justify the call.

It was hard on Margaret and the kids. I got back to Crowthorne from Tel Aviv on the Friday and when I read my letter from the Scottish FA, it said I had to report to Glasgow at 10am the following Monday. I booked myself onto the overnight 'sleeper' from Euston. That was an interesting new experience. I'd never done that before but at that particular stage, my entire way of life appeared to be full of new experiences.

12
BECOMING AN 'OVERNIGHT' SENSATION
(1976)

Strange as it may seem, the first time I ever set foot in Glasgow was in May 1976, when I arrived to make my international debut at Hampden Park.

We had left my birthplace in Banchory when I was only 12 years old to begin a new life in Middlesbrough and although we did occasionally go back to the Highlands to visit relatives, Glasgow for me was just a place on the map. Don't have any doubts about my allegiances, though. I was Scottish to the core and I'd dreamed all my life of pulling on that dark blue shirt. Now, hopefully, I was only a few days away from achieving that ambition. I was counting down the hours.

Just the thought of 'landing' in Glasgow was amazing. Under different circumstances, it would have been a fantastic experience all on its own but I somehow had to clear my head and concentrate on the things that mattered.

Apart from the letter from the Scottish FA telling me I had to report to Grand Central Hotel at 10am on the Monday, I had very little information. I did know that we were playing Wales on the Thursday, Northern Ireland on the Saturday and England the following Saturday. I also knew that all three games would be played at Hampden because, although we should have been away to Northern

Ireland, the game had been switched due to the 'Troubles'.

What I didn't know was that we were going to be allowed to go home for a few days after the Northern Ireland fixture. Consequently, I went equipped to stay for a fortnight! The overnight 'sleeper' from London to Glasgow was an interesting experience. Not a lot of sleeping was done, my mind was too focused on other matters, and it was the weirdest thing when we arrived at the other end. I don't know if they still do it these days with the 'sleeper' but for some reason, although we pulled into Glasgow Central around 5am, they wouldn't allow us to get off the train for at least an hour.

So this was Glasgow! I possibly saw it at its best - a beautiful sunny morning and very few people about. I desperately wanted to go and investigate the city, see some sights and soak up some atmosphere, but two things stood in the way. One was that I couldn't bear the thought of getting lost and arriving late at the hotel. The other was my full-to-the-brim suitcase.

The Grand Central Hotel was literally just around the corner from the station so it meant that I arrived with at least two hours to spare. There's nothing like looking keen. I surprised myself with how nervous I was. That type of thing never normally bothered me too much but I was about to team up with international stars. I was really anxious about meeting them. Would they be prepared to welcome me as one of them?

The Scotland boss Willie Ormond had stayed at the hotel overnight so he was the first person I met when he came down for breakfast. I'd never met him before but he seemed a very shy man who didn't particularly enjoy one-to-one contact. He kept himself to himself. I instinctively felt he wasn't a very good communicator and nothing happened in the months ahead to make me change my mind.

One by one the lads turned up and I needn't have worried. Once a gang of footballers get together, the banter is pretty much the same the world over. Some I vaguely knew because I'd played against the likes of Archie Gemmill, Bruce Rioch and Willie Donachie but most

I'd never met before. I do remember thinking that although we'd been drawn together from all parts, we shared a common goal ... to represent our country with distinction.

A coach took us to our hotel at Seamill, a quiet village on the West Coast, about 10 miles south of Largs, and we spent the rest of the day relaxing. For me, it was all about getting to know my new colleagues and forming relationships. If I was about to go 'to war' with these lads in a few days, it was really important to discover what made them tick. One relationship I formed very easily was with Willie Johnston. We found ourselves 'rooming' together and we instantly clicked.

The Scottish FA had a very nice facility at Largs, so we travelled up to work there on the Tuesday and that's when I got my first firm hint that I'd be making my debut against Wales. The boss said that he wanted me to take all the free kicks and corners. Why would he say that if I wasn't going to play? Even so, nothing more was said to me when we finished training and I think Archie Gemmill, who was our captain, could sense I was feeling a bit frustrated.

He took us all down to the one pub in the village that afternoon. Absolutely no alcohol but lots of laughs and it was a really good bonding session. I'm not sure that Archie actually knew what the team would be to play against Wales but he pulled me aside at one point and said: "If you play on Thursday, just do what you normally do with QPR and you'll be fine." I really appreciated that. Nothing too profound but I just needed someone to say something.

I tried to push it to the back of my mind but the Wednesday was also a big day for me. Liverpool were playing at Wolves that evening so I was about to discover whether QPR would be crowned Football League champions. It was very difficult for me keep up to speed with what was happening at Molineux because the Scotland squad all went to Ibrox that evening to watch Rangers play Dundee. I knew the QPR lads were going to the BBC Studios to watch the Liverpool game live but of course, there were no mobile phones in those days to help me keep in touch.

One of the Scotland backroom staff tapped me on the shoulder at Ibrox to say that he'd heard Wolves had just taken the lead. The next thing I heard was that Liverpool had scored three times in the last 14 minutes and won 3-1.

Football can be a really cruel game. Just one more point might have made all the difference and at that moment, when I heard the result, I really wanted to be with my QPR team-mates to share my feelings with them. Of course tomorrow would be another day. In my case, it might well be the day when I made my international debut. But you have to get so much right over the course of nine months to win the League Championship. Somehow, I just knew that we could never repeat or improve on what we'd achieved in the 1975-76 season.

The magic words were spoken as soon as we arrived on the training ground for a light session on the Thursday morning. "The team tonight will be ...." I'd been given the No. 8 shirt. Fantastic. I was so proud and excited. I haven't got a clue how to describe my exact feelings at that moment but whatever they were, I'll never forget the sense of fulfilment. Big dreams don't very often come true. I'd done it the hard way. It's true that my first League games were in the Second Division for Middlesbrough but since then, I'd worked my way up from the Fourth Division with Notts County. I'd never had a sniff of international honours before at schoolboy, youth or under-23 levels so I really was entering a different world. I knew I would need to call on all my considerable experience to help me cope with the mental and physical challenge.

The big story was not about me. I hardly got a mention in the national newspapers because the only thing that mattered was that Kenny Dalglish had been named as substitute. In fairness, it was a major shock because he was set to equal the Scotland record of 34 consecutive appearances, held by Fifties legend George Young. The players were just as shocked as anyone else that Kenny had not been picked and as far as I know, no official explanation was ever given. All sorts of conspiracy theories were being bandied about, including

Finally, my dream came true. I have my very own Scotland shirt.

the suggestion that the manager had been put under pressure to protect Young's record. Had Kenny gone on as substitute, of course, he would still have equalled the record. He didn't. All very interesting and intriguing but I had other things to concern me.

Concentrate, concentrate - that's what I kept telling myself as the team-coach made it's way through the streets to Hampden. It wasn't easy because there was so much going on and the first people I noticed as we pulled up outside the ground were my mum and dad. I had no idea that they were coming and it meant the world to me! Apparently they'd been waiting there for hours. Why was I not surprised? Dad was obsessional about being early for every appointment he ever had and that's a trait he passed on to me. I have a lot of pet hates and being late is right at the top of the list.

Jimmy and Cathy Sirrel were there as well. How good was that? I'd had hardly any contact with Jimmy for a couple of years but he didn't need to tell me how proud my selection for Scotland had made him feel. In many respects, I was his life's work. I had to play well against Wales. I couldn't let him down.

There were loads of telegrams (they still had them in those days) waiting for me when I got into the dressing room. I scooped them up and took them with me as I went up the tunnel and out onto the pitch. I couldn't wait to take in the scene and it was all that I'd hoped for. It was fantastic that so many people - like my good friend Arthur Mann - had taken the trouble to send me a telegram and the one I remember most was from the headmaster at Banchory Academy.

Ah, the bagpipes. Maybe I had been away from Scotland for a long time but it was still sweet music to my ears as we assembled before kick-off and although you'd never want to hear me sing, I gave it all I'd got when it came to Flower of Scotland. I was sticking to the promise I'd made myself. I was going to savour every moment because you never know what the future might bring.

For the record, our team that day was Alan Rough in goal, a back-four of Danny McGrain, Tom Forsyth, Colin Jackson and

Willie Donachie, Bruce Rioch and Archie Gemmill alongside me in midfield and a front three of Willie Pettigrew, Joe Jordan and Eddie Gray.

We won the game and it was fairly comfortable. Pettigrew put us ahead with a well-taken goal and then a minute before the interval, I made my first meaningful contribution at that level. I floated over a free kick from the right and Rioch timed his run well to score with a header. I ought to have made another important contribution soon after half time but hit the bar when I really should have scored. I was furious! Ninety-nine times out of 100 I would have hit the target and it's typical of me, the obsessive perfectionist, that when I look back on that night the first thing that comes to mind is fluffing a chance. It wasn't too costly because Gray got another for us and although Arfon Griffiths converted a penalty, we won 3-1.

Dad was in his element when I took him and mum into the Players' Lounge afterwards and Jimmy and Cathy also joined us for a drink. I also discovered that my mate Denis Frith had travelled up from London to be at the game and I was annoyed with him for not telling me he was coming, so I could fix him up with tickets as well. Denis was a steward at Queens Park Rangers and was one of the first people I met when I turned up at Loftus Road to sign. He was told to look after me that day - and he pretty much did so for the whole of my time in London. People used to jokingly refer to him as my 'minder' and I suppose he was really. He's a huge presence - no one would ever argue with him - and we just struck up an instant friendship that has lasted ever since. He and a mate had left work early to travel up on the train to Glasgow and he somehow 'blagged' his way into the ground. He said he planned to come back again the following week for the England game. Great effort - and that time I did organise tickets for him.

I didn't think it was a sparkling performance against Wales but we did ok - and no one could say that we didn't deserve to launch our programme for the Home Internationals with a win. Ormond seemed pleased enough. When I saw him being interviewed he said: "Our midfield of Rioch, Masson and Gemmill is one of the best in the business and I think we will go from strength to strength." I was desperate to say to him: "If I was that bloody good, why didn't you pick me earlier?" I resisted. That wouldn't have been a good idea.

There was a quick turnaround for the Northern Ireland game, back at Hampden just two days later, and the boss made a change that came as no great surprise to anyone. Kenny Dalglish was back in the starting line-up and throughout my time as a Scotland player, his name - quite rightly - will have always been first on the team-sheet. He was 25-years-old at the time. For most players, you'd say he was heading towards his prime but Kenny was just scratching the surface. He was the darling of Celtic, still a year away from switching to Liverpool as Kevin Keegan's replacement. Obviously I knew all about his reputation but because he was operating north of the border I hadn't actually seen all that much of him as a player.

First impressions? Yep. I had no problems whatsoever seeing what they were raving about. You couldn't fail to be impressed and what struck me immediately was the quality of his first-touch - not just occasionally but every time. He was a top-notch finisher and I could see strong similarities between him and Stan Bowles. When it came to shielding the ball and holding people off, Kenny was a different class. I really admired the way he dealt with his fame. Everyone wanted a piece of him, which must have been incredibly demanding, but he had a way of being warm and friendly yet keeping people at arm's length. We played golf together on several occasions when we were on Scotland duty and I always enjoyed his company. Not everyone got to experience it but he had a brilliant sense of humour.

Within minutes of watching him work for the first time at close quarters I recognised that here was a special player who could make me look good. And if our midfield department continued to function as well as the boss seemed to think we did against Wales, we'd give him a platform to showcase his skills and maybe even lead us to success.

Kenny came in to replace Eddie Gray and after Archie had given us the lead midway through the first half, I celebrated my first international goal early in the second period. Kenny rolled the ball to me a couple of yards outside the area and a first-time shot with the outside of my right foot found the bottom corner.

Not that I remember it in great detail! You never forget your first goal for your country and the fact that I'd beaten the great Pat Jennings to claim it made the whole experience all the more memorable. That would teach him to pip me for the 'Footballer of the Year' award. The game finished 3-0 and I also played my part in a really well worked third goal. After tricking my way past two players I aimed a pass at Bruce Rioch who'd made a good run into the box. He cleverly allowed the ball to run past him and Kenny was left with only the 'keeper to beat.

Incidentally, I can't move on without mentioning a moment in that match which was to have a huge impact on my life. Rioch missed a penalty - he struck a post - right at the start of the second period and the following week the boss asked for volunteers to take on the job because Bruce didn't want the responsibility any more. It all went quiet as everyone looked at the floor. Someone had to do it and although I wasn't desperately keen, in the end I said I would.

Anyway, I was really happy with life. I thought I'd played a lot better against Ireland than in the opening fixture and overall things couldn't have gone much better. Two wins out of two, and I'd scored one goal and made two others. Now our focus was totally on England.

Once I'd discovered we were being allowed home for a couple of days I booked myself onto the 'sleeper' back to London on the Saturday night. The problem was that having arrived at the crack of dawn at Euston, there was no way I could get back to Crowthorne. The only viable option was to get a taxi and that cost a fortune. In those days, we had to submit our expenses to the Scottish FA after matches. I cringed at the thought of how they might react when mine arrived but I didn't feel I had any alternative.

It was only a brief visit home, just long enough to re-introduce myself to Margaret and the kids, and we really enjoyed our time together. We had plenty to talk about. Monday night, I was on the 'sleeper' back to Glasgow. Talk about London buses. I'd never been on the overnight train, but now I was tucking myself into bed on one for the third time in a week.

The whole atmosphere was different when we reported back. This was the game that really mattered and it certainly carried extra significance from a personal point of view. It was a really big story back in London that I would be going head-to-head with my club-mate Gerry Francis, the England captain. The newspapers were full of it and although I tried to steer clear of all the hype, it was impossible to do that. Victory, of course, would make us the Home International champions and that was the main target. But I was very aware of the importance of the bragging rights as well. Gerry had been 'in my ear' for much of the past year, constantly chirping away about how he'd played the starring role when England crushed Scotland 5-1 at Wembley. I couldn't take another 12 months of that.

The atmosphere at Hampden on the Saturday was something else. The crowd that day was 85,157 and I'd never known noise like it. You could feel the passion and intensity coming at you in waves. Games against England just meant so much to the Scottish fans. The responsibility for sending them home happy really did weigh heavily and you needed to be a strong character not to crumble under it. I must confess that more than once that day, I asked myself why on earth I'd raised my hand when the boss called for a volunteer to take the penalties.

Gerry and I steered well clear of each other before the start. No welcomes, no handshakes, no knowing looks, and although we regularly came into contact during the course of the game you wouldn't even have thought we knew one another. We went about our work in a totally professional manner but as soon as the final whistle went, he was the first player I went to. We gave each other a big hug and normal service was resumed.

Mick Channon put down an early marker when he headed England in front after 11 minutes but we pulled level seven minutes later with the goal from the most unlikely of sources. I scored with a header! Even in my wildest dreams I never thought that could be possible. I'd like to tell you that I often scored goals with my head but anyone with the slightest knowledge of football in that generation knows it wouldn't be true.

We'd actually had a corner on the left-hand side a couple of minutes earlier and big Joe Jordan headed against the bar when I picked him out. For some reason, second time around, I left it to Eddie Gray to take the flag-kick. I can't really tell you why I took up the position that I did. At QPR, if I wasn't taking the corner myself, I'd normally lurk on the edge of the area, hoping to latch onto a half-clearance. This time, a space opened up some 10 yards ahead of that and I decided to fill it.

Joe was again the target, as he always was from set-pieces, and when he failed to make contact I ran in unmarked behind him and - my version - the bullet-like header was unstoppable! I can still see Ray Clemence now, waving his arms around in frustration and screaming: "How the hell can we let him score with a header?" I can tell you that it doesn't get a lot better in life than scoring against England at Hampden Park.

Clemence was a terrific goalkeeper, up-there with Jennings and Peter Shilton as the best of that era. He struggled, though, on that particular day and our winner from Dalglish five minutes after the break was probably the worst goal he ever conceded. Kenny made space for himself to the right of goal but I think he actually scuffed his shot. Maybe that's what fooled Clemence but either way, he allowed it to sneak through his legs and over the line. The game finished 2-1 and it was mission accomplished for us ... we'd won the Home International Championships for the first time since 1967.

Here's another of those little small-world stories. Many years later, when I was on holiday in Australia with my second wife Brenda,

Don Masson heads Scotland's first goal during the match against England at Hampden Park.

standing in reception as we entered our hotel in Cairns was Ray Clemence. We didn't have time for a chat. He was just about to board a mini-bus and head off - but there was instant communication. All I had to do was bend forward and look through my legs! He took it in good spirit and we parted with a laugh.

I'd packed so much into 12 days since walking apprehensively into The Grand Central Hotel for the first time and it had been a fantastic experience. It was 'Boy's Own' stuff and I desperately wanted more of it.

I'd not long arrived back in Crowthorne when I got a call from a man called Reg Hayter. I had no idea who he was but when I started making inquiries, I discovered he was something of a legend in Fleet Street circles. He'd built up a formidable media agency, specialising in sport, and was in the process of spreading his wings. Agents didn't exist in those days but Reg had spotted an opportunity. He wanted to make me a business proposition and we agreed to meet.

Reg persuaded me that I was an overnight sensation and I wouldn't be able to cope with all the demands and requests that would come my way. He and his staff could handle them for me. I wasn't at all convinced that my popularity rating was going to zoom through the roof on the basis of the previous couple of weeks but we agreed to give it a go. He was right, I was wrong.

Sack loads of requests started arriving - mainly from Scotland - for autographs etc and people wanted to meet and offer me deals. I couldn't have coped with it all - nor would I have wanted to - but Reg delegated a couple of staff to look after my affairs and it worked out well. He did a good job for me. He already had a similar arrangement with Bob Wilson, the Arsenal goalkeeper, and as a model for a player's agent going forward, I thought it was ideal.

Quite apart from all the practical help, he got me a lucrative boot deal with Mitre. Their rep came to see me the week after the internationals and agreed to pay me £1,000 a year to wear their boots. That was a lot of money in those days - and there was the chance of bonus payments as well. I got £100 every time I wore their boots in internationals and I think there was also a bonus for live televised matches. If I'm absolutely truthful, I'd always worn adidas and I didn't think the Mitre boots were as good. Occasionally, I still wore adidas but I have to say that the Mitre people couldn't do enough for me. Bearing in mind that I always wore 'rubbers', that presented them with an extra challenge because they didn't produce many of that type. They made them especially for me and I went to their factory in Huddersfield during the close-season for a fitting. They already had the Manchester United pair of Stuart Pearson and Gordon Hill on their books so I was in good company.

It was incredible to think that my performances in three matches could make such a difference. That brief period changed my life to such an extent that as part of what the Hayters people did for me, I even had my own Fan Club. It was crazy. They organised for me to attend various functions - sometimes with Bob Wilson - to open events or present prizes and we were very well paid for doing so. I'd never been comfortable being in the limelight and because I'd always opted out at every opportunity, I was frequently accused of being aloof. That didn't bother me too much. The truth of it was that I just wasn't comfortable meeting strangers and sharing "small talk" but things had changed dramatically.

I think the new take on life was good for me as a person. I could see that if I didn't embrace the fact that more people were recognising me in the street and wanting to pass the time of day, I would have been swept under. There was no going back. Life was different and I had to accept that, and get on with it.

The one thing at that time that was really bothering me was that Margaret and the kids were being neglected. They understood that it wasn't a deliberate thing. I just wasn't able to devote more time to them with so much going on. I was determined to try and make it up to them during the summer period but by the time I'd returned from Scotland, there was less than a month to go before I had to report back for pre-season training. I had to organise something quickly ...I desperately needed a holiday.

Gerry Francis had a couple of mobile homes in the South of France and offered to let me have one for a week. Great! That was just what we needed - at least I thought so at the time. We packed the kids into the back of our yellow Triumph Dolomite, and off we went. The Dolomite was very fashionable at the time. No disgrace in being seen in one of those - despite the colour! But it was hardly ideal for driving the length of France with four people on board and it took us two days to get there. Consequently, it also took us two days to get back - so there wasn't a lot of holiday time in the middle.

At least we were able to be together again and share some lovely experiences that have regularly raised a laugh over the years. It also enabled me to clear my head and get ready for exciting new challenges.

It's smiles all round and with very good reason. The Queens Park Rangers squad who enjoyed the club's best-ever season in 1975-76.

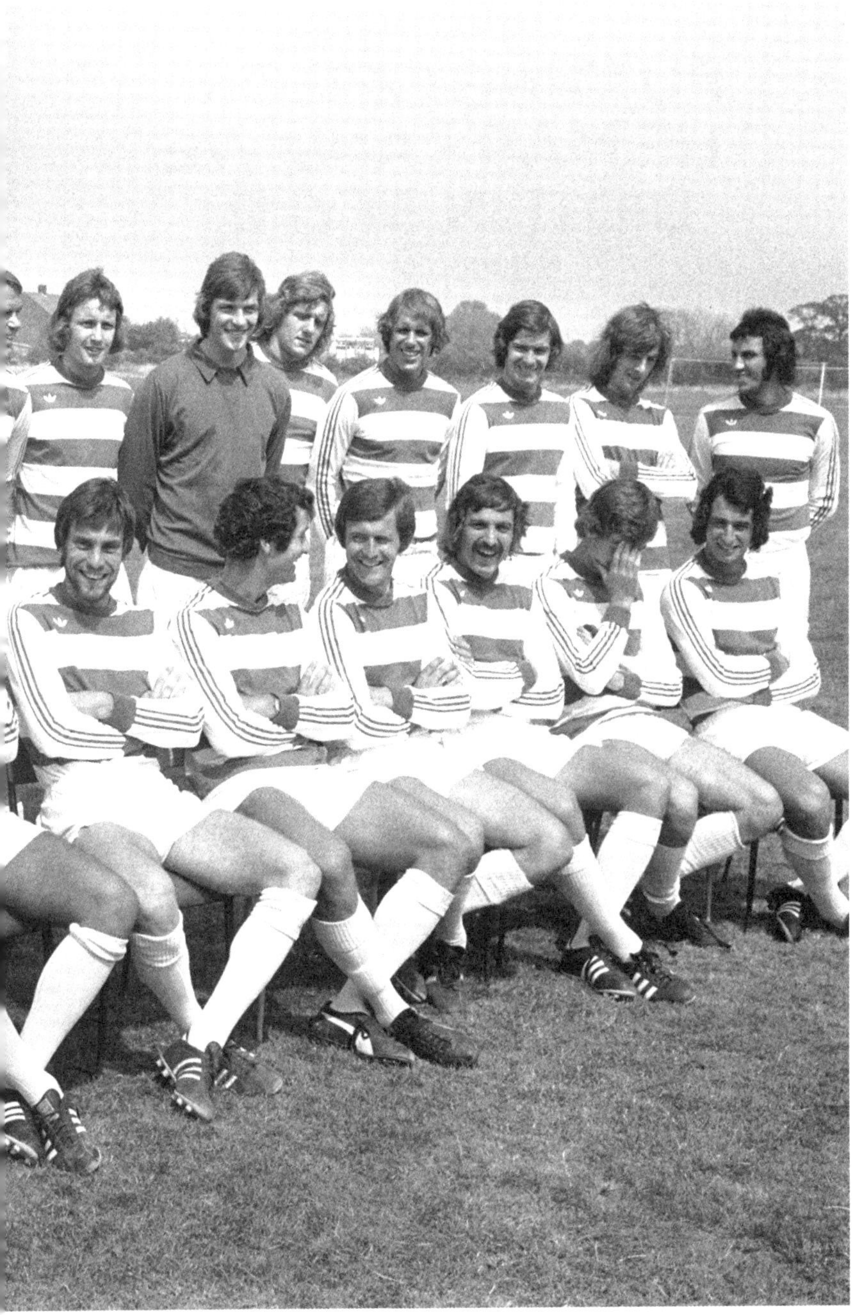

13
PUTTING QPR ON THE MAP – AND WE DID IT IN STYLE
(1976-77)

Bloody penalties! Every chapter of my life seems to reach a point where a spot-kick plays a prominent role in deciding my direction of travel. The 1976-77 season was no exception. This time, Queens Park Rangers lost a penalty shoot-out in the UEFA Cup and we were eliminated at the quarter-final stage.

You could say we had only ourselves to blame for getting backed into a corner by AEK Athens - and you would be right. We easily beat them 3-0 at Loftus Road in the first leg and at least the penalty theme was positive on that occasion because Gerry Francis converted two in the first 11 minutes. We dominated the game and were annoyed that we didn't win more convincingly. Even so, we'd seen nothing from the Greeks to suggest they were capable of coming back from that. All we had to do in the return was score and they'd need five goals to beat us. They'd never achieve that.

But three things happened to undermine our position of strength. The first was that we boarded the flight to Athens without three England internationals - Francis, Dave Clement and Dave Thomas. Secondly, we didn't manage to score a goal and the third was that AEK confirmed what we'd already discovered from previous rounds. The continentals were a totally different proposition when you played them on their own patch.

They did stage a comeback. They beat us 3-0 and when extra

time couldn't settle it, we were into the dreaded penalties. A couple of minutes before the end of extra time AEK pulled off a masterstroke. They changed their goalkeeper because they felt the substitute was better at dealing with penalties and it proved to be a match-winning move. Frank McLintock led from the front, as always, and tucked away our first penalty. So did I when I went second, but Peter Eastoe's effort was then saved. The contest went on - and on. AEK converted their first six kicks and it reached the stage where we were trailing 6-5. David Webb would have to score to keep it going. I'm the last person to criticise anyone for missing a penalty. It happens. 'Webby' wasn't in our team to score penalties and although he was upset, there were no recriminations from us. It was a collective thing. We shouldn't have allowed ourselves to get into that situation.

It meant, though, that the European adventure was over and we were bitterly disappointed.

We'd fancied our chances of going all the way. There were some very strong clubs in the competition - the likes of Barcelona, Juventus, Athletic Bilbao and Manchester United - but we felt from the outset that the style of play Dave Sexton had developed made us well-equipped to take on the best. Above all, we were keen to enjoy ourselves, put Queens Park Rangers well and truly onto the European football map and give the travelling fans good reason to be proud of us.

Stan Bowles never needed a second invitation to enjoy himself and he took SK Braun to the proverbial cleaners in our first round tie. Based in Bergen, Norway's second-largest city that sits on the country's west coast, SK had no idea how to contain him. Stan scored a hat-trick in the home leg. I got the other one in a 4-0 success and he was our three-goal star again in the return, when we trounced them 7-0. In all, Stan scored 11 goals in the course of our eight-game UEFA campaign and he was in his element, showcasing his skills across Europe.

Next up we were drawn against Slovan Bratislava and it was another of those incredible 'small world' stories. I'd never been to Czechoslovakia before, nor had I visited a communist country. Suddenly I found myself going there twice to play in the space of a week.

The draw for the qualifying stages of the 1978 World Cup had placed Scotland in a three-team group with Czechoslovakia and Wales. Only the winners would go through and as Czechoslovakia had won the European Championships two years earlier, they were clear favourites. They certainly were when they began the campaign by beating us 2-0 in Prague. We gave a decent account of ourselves but conceded two goals in the space of three minutes straight after half time and overall I think the score was a fair reflection. It wasn't all over by any means. In theory, we'd got the hardest of the group games out of the way but we would have to win all the others if we were going to have a chance of spending the summer of '78 in South America.

Five of the players in Czechoslovakia's starting 11 were from Slovan Bratislava. That was a measure of what we would be up against when I went back there the following week with Rangers. Although we were treated well enough - no complaints on that score - I can't say that I really took to the communist way of life from the little bit I experienced. It was, though, a good life-lesson. It helped me appreciate what we have going for us in this country. Slovan were a decent side with some skilful players but so were we. We drew 3-3 in Bratislava, with Stan getting another couple, and two weeks later it was Don Givens' turn to hog the limelight as his hat-trick inspired us to go through with a 5-2 win in London.

The fans were loving it, QPR on the 'big' stage for the first time in their history, and loads of them fancied the trip when we were drawn against FC Cologne. The Germans were going to be a very different proposition. We were totally aware of that. Their team was sprinkled with top-quality international players and we were about to be tested like never before.

The first leg at Loftus Road couldn't have gone better for us. We won 3-0 with goals from Givens, Webb and Bowles and for me, that ranked as our best display in the competition. Despite that, I still felt very strongly that we had it all to do if we were to reach the quarter-finals. There was sure to be a reaction from the Germans - and eventually there was. It was just what the doctor ordered when I grabbed an early goal in the second leg. Surely with a 4-0 advantage, we would have no problems progressing? Wrong. They absolutely pulverised us and if Phil Parkes had not produced one of the finest displays of his career, we would undoubtedly have been eliminated. Cologne clawed their way back into it with three goals - including two in the second half from star striker Dieter Müller - but the player who really impressed me was Wolfgang Overath. A left-sider who had figured against England in the 1966 World Cup Final, he was quite magnificent. I reckon his performance that night was as complete as I ever saw from a midfield player. In the end, we made it through by virtue of my 'away' goal and it was hugely satisfying to know that the top clubs will have been looking at that result and saying: "Wow! Who are these Queens Park Rangers?"

A big moment for me and for QPR. This goal against FC Cologne in Germany took us to the UEFA Cup quarter-finals.

Incidentally, Dave Sexton told me on the way home that Cologne had made inquiries about signing Givens and me. He quickly added: "Don't get too excited ... we've told them that neither of you is for sale." It was a QPR tradition for several years that we went to the outskirts of Cologne in pre-season to live and work at an excellent facility that was ideal for what we wanted. From what I'd seen of the city it looked really nice. And from what I'd just seen of the likes of Overath and Muller, I would have strongly fancied the idea of working with them. This was still a few years ahead of Kevin Keegan and Tony Woodcock going across to sample life in Germany. They made it work and I'm sure Don and I could have done the same. No point in moaning about it. As I've repeatedly said, the club owned us body and soul and if they said we were not for sale, that was the end of the matter.

Once again with the UEFA Cup there was no happy end to the story as we fell at the next hurdle. Frustrating, devastating ... call it what you like. But we'd done English football proud. The challenge now was to put the experience we'd gained from broadening our football education to the best possible use, and earn the right to do it again. That was going to be a very tough 'ask' because in the League, we'd failed fairly miserably in our attempts to pick up where we left off the previous season. I cannot say that came as any surprise. To give ourselves a realistic chance of improving on our exceptional performance in 1975-76 we would have needed to bring in three or four internationals during the summer. As it happened, we didn't make a single signing of any substance and to compound the situation, we lost the services of one of our most influential players.

It actually couldn't have been worse. I had no idea about the politics behind the scenes, that was none of my business, but we were all surprised and disappointed that no attempts seem to have been made to strengthen the squad. We'd managed to get away with operating on a 16-man first-team squad the previous year but no way could that happen again - especially with the extra demands that playing in Europe would bring. Ours was not to reason why!

It seemed as if I'd hardly arrived back from our family break in the South of France when I was packing my bags again and heading off to Germany to the two-week pre-season training camp. I loved it. It was certainly no holiday but as they say, a change is as good as a rest. From memory, we played three games while we were there - against Essen, Munster and Borussia Monchengladbach - and won the lot without conceding a goal.

I'd learned over the years that it was always a bad thing to read too much into pre-season results but maybe that sequence of wins influenced the thinking of the powers that be. Maybe they thought they could, after all, get away without investing in new players. If so, it very quickly became apparent that it was a mistake.

Gerry Francis developed the back injury that was to have a major impact on the rest of his playing career. He didn't play his first League game of the season until February 12. He was our captain and midfield powerhouse. Losing him for all that time was massive. The creative blend between Francis, Bowles, Hollins and me was crucial to the scintillating style we'd adopted at Rangers and without Gerry, we struggled to fire on all cylinders. Don't get me wrong. Most of the time we did okay but compared to the previous season, that little bit extra was missing.

Talk about a reality check. With no Francis or Webb in the side, we were embarrassingly thumped 4-0 at home by Everton on the opening day of the season. If I'd been the superstitious type I could have explained it away by saying it was because I wasn't wearing my No. 9 shirt. I'd got used to that the previous year and loved carrying it around on my back. For whatever reason, Dave put me down on the team-sheet to wear No. 5 against Everton. In those days, of course, there were no such things as squad numbers. Outfield players just wore 2-11, normally reflecting the positions they filled. But that wasn't the case for me that season because although I always did the same job, over the course of the campaign I wore numbers 5, 6, 7, 8 and 9. One more and I could have won the Lottery!

We also lost at West Ham two days later, then drew at Ipswich and we were four games in before we notched our first victory of the season, at home to West Brom. I'm sure that having big 'Webby' back in the heart of the defence was a factor in that result and the following week, Dave reacted to the loss of Francis by finally making a signing. Eddie Kelly, who had figured in Arsenal's 'Double' success a few years earlier, arrived to strengthen our midfield. He was an experienced player who had been captain of Arsenal and in theory he was a like-for-like replacement as an attacking midfielder. I didn't envy him though, because he had really big boots to fill. We had worked hard for more than a year with Gerry, in training and matches, to develop an understanding that fitted with our 'Total Football' philosophy. It wasn't realistic to expect Eddie to drop straight into that role. It was going to take time.

He marked his debut by helping us beat Aston Villa in mid-September and the following day, I was back on the overnight train. Scotland had a friendly against Finland at Hampden. I'm not sure how much Willie Ormond will have learned from it because we strolled to a 6-0 win but I suppose there were plusses. It was good to have the group back together again for a couple of days and for me, I was able to justify my fairly reluctant decision when the boss had asked for a volunteer to become our penalty-taker. There was no great pressure involved. We were already two goals up when the spot-kick was awarded and I tucked it away with the minimum of fuss.

Here we go again, back on the 'sleeper' for my return journey and this time it was with a twist. The Scottish FA were not happy about me claiming on my expenses for a taxi to take me from Euston Station to Crowthorne when I got back from the Home Internationals. I was told that in future, I had to use the train for the second leg of my journey. That meant I had to get myself from Euston to Paddington at the crack of dawn, catch a train to Reading and Margaret had to drive up from Crowthorne to get me. What a joke. It added an irritating hour or so onto what was already the best part of an eight-hour journey - all for the sake of a few quid.

From a personal point of view, I was happy enough with the way I was performing - and so was Dave. In fact, he collared me one morning and told me to make myself look respectable (that always mattered to Dave) after training because we were going to see the chairman. Interesting. I had no idea what that was all about but he spelled it out as we made our way to Jim Gregory's business headquarters in Roehampton. He wanted me to have a pay-rise. He thought I should be elevated to the same level as our other senior players.

The meeting didn't take long. Dave stated his case very eloquently and the chairman sat behind his expansive desk, taking it all in. Dave explained that in his opinion, I'd given excellent value in return for the £100,00 fee Rangers had paid to Notts County. I'd played in every game since I signed, had played a prominent part in the club's best-ever season and was now an established international. Once he'd finished, the chairman took a deep breath and didn't mince his words: "No," he said firmly. "That's my answer. There will be no adjustments to the contract Don signed when he joined us. " Then he turned to me and said: "If you don't like it Don, I will play you in the reserves for the next two years until your contract expires."

It was nice to be appreciated. This had all come about on Dave's initiative. I hadn't made any of the running at all but it showed yet again how the club held all the aces. Maybe it was a pity that they didn't fancy selling me to Cologne! I just stood up and said: "Thank you Mr Chairman," and walked out of his office. I also stressed to Dave how grateful I was to him for trying. What went on that day told me a lot about both men.

Matches were coming thick and fast. The UEFA Cup was in full swing by then and we were making good progress in the League Cup, easing our way past Cardiff and Bury in our first two games. It meant we were playing Saturday-Wednesday-Saturday every week and when you add in all the travelling this entailed, there was virtually no time for doing any quality work on the training ground. Nor was there any time for recovering from the minor injuries that are always an occupational hazard for footballers.

At least, though, we were picking up points on a more regular basis and we would have got a terrific win at Manchester City had I not smashed a penalty into orbit. I'm pretty sure that was the first one I ever took for Rangers. I never normally got a look in because Stan and Gerry were 'on' them but neither was playing on that occasion. I could sense the eyes of the other lads all looking in my direction when it was awarded. There were 40,751 people at Maine Road that day and I provided them with their highlight. No one seems to remember that Dennis Tueart also missed a penalty in that game. It's totally random, I know, and I cannot start to explain why but a brilliant picture of me missing that penalty appeared on the cover of a single by Phil Collins' band, Genesis. No one ever contacted me or tried to tell me how that had come about. Not that they had to, of course, but I would like to have known their thinking.

Incidentally, I'd made arrangements to stay overnight in a central Manchester hotel after that game because the following day, I would be working for Mitre as part of my boot deal with them. I'd fixed up for a night out with Asa Hartford, my Scotland team-mate who was then playing for City. When he turned up to collect me from the hotel, who should be with him but Joe Corrigan - the City goalkeeper whose crossbar I'd just cleared with a good few feet to spare. It was just as well there weren't any national newspaper photographers knocking around as we hit the town. The mind boggles over what they might have made of that. We had a brilliant night - so good, in fact that Asa decided not to try and make it home and made use of the spare bed in my room. The following day, a couple of the other 'Mitre men' - United stars Gordon Hill and Stuart Pearson - picked me up from the hotel and took me to the NEC, where we spent the day working on the Mitre stand at a massive football exhibition.

We had a really rocky patch building up to Christmas and after a run that saw us win just two games out of 11, we were plunging towards relegation trouble. Our cup results were probably creating a false impression. We were briefly back to our old selves when we went

GENESIS
Spot The Pigeon

Match Of The Day
Pigeons
Inside And Out

to West Ham and won 2-0 in the League Cup, thanks to a Bowles tap-in and a brilliant solo effort from Dave Clement, and then managed to beat Arsenal 2-1 to book our place in the semi-finals. Our UEFA Cup hopes were also still intact - so it wasn't all bad.

Actually, it was. We were struggling desperately to find a consistently good level of performance and I'm sure that was influenced by the fact that we had such a heavy workload and such a small squad of players. Back-to-back wins over Tottenham and Everton gave everyone a lift but the biggest boost came when we heard the news that Francis felt ready to return. His troubles had been going on since pre-season and all sorts of jabs and treatment couldn't solve it. Eventually it was diagnosed as a problem with the sciatic nerve and as anyone who has suffered from that will tell you, it can be excruciatingly painful. It certainly won't allow you to play professional football and once the medical people got to the root of the problem, Gerry was told that resting it was the only solution.

Meanwhile, we battled on without him as best we could until February 12, when he made his comeback at West Brom. We drew 1-1, Gerry got the goal and it was the first time that season that the established 'Runners-up' team found themselves together again. Sadly, he was only back for half-a-dozen games before the injury ruled him out again.

Realistically, the cup competitions represented our best hopes of success. It was essential that we pick up enough points to steer well clear of the relegation battle but we were all agreed as we got to the turn of the year that the cup competitions were our priority. From my point of view, we'd narrowly missed out on a League champions' medal the previous year and I was desperate to get my hands on something concrete to show for the brilliant time I'd had at Loftus Road. The clock was ticking. I wouldn't get many more chances.

We had Wembley in our sights in the League Cup. All we had to do was beat Aston Villa to book a dream day-out and as we'd already done that in a League fixture earlier that season, we knew it wasn't beyond us. The first-leg of the semi-final was a bit of a non-event. To be fair to Villa, they came looking for a draw at Loftus Road and did a job on us. We just couldn't break them down but a goalless draw wasn't the end of the world. It simply meant we would have to up our game at Villa Park a fortnight later - and we had every incentive to do so.

John Deehan gave Villa the lead in the second half and after Gerry equalised to take the game into extra time, Deehan nudged them back in front again. It looked like curtains for us when Givens had a penalty saved but with just two minutes left, Eastoe grabbed a dramatic equaliser.

In those days, you didn't go to penalties to settle things. You played again on neutral territory and six days later we travelled up to North London to try again at Highbury. The pitch was a real mud-heap. They often were in that era, you didn't expect otherwise, but the surface contributed to a goal that sent Villa on their way to Wembley. It was still goalless and we were giving as good as we got when I mis-controlled the ball. It bobbled just as I went to trap it and Dennis Mortimer seized on my mistake. He threaded a pass through for Brian Little, who fired them in front - then scored twice more to crush our hopes.

It was all my fault. Failing to control the ball, as I did, was a criminal offence in my eyes. You didn't do that type of thing at top-flight level and I was desperately upset about letting everyone down. I was completely intolerant of my failings at the best of times and this was a crushing blow to me. People were right to point out that the other two goals in a 3-0 defeat were not my fault. That was absolutely no consolation. The first goal was the critical moment of the match and like I've already said, it was completely down to me. I'd just blown the best chance I was ever likely to get to appear in a Wembley final. People say that losing a semi-final is the most painful defeat you can suffer. I certainly wouldn't argue with that.

Dave Sexton pulled me aside after the game and said he wanted me to have a break. He could see I was really upset and my batteries desperately needed to be re-charged. He said he was 'resting me' for the home game against Leicester the following Saturday - and Stan as well. He didn't want to see us until the Monday but made it clear we should get ourselves mentally prepared to play against AEK Athens in the UEFA Cup quarter-finals.

Part of me wanted to say: "No ... I want to play against Leicester."

I was really proud of the fact that I'd made 114 consecutive appearances in League and Cup games since joining Rangers. I didn't want that record to end but I very quickly saw sense. Dave had weighed up the situation in his usual methodical manner and decided that was the way to get the best out of me. It meant that I had five whole days to act like a normal family man. From memory, I didn't do anything special. That would have defeated the object. I just spent quality time with Margaret and the kids and it did me the world of good. Believe me, Queens Park Rangers were uppermost in my mind at that time but I was also conscious that as soon as our League and Cup programme came to an end, I'd be back on international duty. Aside from the Home Internationals, we had a three-game trip to South America coming up. We hadn't yet clinched our place at the World Cup Finals in Argentina but the thinking was that if we made it, that trip would give us a good idea what to expect the following summer. The key thing was that my season was far from over. I needed to prepare myself mentally as well as physically for what was to come.

I knew it was a case of 'needs must' but I wasn't seeing enough of Crowthorne and the family for my liking. When I did get the chance to relax and socialise, I greatly valued the company of our neighbours, Bill and Sheila Fox. They were Scottish, so I had a natural bond with them, and we really enjoyed each other's company. They started coming to home games at Loftus Road and it became our regular routine that afterwards we would go to our favourite Italian restaurant in Shepherd's Bush. Neil also got on well with their sons, Derek and Graham.

Margaret became good friends with the wife of Ray Dorset, the leader of Mungo Jerry, the rock group who enjoyed great success in the Seventies. He used to turn up in a bright blue Mustang - there was no mistaking him. Another who became a good friend was the actor Tony Selby, who appeared in many television programmes - including Doctor Who - and starred in the RAF National Service comedy series, 'Get Some In'. We used to go to the recording studios in the West End to watch his shows being made and it was fascinating to see how they went about it. Watching television became a different experience after that.

The break from football, brief as it was, did me good. I came back to play my part in the 3-0 win over AEK Athens and although, as I've already explained, there was no happy ending to our UEFA Cup campaign, we had to knuckle down and haul our way clear of the threat of relegation. We really were in trouble by the time we went to Middlesbrough in April and it must have been the familiar Teesside air that inspired me to make an important contribution. I had to call in a few favours to get enough tickets together to accommodate all the family and friends who wanted to be at Ayresome Park that day and I gave them something to remember. We ran out 2-0 winners and after setting up the first goal for Ron Abbott, I helped myself to the second. The ball came back off the crossbar after I'd chipped the goalkeeper and I managed to get there first to convert the rebound.

Quite unusual for Rangers but we flew up to the match and my mum and dad came to Teesside Airport afterwards to see me off. They had to collect my three-year-old nephew, Dean Atkinson, along the way because they were baby-sitting him that night and he turned on a 'one-boy' show for the lads while we were waiting for our flight to be called. His rendition of Jimmy Osmond's 'Long Haired Lover from Liverpool' was word-perfect, complete with all the actions. The players absolutely loved it. They saw a star in the making because Dean went on to have a good career in show business and was doing a ventriloquist act on cruise ships before Covid-19 came along.

That win at Middlesbrough gave us a much-needed boost and we got another one the following week as Eastoe scored twice when we crushed Manchester United 4-0. We could still do it ... shame we didn't do it often enough. To underline the point, we failed to win any of the next five matches. We were looking over our shoulders by then. We needed to get a grip - and quickly. But to do that, we'd have to dig really deep. By the time we arrived at the start of May we still had six more League matches to play and they had to be crammed into the space of 17 days.

It was a massive test of our character and I'm pleased to say we were not found wanting. Wins over Leeds and Ipswich and draws against Villa and Birmingham meant we completed the season in respectable fashion. But although our final mid-table position of 14th looked reasonably comfortable, we were kidding ourselves if we thought that.

I have no idea what the record is for the number of appearances made in a season but I must have mounted a good challenge for it. That Leicester clash was the only League game I'd missed and if you add in eight UEFA Cup ties and nine games in the League Cup and FA Cup, that makes 58 appearances for Rangers. On top of that, by the time I headed off for the shortest of summer breaks at the end of June, I'd also taken my tally of Scotland games that season to eight.

It was a summer of real change for Rangers. I knew that Frank McLintock, a great man and a great player, had decided to bring his 20-year career to an end. I was really going to miss him and by the time I returned to Loftus Road, after flying half way around the world and back again, we also had a new manager. Dave Sexton, such a huge influence on my career, had moved north to take charge of Manchester United.

Chapter 14
MORE 'HOME' SUCCESS - THEN TO THE MARACANA
(1977)

It was time to change track and I did it with schoolboy enthusiasm. All being well, I'd add six more Scotland caps to my collection before I closed down for the summer and in the process, I'd get the chance to appear at some iconic stadiums and match myself against some of the best players in the world.

The first target - and it was massive in my mind - was to help Scotland win the Home International Championships for the second successive year. That hadn't been achieved since 1963. I really wanted to be a part of making that happen again and give Scottish fans good reason to feel proud of us. Then, the plan was to fly to South America and play Chile, Argentina and Brazil on a tour designed to prepare us for the 1978 World Cup Finals.

How exciting was that? It was the stuff of dreams for a professional footballer - especially one who was striving in every way he knew to make up for lost time.

I'd played 58 games for QPR that season - plus a World Cup qualifier in Scotland - and I think some people were expecting me to complain about being shattered. There was absolutely no chance of that happening. I just wanted to play at every opportunity and especially so if it involved representing my country.

I was lucky. Being naturally fit helped me to shrug off the affects of a strenuous club season and in the main, I managed to steer clear of injuries. I'm so envious of the likes of the great Tom Jones, still strutting his stuff in his Seventies. He chose a career-path that enabled him to do that. It doesn't work for professional footballers. I knew that at the age of 30, at best I'd got another three or four years of top-level football left in me. I didn't want to waste a single day. By the time I got to 50 I was already saying I'd give anything to be able to chase a silly football around again and every day I'm still saying the same thing now.

There were no guarantees when the players assembled to prepare for the Home Internationals that I was going to play in the opening game against Wales because I'd missed the previous two matches - and Scotland had won both of them.

The first, the previous November, was the World Cup qualifier against Wales at Hampden Park and I missed it because of injury. Terry Yorath, who just happened to be the Wales captain, had managed to leave his mark on me when we'd played at Coventry the week before the international. He'd been at me all game, as he always was, and eventually caught me on the ankle. It was badly swollen and I had to withdraw from the international squad. My old mentor Jimmy Sirrel had an interesting theory about that type of thing. He always argued that you should take it as a compliment. It meant, he said, that an opponent couldn't match you for ability so he needed to resort to more primitive methods. Incidentally, we won that game 1-0 when Ian Evans turned the ball into his own net after good work by Danny McGrain and Kenny Dalglish so our hopes of qualifying were still alive.

I'd also missed the friendly-match win against Sweden in April because QPR had a League game the night before. So, by the time I reported for duty again nothing was certain - especially as there had been a change at the top. Willie Ormond had resigned and Ally MacLeod was brought in to replace him.

Without really understanding the ins and outs, I think Ormond found the pressures hard to take and believe me, it was a genuine pressure job. Scottish fans - and the media - are so passionate about their football that they always set the bar incredibly high in terms of expectation. That could be really difficult to live with at times. Ormond does, however, deserve great credit for two things in particular. The first was that he'd guided us to success in the Home International Championships the previous year, the second was that he'd picked me!

Was MacLeod a good appointment? I really couldn't have an opinion at that time because our paths had never crossed. I did remember as a 13-year-old seeing him on television, playing on the losing side for Blackburn against Wolves in the FA Cup Final. Also, bearing in mind that I was an Aberdeen fan, I knew he'd been 'our' manager for a couple of years before taking on the Scotland job. As for whether he was best qualified to lead Scotland's World Cup campaign, it seemed to me that he still had a lot to prove. He made a big point at our initial team meeting of telling us that he was "a winner". Nothing about his CV actually suggested that.

Anyway, there was a blank piece of paper between us. It was up to me to convince him I should be part of his long-term plans. Equally, it was up to MacLeod to show that he could find a way to get us to fulfil our potential. I'd seen enough during my fairly brief international involvement to realise that he was inheriting a very talented squad of players. Some were already well-established, others like me were straining at the leash, and there were a load of very promising youngsters knocking on the door. Overall, it was arguably the best talent base Scotland had ever had - certainly the best for many years. The new boss had 12 months to develop the squad, ensure that we clinched a place at the World Cup Finals and get us in the right shape to go to Argentina and perform.

It was clear that he wanted to assert his authority from the start and he did it in a way that shocked all of us, none more so than Archie Gemmill. He announced at that initial team meeting there would be a change of captaincy. Bruce Rioch was to be the new skipper and I was the vice-captain. Archie was fuming and I did feel sorry for him.

From what I could see of it, he'd done a decent job. From my point of view, though, it was a good start. It suggested that MacLeod saw me as a key part of his plans and I was delighted.

It was going to be fascinating to see how he approached the challenge and in theory, the situation was ready-made for him. By the time we'd finished the Home Internationals and our three-game tour, he ought to have a sound perspective on every member of his squad, as a player and a person. It would be a brilliant learning period for him - a chance to consider his options and put some building blocks in place leading up to the World Cup.

By then, I'd got a better understanding of what an international manager's job entailed. It wasn't at all easy and I didn't envy him. Normally before an international, players would turn up from all parts of the UK, often carrying a knock they'd picked up in the previous day's League game and having invariably made a lengthy journey to meet up with the squad. Getting any quality work done before the game was virtually impossible. Depending on what day the game was played, you might manage a couple of light training sessions and then, straight after the game, the players headed off in their different directions. It would then be weeks, if not months, before the manager saw them again. How do you work on tactics and patterns of play? The answer is that you simply couldn't.

It's different today but back in the Seventies, the argument regularly put forward was that we were international footballers and therefore shouldn't need to be taught how to play the game. Maybe there was truth in that but the difference between winning and losing, especially at the top level, is all about fine margins. It's about finding a way to get a slight advantage over the opposition and that comes from building relationships with your colleagues through working regularly on the training ground.

If we could find a way to get past Czechoslovakia in the qualifying group and clinch our place at the World Cup Finals, the general feeling was that we had enough talent in the squad to make a real impact. I was fascinated to see how Ally was going to handle it. He couldn't afford to waste the next month.

We had a fairly settled team building up to the Home Internationals and he largely stuck with it. First up we played against Wales at Wrexham and it was an inauspicious start to the new regime. We drew 0-0 and the fact that I cannot recall a single thing about it probably tells you everything. One point in the bag but it almost certainly meant that if we were going to retain our title, we would have to beat Northern Ireland and England.

We comfortably beat the Irish at Hampden, Dalglish scoring twice in a 3-0 success, and then journeyed south for a day that I seemed to have been waiting for all my life. I'd never been to Wembley, not even as a spectator. There had been talk of QPR using the stadium for our UEFA Cup quarter-final against AEK Athens because the Loftus Road pitch was in such a bad way but for whatever reason, it didn't come off. That route to Wembley had been closed off to me and so had another one when I cost us the chance to go there for the League Cup Final. I was really fortunate because I still had one more option that could lead to me appearing at what has always been regarded as the home of football.

We stayed overnight at a hotel in Harpenden, just off the M1 and a few miles south of Luton, and I was in for a pleasant surprise. Graham Smith, the adidas product director had come to catch up with a few of the lads who wore their boots and I was delighted to see him again. All those years earlier, when Bob Worthington and I signed for Notts County from Middlesbrough, Graham was there as a part-time goalkeeper. The three of us shared an attic room in a West Bridgford hotel. It was brilliant to see him again and I was pleased that he'd done so well for himself. He went on to become a director at Chelsea and launched his own business that became big in The States as well as the UK.

So here I was, the little lad from Banchory, waking up to find that I was just hours away from taking on the 'Sassenachs' on their own battleground. What a responsibility that was! I was very aware of the huge sacrifices many Scots would have made to get themselves to Wembley, saving up for two years to raise enough money to cover the costs. Match tickets were absolute gold-dust, and the whisky flowed in abundance.

It took ages to get to the ground. Even with a police escort our progress was slow but once I got the famous Twin Towers in my sights, I tingled with excitement. There wasn't a hint of anti-climax. It was everything I'd dreamed of and I couldn't wait to get off the coach and find out more. I can remember it as if it was yesterday. I strolled up the tunnel with big Gordon McQueen - 'Go-Go' as we used to call him - and when we got out into the sunshine, Scottish fans were everywhere. I don't think segregation was in force within football grounds at that time but if it was, it failed miserably. They really made their presence felt and I said to 'Go-Go': "If we can't perform for these people, we want shooting."

When it came to the pre-match talk the manager didn't have too much to say. He really didn't need to say anything. The whole experience was self-motivating and as Wales and Northern Ireland had drawn their game the previous evening, we knew that victory would give us the title again. I do, though, remember one amusing little incident. As Ally finished talking he asked if anyone had anything to add. There was silence for a couple of seconds and then Kenny Burns piped up. He was one of our substitutes and said: "Yeh! If we're winning comfortably with 10 minutes to go, can I go on and nail Trevor Francis?" That helped to break the tension. Burns and Francis were Birmingham City colleagues at the time and it was no secret that they hated each other. Ironically, of course, Brian Clough brought them back together later in their careers to help Nottingham Forest win the European Cup. By that stage, they were on much better terms.

What an incredible feeling it was walking up that tunnel and out into the June sunshine. It was a really warm day, sure to test our stamina, but I wasn't going to let a minor thing like that affect me.

It was a decent game, fairly nip and tuck, but I don't think we were second-best at any stage. We went in front a couple of minutes from half time when 'Go-Go' got up brilliantly to head in an Asa Hartford free kick, then stretched our lead on the hour. Willie Johnston crossed from the by-line and although Kenny Dalglish's first attempt was blocked after Bruce Rioch knocked the ball back across goal, he managed to scramble in the rebound.

The fans were in dreamland and despite Mick Channon converting a late penalty to make it 2-1, we had achieved what we set out to do. Sadly, we couldn't organise a lap of honour - which I would have really treasured - because of a wholesale pitch invitation when the final whistle sounded. Literally thousands poured on, carried along on a wave of jubilation, but what happened next possibly didn't show them in the best light. Some fans snapped a crossbar by swinging on it and hundreds went home with a chunk of Wembley turf for a souvenir.

I actually didn't finish the game because Ally took me off in the closing stages. He was paid to make such decisions so no complaints from me. Anyway, it put me in a better position to run for cover as soon as the pitch invasion began. I remember seeing the edited highlights of the game later that night and when the panel were discussing it afterwards, Tommy Docherty gave me a classic back-handed compliment. Like all true Scotsmen he was getting carried away by it all and said: "We could even afford to take Don Masson off and still win!"

I don't know to this day how he managed it but when I finally emerged from the happiest of dressing rooms, my son Neil was standing outside waiting for me. How did he do that? Apparently he just said "Don Masson is my dad" - and the steward let him come down the tunnel. Anyway, I was delighted because it gave me the chance to take him into the dressing room and give him a memory that he still treasures. He also had another souvenir because I'd swopped shirts at the end of the game with Ray Clemence, so I was able to give him a sweaty yellow jersey with a red No.1 on the back. Margaret had grabbed a souvenir of her own as she and Neil battled their way through the ecstatic fans to reach the mouth of the tunnel. She somehow got her hands on a chunk of turf and was really pleased with herself. I suggested it might be best if she hid it away until we got home!

It was utter chaos but we did eventually reach the Players' Lounge. Everywhere we turned people wanted to slap our backs and get our autographs. For one of them, I made his day. I was carrying my boots and I handed them to him. I think he thought at first I was just letting him touch them and seemed happy enough about that. The look on his face when I told him he could keep them was priceless. I hope he still had them by the time he got home.

This time I didn't have to use the 'sleeper'. Margaret had driven up to Wembley with Neil, my sister Joan and her husband Dave, so it only took an hour or so to get home once the traffic had eased. Forgive me if I say that I got a real buzz of satisfaction from looking at the glum English faces along the way. So often in the past it will have been them doing the gloating. It was nice to know I'd helped to balance the books. There was only one problem with that journey. Neil insisted on wearing Clemence's jersey in the car and by the time we arrived home, we needed to have all the windows wide open.

The Queen's Jubilee Celebrations were in full swing in June 1977 and when we got back to Crowthorne there was a big Street Party going on. The atmosphere couldn't have been more different to what I'd just experienced but it was brilliant all the same. I was surrounded by lovely people, just wanting to enjoy the occasion. We were very lucky to have them as neighbours.

I needed some time to take stock of all that was happening and was grateful that we had a few days off. My diary said that after playing England at Wembley on June 4, my next game would be against Chile in Santiago on June 15. I always found that after a particularly hectic period it was every bit as important to clear the mind as it was to prepare the body. After three or four days in Crowthorne with Margaret and the kids I was ready to go again.

We were flying out from Prestwick so it meant another trip on the London-Glasgow 'sleeper'. I didn't mind. People used to say that it must have been a real pain but that wasn't how I remembered it. That was all part of the adventure for me - and what lay ahead was a special adventure.

Next stop Chile and although I cannot recall how long it took to get there, it seemed like forever. We landed in Recife, Brazil's fourth largest city, to refuel the plane and then on to Santiago. The fact that Scotland had agreed to play in Chile was hugely controversial. The Government had been overthrown a couple of years earlier and Augusto Pinochet had been installed as President of the military junta. There were all sorts of horrible stories about the treatment being dished out to anyone who voiced their disapproval. It was claimed that more than 3,000 people were executed and as many as 80,000 interned.

Living in the south, I was slightly out of touch with all the discontent being shown in Scotland. People felt very strongly that we shouldn't be going there and by doing so, we were accused of condoning the actions of the military regime. The media labelled it 'The Match of Shame' and The Scotsman newspaper even produced posters that read: 'Don't Play Ball with Fascists'.

The whole thing was way out of our league. I can hold up my hands now and say that I should have made more of an effort to discover the full facts but it was down to the Scottish FA. I don't ever recall them asking for my opinion about whether I wanted to go - as an individual or within the group. We assumed they had taken best advice before deciding to go to Chile and trusted them to protect our interests. Realistically I don't know how we could have done anything else.

None of us was completely happy about the situation and the second we landed in Santiago we realised it was a mistake. There were soldiers with guns on every street corner and the underlying tension was incredible. It reflected what had gone on over the previous three years. Throughout our time there, a 7pm curfew was strictly enforced across the city.

We just wanted to get the game played as quickly as possible and leave but when we arrived at the National Stadium, the whole thing was vividly brought home to us. We'd been told the stadium had been used as a detention centre and many of the atrocities had taken place there. It was easy to believe that. The dressing room walls were littered with bullet holes and as we sat there, waiting to take the field, you couldn't help but imagine the horrific scenes that had probably taken place within those confines. It affected us all - it couldn't fail to - and under the circumstances, we were incredibly professional. We won the game 4-2.

Next stop was Buenos Aires, the capital city of Argentina, and I really liked it. No doubt I was so relieved about leaving Chile behind that it influenced my thinking but we were made to feel incredibly welcome. We were based in a classy part of the city and when we wandered around the shops I couldn't believe the quality of the clothes. The leather items were the best I'd ever seen. Thank goodness Margaret wasn't there with her credit card! When we arrived we found that the England team were staying in the same hotel, having just played Argentina and managed a 1-1 draw. There wasn't time for much contact between us because they were just heading off. Mind you, they wouldn't have been keen to hang around and be reminded about our trip to Wembley.

We were only in Buenos Aires for a couple of days, so there was no time to really explore the area outside of the city but as I remember it, we had a great time. They were a really good set of lads who mixed well together and I'm sure that was part of building the belief we could achieve things.

The match finished 1-1 in front of a crowd of 54,000 and although it was stupid to read too much into that, we got a bigger boost from the result than they did. As the host nation for the following year's World Cup, Argentina were favourites to win that competition so drawing a warm-up game with little old Scotland was seen as a bad result. On the reverse side, we came away seeing it as evidence we could live in

The Scotland team about the take on Argentina. Back row: Kenny Dalglish, Willie Johnston, Alan Rough, Willie Donachie, Danny McGrain. Front row: Martin Buchan, Lou Macari, Archie Gemmill, Asa Hartford, Don Masson, Tom Forsyth

that company. The experience was invaluable. I opened the scoring from the penalty spot after 77 minutes and Argentina equalised from a penalty three minutes later. Let's just say that our award was far more justified than theirs!

Two other things of note I can recall. The first was that I was really impressed by the busy little central midfielder who was directly opposed to me. I'd never heard of Ossie Ardiles before but I wasn't the slightest bit surprised that he went on to have a huge impact in the English game. He was my type of player, neat and tidy with great passing ability and a fantastic engine. We certainly covered some miles between us in that game.

The other thing was that Willie Johnston's famous short-fuse let him down again and this time, he feared it would have very serious consequences. In fairness, the full back, Vicente Pernia, had been kicking him up hill and down dale and midway through the second half 'Bud', as we always called him, could take no more. He caught him flush with a beautiful right-hook. Both of them were sent off.

As usual, I was sharing a room with him and he was really up tight when we got back to the hotel. He was convinced that incident would cost him the chance of going to the World Cup. He'd had a few in the bar to drown his sorrows and I left him wandering around the hotel when I went to my bed. Some time later I got a call from Ally MacLeod asking me to go and see him in his room. Apparently a member of the hotel staff had rung to say he needed to deal with one of his players. 'Bud' was with Ally when I got there, really upset and apologising non-stop for getting himself sent off. Ally dealt with it by saying: "'Bud' ... your name will be the first on my team-sheet when we come back to Argentina next year."

That was good enough for 'Bud' - and for me. We were asleep within minutes. I never did find out whether Ally really meant what he said or if he was just desperate to defuse the situation.

We were soon on the move again, off to Rio de Janeiro ... the most wonderful place I've ever visited. We were there to play football, of course, against everyone's second-favourite international team, but it was really difficult to give it our full attention. To start with, we were based right alongside the world-famous Copacabana beach and everywhere you looked for pretty much every minute of the day there were beautiful sun-tanned women. The beach itself is a vast area and it needs to be because it attracts incredible crowds of people every day. We trained on the beach a couple of times and fortunately, they were just light work-outs. When you saw what some of the Brazilians all around us were capable of doing with a football, we didn't want to be embarrassed.

We managed to find time to fit in a trip up Sugarloaf Mountain in the cable-car and also took the team bus to visit the famous giant statue of Christ the Redeemer. Sitting at the top of Corcovado mountain, the incredible statue towers over the city. What a view ... simply sensational. And if you're talking about tourist attractions, you have to include the Maracana Stadium on that list. It wasn't completely full when we played there - the attendance was 60,763 - but it was still an unforgettable experience.

I don't know what it's like today but at that time the dressing rooms were down in a dungeon area and you climbed the steps to be greeted by a wall of noise. What also greeted me when we went out to inspect the pitch before kick-off was a board that had 'Masson' printed on it in huge letters. I thought for a split-second they were giving me a special welcome and said to 'Go-Go' McQueen: "You couldn't make it up!" It turned out that it was some sort of promotional thing, nothing to do with me. Never mind ... it gave the lads a laugh.

The other thing that really got our attention was a display of football skills the likes of which I've never seen in my life. I don't know if you ever saw the Coca Cola advert, where a young Brazilian performs astonishing things with the ball? It was him, and he was putting on a pre-match exhibition for the crowd. It was amazing. No way could I have done the things he was doing. 'Go-Go' was blown away by it and he kept saying: "I want to adopt him now and take him home with me!"

The match was a disappointment. We all knew it was likely to be a one-off experience so we were anxious to do ourselves full justice. Sadly, it didn't work out that way. We lost 2-0 in a match that kicked off late because of the extreme heat but that scoreline flattered us. The truth is that by then, we'd run out of steam. We were down to the bare bones because several of the lads had injuries and it was almost a case of anyone who is fit can play.

Brazil included the likes of Edinho, Cerezo, Paulo Cezar and the great Rivellino in their line-up. Marvellous players and I felt honoured to be on the same pitch.

We were due to head for home the following morning and having had a few drinks, a group of us decided we wouldn't bother to go to bed. At 5am, as soon as the sun came up, we went for a game of tennis. None of us was focusing too well but we discovered the secret. What we had to do was hit the middle one of the three balls we could see!

It was helpful for me that our return flight landed at Gatwick. The Anglos got off there and the others flew on to Glasgow. How lucky was I? I've always thought that travel broadens the mind and I'd been paid to do a whistle-stop tour of South America, staying in the finest hotels. The experience was fantastic but in football terms, it felt just like an end-of-season trip rather than preparation for taking part in the biggest event in world football.

It would be wrong to say there was no real point to it because at least we gained an insight into what we could expect if we qualified for the World Cup finals. How much closer it had taken Ally MacLeod to deciding his best 11 players and how he could best use them, I really wasn't too sure.

15
STAYING COOL TO CLINCH OUR WORLD CUP TICKET
(1977-78)

It was a feeling I could never have expected to experience. Let's be honest, how could I seriously allow myself to think that at one point in my life - however briefly - I would be the most popular Scotsman in the world? At the precise moment when I scored a crucial goal in our World Cup qualifier against Wales, I reckon that's where I figured in the rankings.

Over the years, people by the thousands have regularly painted a picture for me. They remember very clearly where they were and what they were doing at that moment of high drama. Huddled together in the pubs and bars, factories and front rooms, most have said they were struggling to cope. They didn't know what to do for the best as I set up to take a crucial penalty. There were only 11 minutes left of a game we had to win to qualify for the World Cup Finals. It was goalless and on a proverbial knife-edge. Even members of my own family who were at the game, couldn't bear to look. Only my dad, I was told, had total faith in me to do what was required. When the ball hit the back of the net to edge us in front and carry us within touching distance of a trip to Argentina, I could feel the love.

It's a great shame that we're not able to just 'stop the clock' in certain situations. I wanted so much to savour that moment. Unfortunately, that's not the way life works. You have to move on and in our case, on that unforgettable night, we still had work to do before there was genuine reason to celebrate. The Welsh lads still had time to hit back and ruin everything. But three minutes from time, Kenny Dalglish put paid to those concerns with a magnificent flying header from Martin Buchan's superb cross.

We were so proud of ourselves. Against all the odds, our little nation with a tiny population had come out top of our qualifying group. We could make plans to embark on what we fully expected would be the adventure of a lifetime.

So how exactly did I feel when we were awarded a penalty that, by anyone's standards, stemmed from a decision that was ultra-controversial? Well, look at it this way. I was our captain on the night because Bruce Rioch was not playing. I was also our designated penalty-taker. In other words, much as I might have wanted to, there was absolutely no scope for ducking out of it. Not that I was ever going to do that - no one has ever been able to accuse me of shirking my responsibilities. It was all down to me against Dai Davies, the experienced Wales goalkeeper. Simple as that. And the prize to be claimed by one of us was absolutely immense.

To answer the question ... I actually felt okay. Of course it was tense and the noise was incredible. On top of that, the Welsh lads were understandably aggrieved about having the penalty awarded against them when it appeared to be Joe Jordan who had handled a long throw from Willie Johnston. Joe has never admitted it to this day but let's just say that we quite probably wouldn't have got away with it in the VAR era. I had to stand around while they made their feelings known to the referee. That was hardly ideal... I just wanted to get it over with. All credit to them, they didn't add to the pressures by having a go at me. I somehow had to put 'blinkers' on until all the fuss had died down and focus on what had to be done.

Talk about an understatement. The TV commentator said: "I think Don Masson is fully aware of the significance of this." Too bloody right I was.

I'd already made up my mind where I wanted to put the ball, and stuck to the plan. Fortunately, Davies made the wrong choice ... that always helps. In such a key game the first goal was clearly going to be critical. Once we scored and our fans upped the volume, we could sense the Welsh lads feeling it wasn't going to be their night. It was really hard on them and I'm sure they must have been thinking the Welsh FA had left them to tackle us with one hand tied behind their backs. FIFA had ruled the tie couldn't be played at Cardiff's Ninian Park - their normal venue for international matches - as a disciplinary measure, following crowd trouble at the recent game against Yugoslavia.

We all expected it to take place instead at Wrexham - and we were dreading that. We'd played there the previous year in the Home Internationals and didn't like the stadium, the pitch or the hostile crowd. I couldn't believe it when I heard the tie had been switched to Anfield. That played right into our hands. No doubt the Welsh FA will have seen an opportunity to cash in on a massive occasion for both countries. They were right in that respect because there was a capacity 50,000 crowd on the night and plenty of disappointed

A moment that united the nation. Converting the famous penalty against Wales at Anfield projected us towards the World Cup Finals.

punters outside. But they'd handed us the initiative. Our fanatical fans snapped up well over half the tickets and succeeded in turning it into a home game for us. As soon as we emerged from the tunnel and soaked up the warm reception, we knew we were in business.

The situation in our group was that Czechoslovakia, the reigning European champions, had opened up with home wins over both Wales and us. They were clearly in the driving seat, even though we'd revived our hopes by narrowly beating Wales at Hampden.

It meant that when the Czechs came to Hampden in September, it was a must-win game from our point of view. The stadium was rocking with 85,000 people inside and I picked a great night to produce what I regard as my best-ever performance for my country. It was just one of those nights when everything I seemed to try worked out for me and I was at the heart of an outstanding team performance. Jordan and Asa Hartford put us 2-0 up before half time and Dalglish stretched the lead midway through the second period. It seemed of little significance when the Czechs got a late consolation to make it 3-1 but was it? Goal average could be all-important.

Wales confirmed that by doing even better against the Czechs. They beat them 3-0. It was a terrific result for them - and also for us because it threw the group wide open. And just to prove my earlier point, they achieved it at Wrexham's Racecourse Ground.

I got a lot of praise for my efforts against the Czechs, not least from the manager. People told me that every time he did an interview he would say, in that excitable way of his: "What about Masson?" It was nice but players don't need to be told when they've done well. No one knows better than they do.

I did, though, find myself very much in the limelight over the next few days. It seemed as if everyone in the media wanted a slice of me, and that included Brian Moore and Bob Wilson. This time I didn't take the 'sleeper'. I stayed over at the Grand Central Hotel, lapped up the fantastic atmosphere that our result had generated across Glasgow, and travelled back to Crowthorne on the Thursday morning. I went into training with QPR on the Friday and there were messages waiting from both the major television stations. They wanted to interview me on Saturday morning.

To be honest, I could have done without it. Admittedly I was still running on adrenaline but was very conscious of the need to get myself 'tuned in' for our big local derby clash with Chelsea. I guess in today's world, the club would have denied me permission to do the interviews but Rangers gave me their blessing. The plan was for a taxi to pick me up from Crowthorne and take me to the ITV studios, then hang around while I recorded a piece with Brian Moore. It then whisked me away to the BBC Television Centre at Shepherd's Bush where I was live on Football Focus with Bob Wilson. As a former Scotland goalkeeper, he was really 'up' for the piece and it went well.

The taxi was still waiting and our next stop was White's Hotel on Bayswater Road, our normal venue for the pre-match meal before home games. The trouble was that the traffic was really building up by that stage, with all routes leading to Loftus Road, and I arrived just as the other lads were heading off to the ground. No big deal. We played well that day in a cracking atmosphere and I scored our goal in a 1-1 draw.

From an international point of view, things were going great for me and the week before we took on Czechoslovakia, I'd achieved another of my life's ambitions. We were off to play East Germany in a warm-up game and as Rioch was missing, I got to captain my country for the first time. It was a poor game in a soulless stadium and we lost 1-0. But no one would ever be able to take away from me the fact that I'd been the captain of Scotland. I'd led our troops into battle. It was such an honour and a claim to fame that I treasure very dearly.

That whole trip was actually a fascinating experience. The Berlin Wall was such a dominant feature with its bared-wire fences and huge spotlights, and having flown into the West of the city, we had to transfer to the other side. The only way to do that was by going through Checkpoint Charlie and how intimidating was that? It was just as you see it on the films ... gun-posts, binoculars, aggressive-looking soldiers,

SCOTLAND
'BRITAIN'S BEST'

1978 World Cup qualifying tie
WALES (0) 0 v. SCOTLAND (0) 2 at Anfield

TO THE wild delight of their supporters in the 50,850 Anfield crowd, Scotland won the battle of the Celts to surge into the 1978 World Cup Finals as Britain's sole representatives for the second successive time.

But the fire of the brave Welsh dragons blazed for a long while afterwards because of the controversy of the late, disputed penalty decision by referee Wurtz.

At first it appeared a Welsh fist had punched the ball away following a throw-in from Willie Johnston.

But later a television slow motion replay suggested that Scotland's Joe Jordan could have been the culprit—although he fiercely denied it.

Whoever was responsible, it was still a pity such a sad incident should have helped to decide the outcome of one of the most passionate matches in World Cup history.

Don Masson's converted penalty-kick was greeted by "We're going to Argentina" by the jubilant Tartan Army packed on the terraces.

A superb goal by Kenny Dalglish three minutes from the end made certain of that, but it had been Wales—a team half composed of players from outside the First Division—who had played the more constructive football, and created the better chances.

Although hard-hit by injuries, the gallant Welsh exposed Scotland's deficiences in defence, particularly John Mahoney and the penetrating left-wing dashes of Wrexham's Mike Thomas.

Terry Yorath was an inspiring captain and Leighton Phillips a commanding centre-back.

Scotland's stars were Lou Macari, Asa Hartford and goalkeeper Alan Rough, who made several splendid saves. One, at full stretch to finger-tip a John Toshack lob on to the bar, was world class.

Scotland began as though they were going to over-run the Welsh Three corners in the first 70 seconds had them reeling.

But gradually, Phillips and Norwich City's fine young full-back David Jones, stifled the threat of Dalglish and Jordan.

Then Wales surged forward themselves and Rough came to the rescue with saves from Toshack, Thomas and

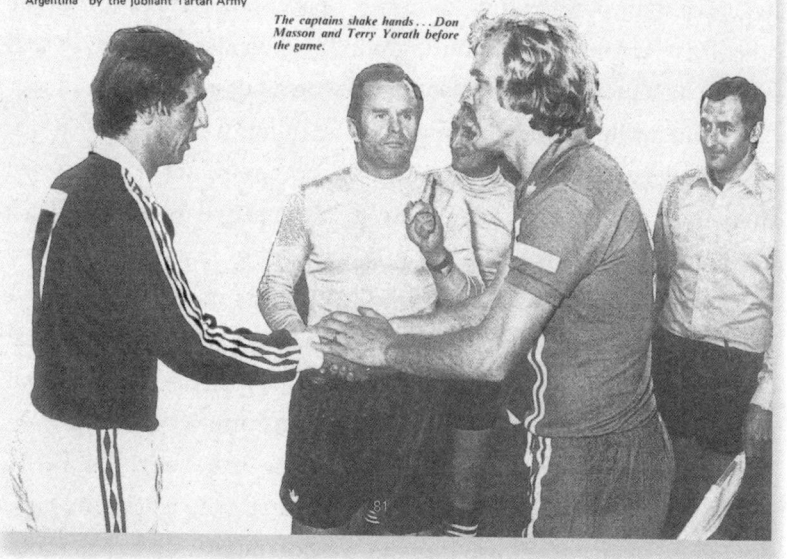

The captains shake hands...Don Masson and Terry Yorath before the game.

you name it. When we arrived in East Berlin I was stunned by the difference in the way of life. I'm glad I got chance to see it for myself because I wouldn't have believed it otherwise. Like everyone else in the summer of 1990, I watched in astonishment as the Wall was being dismantled, happy that it was going to offer a much better way of life to half the population of the city.

Before I move on I'd just like to go back to that great night at Anfield. The icing on the cake for me was that so many family members and close friends were there to share in our success. The only one who was missing was my mum. She was really upset that she had to stay behind in Middlesbrough, where she was on duty at the doctors' surgery, handling the night-time phone calls. It was a shame but it couldn't be helped. Margaret was there, so was my dad, my sister Joan with her husband Dave and our good friends Bill and Sheila Fox. My mate Denis Frith travelled up from London and I was pleased that I also managed to sort a couple of tickets for two former Notts County colleagues, Arthur Mann and Gordon Mair. A couple of passionate Scots, they were up behind the goal at the Anfield End, where I converted the penalty. I never did ask whether they hid behind their hands!

A good home: my No.8 shirt from the Wales game now resides in the living room of Neil Mann - son of my pal Arthur - in Sydney, Australia.

My family came back to our team hotel on The Wirral afterwards, so did Bill and Sheila, and when I introduced them to the jubilant Ally MacLeod, he asked where they were staying. They actually didn't have anywhere to stay and were probably going to head for home but Ally wouldn't hear of it. A lot of the players who lived in and around Manchester had opted not to stay the night. That meant their rooms were available and Ally insisted my 'party' should make use of them. I really appreciated that and Joan and Dave have dined out on it for years. I'm not sure that it was true but they tell everyone they stayed in Kenny Dalglish's room.

I was on top of the world the following morning as we drove back to Crowthorne. On the surface things could hardly be better and as lovely people kept telling me, I was getting my rewards for all the hard work I'd put in over the years. Now I could look forward to "selling myself" - as Jimmy Sirrel would say - on the biggest stage in world football.

I never lost sight of the fact that there was incredible competition for the midfield places. In fact, I doubt whether Scotland ever had a better choice in that department. There were six obvious contenders - Bruce Rioch, Asa Hartford, Archie Gemmill, Lou Macari, Graeme Souness and me - and others were also starting to emerge. In terms of ability, I think there was very little to choose between us. We had different strengths and weaknesses and Ally's job was to decide which of us would blend together the best. I'd certainly played my part in qualifying for the finals and as things stood after the crucial Wales game, the central spot was mine to lose. But that was in September. Would it still be the same by the time we boarded the flight to South America seven months later?

I needed to stay fit and maintain my standards. They were the two obvious targets. Meet both of those and I should be fine.

It wasn't as simple as that. Oh no. For the first time in a very long time, I lost my grip on things and everything started to unravel. In fact, it had already started by then. In mid-July to be precise, when

Manchester United announced that they had appointed Dave Sexton as their new manager. I don't need to explain how important Dave had been over the previous three years, not just to me but also to Queens Park Rangers as a whole. He'd been the architect of the best two seasons in Rangers' history and as much as we tried to shrug it off, we all knew that losing him would massively influence our fortunes.

We'd already said goodbye to two key players. Frank McLintock had retired and Dave Thomas had been allowed to move to Everton. It was difficult not to fear for the future when we clocked in for pre-season training and Dave was not there to lead us. There's no way that he could have turned down Manchester United and he fully deserved to have a crack at one of the biggest jobs in football. If he did stop to think for a second, I'm sure he would have told himself that he'd taken Rangers as far as he could. What we'd achieved over the previous two seasons with such a small squad of players was incredible. We hadn't actually won anything but had earned the respect of fans across the land by the way we went about our work. In our heart of hearts, though, we all knew it was unrealistic to think we could top that and Dave will have known that better than any of us.

I was very sorry to see him go but these things happen in football. It doesn't have to be the end of the world but if you are going to take it in your stride, the decision-makers have to step up. It's stating the obvious to say that they have to make the right moves and understand what the implications of their decisions will be.

I was shocked when I heard that Jim Gregory had given the manager's job to Frank Sibley. He was just 29 at the time, a fair bit younger than me, and I didn't get it. To my mind, Rangers needed to carry out a comprehensive re-building operation and with comparatively little money to spend, it was a job for an experienced pair of hands. Let me make it clear that on a personal level, I had absolutely no problem with Frank - and nor did the vast majority of the players. He had been Dave's assistant since I arrived at the club and was a popular figure in the dressing room. But Dave was very 'hands-on'.

He did all the training and coaching himself, and controlled every aspect of the build-up to matches. Frank had very few opportunities to show what he could do. It would be a massive step up for him.

A knee injury had tragically ended his playing career at QPR when he was just 23 and he had done well to make a fresh start. After coaching the youth team and reserves he landed the post as Dave's No. 2 and in the chairman's eyes, was clearly being groomed to become the manager. But it all happened too quickly and the way things panned out, we all felt very sorry for him. To be honest, I don't even think he wanted the job. He knew it was too big for him. He was out of his depth.

I'm really testing my memory but if I recall things correctly, we went to Belgium in pre-season that year to play in a four-team tournament. Apart from the hosts, there was a Russian club taking part - they were two weeks ahead of us with their fitness and ran us ragged when we played them - and also Derby County. By way of coincidence, Derby were in precisely the same situation as us.

Colin Murphy was their manager at the time and it had come as a shock to everyone in football when he'd landed the job the previous November. Here was a man who had never played the game professionally and had been reserve-team coach at the Baseball Ground. Suddenly, he was put in charge of a fantastic group of players who had won the League Championship twice in the previous six seasons. We stayed in the same hotel as Derby while we were in Belgium and after one of the games I was in the bar, chatting over a drink to my Scotland colleague Archie Gemmill. It wasn't a 'boozy' session in any shape or form but Murphy came across to him in quite an animated way and told him to get to bed. Archie just swotted him away before shaking his head at me, and saying: "He's got no chance".

I don't know Murphy so I have no axe to grind with him and I should point out that he enjoyed a long career in lower league management, which included successes along the way. But it was ridiculous for Derby to put him under such strain when he was clearly not qualified to take charge at that time. A month into the new season he was sacked and ironically, a few weeks after that, I moved to the Baseball Ground.

Sibley was subjected to an identical situation. I certainly wasn't the only one who realised at an early stage that it could only end in tears. Try as we did to stay positive about things, the buzz had gone. That inner belief we'd all had, that together we could beat anyone, had gradually evaporated.

Our only new recruit that summer had been my good friend David Needham, who followed what was becoming an increasingly well-worn trail from Notts County. He was well overdue to move into the First Division, having proved himself over many years to be arguably the best central defender beneath that level. He was a terrific athlete, outstanding in the air and he could certainly play. I had no doubt that he would cope with the extra demands of top-flight football but it wasn't quite as straightforward as that. He was stepping into the shoes of Frank McLintock and he was such a hard act to follow.

In many respects, our careers were following the same course. Dave was 28-years-old, just as I was when I moved to Rangers, and had played 429 senior games for County. Like me, he was desperate to prove he could 'do it' in the First Division but that's where the similarities ended. While I was becoming what Dave Sexton described when I signed as the 'final piece of his jigsaw', Dave was joining a club that was in decline.

We roomed together for away games and that gave us plenty of chance to discuss the situation. To be fair to him, he never moaned about the state of affairs but I did feel sorry for him. As with me, County had turned down numerous offers for him over the years and when they finally allowed him to move on, he'd joined a team that had totally forgotten how to win matches. Mind you, I didn't need to feel sorry for long. Four months into the new season, he was back in Nottingham, playing his part in Forest's incredible run of success under Brian Clough and Peter Taylor. By the time he'd finished, he'd helped them win the League Championship and European Cup, and played at Wembley in the League Cup Final. I wish I could say the same!

We struggled from the off. We lost at home to Aston Villa on the opening day, then at Wolves in midweek before getting our first point of the season when Needham's goal gave us a 1-1 draw at Norwich. Things didn't get a lot better.

I was dipping in an out to some extent during September and October because of my Scotland commitments but I was reasonably happy with my club form. I scored in three successive games at one stage as we drew with Chelsea and Bristol City and narrowly lost at Birmingham, but we were a pale shadow of the QPR I'd known. We won only one of our first 12 matches and at that stage, we were sitting one place above the relegation zone. The writing was on the wall. Things were starting to change and a crushing 5-1 home defeat by Everton appeared to force the issue.

Sibley - presumably under orders from above - had decided he needed to reduce the average age of the squad. Apparently that was part of the reasoning behind Thomas' move to Everton, which hadn't made sense to me, and Dave Webb went to Leicester seven games into the season. I don't need to explain how important the McLintock-Webb partnership was to our success and now we'd lost them both. On top of that, Gerry Francis was still having major problems with his back injury. He scarcely played and we were getting to the stage where we were almost unrecognisable from the 'Runners-up' team.

Come the end of the season, Rangers avoided relegation by just one point and what shocked me most was the contribution of Stan Bowles and Don Givens. Knowing what terrific players they were, it was inconceivable that Bowles scored only six League goals in 40 games, and three of those were penalties. Givens' record was four goals from 37 League games. How could that possibly be? Maybe it was simply that without Dave Thomas and me, and Gerry for most of the time, their supply-chain had ceased to function.

The speculation about me started in mid-September, after Tommy Docherty dropped it out to the press that he fancied signing me. He'd replaced Murphy as manager of Derby County a few weeks

Joining Derby County should have been a great move for me but it turned into a nightmare.

after being sacked by Manchester United, and the national newspapers made a big deal of the fact that I was his No. 1 target. It wouldn't be fair to name them but I got calls when the story broke from two of my Scotland colleagues and both wanted to say the same thing... "Don't do it!"

They were warning me off from signing for Docherty but I had to tell them: "You're too, late. It's already a done deal."

Before I move on, I have to reflect on my time with QPR. I'll always be grateful that they gave me what I was looking for - a platform on which to prove I could hack it at the top level - and I have nothing but happy memories of my time at Loftus Road. I loved living in London, exploring all the touristy areas, and I worked with some great people - on and off the field. I was reluctant to leave and Margaret and the kids certainly didn't want to leave Crowthorne. But when decision-day arrived, it was clear that Sibley and Gregory felt my time at Rangers had run its course. They'd agreed to a straight-swop deal that would involve Leighton James, Derby's Welsh international winger, moving the other way. The valuation they placed on it was £200,000 and I was pleased about that because I could walk away with my head held high. During my three years with Rangers I'd chalked up 130 League and Cup appearances and only once in that period was a team-sheet pinned up without my name on it. That was the day when Dave Sexton rested me ahead of our UEFA Cup quarter-final against AEK Athens. I'd helped them enjoy the two best seasons in the club's history - and then they doubled their money on me when I left.

I was grateful for those calls from my Scotland mates but surely the picture couldn't be as bad as they were painting it. Yes, it could - and it didn't take long for me to discover that.

I had to be interested when I heard that Derby wanted to sign me. I sat down and made a list of the reasons why I should join them and reasons why I shouldn't. At the very top of the list of 'pros' was that I was concerned about what QPR's sudden collapse was doing to my World Cup prospects. I was paranoid about the competition that existed for midfield places and if Ally McLeod thought QPR's losing habit must be affecting my form, it could have consequences.

Gerry Daly, the talented Irishman, was already at the Baseball Ground and when I opened negotiations, Docherty told me he was also close to clinching a deal to sign Bruce Rioch from Everton. That was a popular move because Bruce had helped to win the title in a previous spell with Derby and as Scotland's captain, the chance to work with him in midfield on a regular basis could only be positive.

So that was two big ticks in the 'yes' box and I also felt that if I did have to move Margaret and the kids - and me - away from Crowthorne, at least it would be back to the East Midlands, which we knew and loved. We could even go back to living in the Nottingham area because it took less than an hour to get to Derby.

The other really big thing for me was that Derby had some fantastic players and I was excited at the thought of working with them. When I looked through the names - Roy McFarland, Colin Todd, David Nish, Charlie George and Daly - I thought: "How can Derby not be in contention to win the title again?" Add Rioch and me to that lot, and we could be formidable.

The only negative I could think of to go in the other column was the state of the Baseball Ground pitch. It was totally beyond me how Derby under Brian Clough and Dave Mackay had played as well as they did on that surface. I had to remember that it didn't stop them from being successful. It wasn't easy to put QPR behind me but it had to be done. Everything pointed to the fact that I was starting a brilliant new chapter in my life that would act as the perfect prelude to representing Scotland in the World Cup.

Alec Stock, an institution at QPR, did me a big favour when the story broke about me moving to Derby. He'd been the manager at QPR in the Sixties when they achieved that remarkable 'double' of getting promoted from the Third Division and winning the League Cup and he'd recently returned to Loftus Road as a director. He was aware that I was about to talk business with Mr Docherty and when I asked him if he knew of anyone who could help with my negotiations, he recommended that I speak to a financial advisor based in Birmingham. Don't forget that we were still in an era when football agents didn't exist but Alec told me the man was a West Brom fan and had done a good job acting for Bryan Robson. It was a bit of a gamble because the first time I ever met him was outside the Baseball Ground, a few minutes before we went in to talk terms, but he didn't let me down. He handled things really well and I was delighted with the deal that I got.

Docherty could not have been more pleasant and welcoming so what was all the fuss about? Well, my Scotland mates told me that was par for the course. He's always very pleasant when you first arrive but within weeks he will turn on you and make life very uncomfortable. That's the way he operates. At the time, I was happy to give him the benefit of the doubt but within weeks, I just wished they had rung me a couple of days earlier.

Margaret and I were booked into the Bridgford Hotel on Trent Bridge for a couple of nights and it was a nice gesture from Docherty that he gave me a few days off to get my domestic arrangements sorted. Unbelievably, they fell into place like clockwork. We went to Burton Joyce, where we used to live, to catch up with our good friends John and Daphne Mounteney and told them we were considering moving back to that area. They knew that a dentist living not far from them was planning to emigrate to New Zealand but as he wasn't going until six months later, the house wasn't yet on the market. We didn't need immediate access because Margaret would be staying in Crowthorne with Neil and Jayne until a move fitted with schooling so we made arrangements to go and view the house. Margaret instantly fell in love with the brand new kitchen they'd installed and before we left, we'd shaken hands on a brilliant deal. Because the house hadn't gone on the market, there weren't even any estate agency fees involved.

I signed in the mid-October and then took up residence in the Midland Hotel in Derby until early in the New Year. It meant making regular trips to Crowthorne, of course, but there was a bonus where that was concerned because Derby were sponsored by the local Saab dealer and all the players got a nice car.

Initially, things were great. The week after I'd made my debut in a 2-2 draw at Norwich, Bruce Rioch did join us and Docherty, as he normally did, fed the newspapers a great line when he described his midfield department as "the three Van Goghs". The players made me really welcome and there was so much talent within the group. I was going to love working with them. I remember being on a Scotland trip when a gang of us were discussing the merits of McFarland and Todd as a central-defensive partnership and we were baffled as to why they didn't pair up automatically in the England team. Once I saw them in action at close quarters, they were even better than I'd thought.

It was immediately clear, though, that things were very different compared to life at Queens Park Rangers. It was all to do with the manager. We never saw him until the Saturday lunch-time when we arrived for the pre-match meal. Frank Blunstone did all the work. I liked Frank, as did all the lads. He was a real 'football man'. He'd played more than 300 times for Chelsea, won five caps for England, and had been Docherty's assistant at Manchester United before following him to Derby. He was a hard worker, good at what he did ... but he wasn't the manager.

I know that people work in different ways. I 'get' that - but I'd gone from one extreme to another. Jimmy Sirrel and Dave Sexton were incredibly 'hands on'. They controlled everything and were so methodical in preparing us for matches. We worked hard on set-ups for free kicks and corners, and analysing the strengths and weaknesses of the opposition. We were made as ready as we could be to face the challenge in front of us. You always knew with Jimmy and Dave that if we failed, it wouldn't be through lack of trying.

There was none of that with Derby. It was very much the turn-up-and-play mentality and football had moved on from those days. I was fully expecting before the game at Norwich that Docherty would 'hold court' but it never happened. The lads could see that I was in a state of some shock and they found it highly amusing. Less than two hours before kick-off, we didn't even know the team. Colin Todd eventually explained to me that the team was never announced. You found out whether you were playing when you walked into the dressing room. If your boots were in your changing position, you were 'in'. I just shook my head in disbelief.

There was more to come. Fifteen minutes before kick-off, Docherty would finally appear, throw an imaginary ball into the air and say to McFarland: "Mac, get 'em out and push 'em up. We're better players than them and a better team. Go out and prove it." And that was it. My mouth must have dropped open and when I looked at 'Toddy', he burst out laughing. The players had been studying me, waiting to see my reaction. I hadn't let them down.

The 'Van Goghs' took time to settle but fairly quickly, we embarked on a run that sent us zooming up the table. We only lost once in 10 games from mid-November and having arrived in 10th place at the turn of the year, there was still time for us to at least push for a place in Europe.

Instead of going forward, we slipped backwards and that was certainly true on a personal level. Just as I was warned it would do, my relationship with Docherty soured very quickly. I don't know if that had been Docherty's style of management at his other clubs but it seemed to me that the way he conducted himself at Derby was a joke. He did nothing whatsoever to help, inspire or guide the players. Then again, it would have been virtually impossible for him to do that because we hardly ever saw him.

All he seemed to be interested in was wheeling and dealing. Players were constantly coming and going and I don't know who benefitted from that. It didn't seem to be the football club. I'm told he oversaw 30 transfer deals in the space of a year and many Derby fans will tell you that in that time, he ruined much of the good work that Clough and Mackay had done.

What really got to me, though, was the disrespect he showed us. He was usually fine to my face on the rare occasions we had any contact but he seldom missed an opportunity to have a go at me behind my back. He always seemed to be looking for cheap laughs in the newspapers and a good friend of mine, who is a big Forest fan, couldn't wait to let me know what Docherty had said about me during an after-dinner speech at the City Ground. Apparently he really slaughtered Bruce and me, saying that there was no way we should be going to the World Cup with Scotland. So much for the unwritten rule that says managers are always loyal to their players.

I wasn't the only one who was having a problem. Charlie George was so angry over something Docherty had said about him in the papers that he decided to confront him. He told us afterwards that he'd 'lost it' during the heated discussion and had pinned him against the wall.

It was no consolation but at least I had a natural ally - someone who understood exactly how I was feeling. Bruce was fined two weeks wages and also transfer-listed after having a major bust-up with Docherty in public. He was also fined for allegedly leaving the pitch without permission when he was injured.

The relationship between us and him couldn't have got any worse and I think it revealed a lot when Bruce and I were asked to fly to Glasgow to do some television stuff ahead of the World Cup. Just as an aside, that was a horrible experience. We went on a little three-seater plane from East Midlands Airport that wobbled about all over the place in the strong winds, did the work and then flew straight back again. But the key thing is that we didn't bother to ask for permission to make the trip because we knew it would be denied. That hardly helped the situation with Docherty - but we were past caring. That story just shows how bad things had become. At any other time before I went to work for Docherty I would never have dreamed of doing that without permission.

My form dipped dramatically on the back of what was happening. It was blatantly obvious that he didn't like me and didn't want me at the club. Although most of the time he kept picking me for matches, I had no respect whatsoever for the man. I didn't want to play for him. I always try to see the best in people but I couldn't do that with him.

I needed to go all the way back to my days with Middlesbrough to find the last time I felt remotely that way. What I'd learned in the meantime was that in order to get the best out of me, I needed to feel wanted.

It was such an important stage of my career and I cannot tell you how miserable the whole thing made me. I was working for a very good football club, surrounded by outstanding players and should have been having the time of my life. One man was ruining everything and I felt very bitter about it. I have no idea why but he seemed to have an agenda. He had been through the same thing at Manchester United with Denis Law and Willie Morgan and now he really had it in for Bruce and me.

Under the circumstances, the Derby fans were brilliant with me. I couldn't have complained had they not been because for most of my time at the Baseball Ground I failed by some distance to do myself justice. It certainly wasn't through lack of effort and I got the impression that the players felt sorry for me. They understood what I was going through.

I won't go on about all the irritating little things that were happening to eat away at my confidence - I'll just give you one example. We were playing a testimonial for Brian Clough at the City Ground and at that stage, I was back living in Burton Joyce, which is a village on the outskirts of Nottingham. As anyone would in that situation, I asked for permission to go straight to the ground. My request was denied. I had to drive all the way to Derby, go back to Nottingham on the team-coach, travel back to Derby to collect my car and then drive back to Burton Joyce. There's a lot more I could say but what's the point? Some things are best left unsaid.

I didn't play in the last four games of the season - nor did I deserve to the way I'd been playing. I was a worried man. At that moment in time I needed to be in the form of my life. Instead, I was more short of confidence than I'd ever been. Even when I was stuck in the reserves at Middlesbrough my self-belief remained intact. It was just the others that were wrong!

Years later, when I had the Gallery Hotel on Radcliffe Road, which is less than half a mile from the City Ground, I got a call from Les Bradd. He was working in the Forest commercial department at that time and said Tommy Docherty was speaking at a dinner they'd organised. Could we put him up for the night? I'd do anything in the world for Les - except one thing. There was absolutely no chance of that happening.

I was actually at Forest the last time I saw Docherty. I was there as a guest and when he saw me, he came across the room, bracing himself as if to give me a hug. That didn't happen either. I would never forgive him for the way he'd treated me.

16
RIGHT AT THE HEART OF ONE BIG TALE OF WOE
(1978)

"Ladies and gentlemen. We have a celebrity with us tonight. His name is Don Masson and he missed a penalty against Peru in the World Cup." That's how I was introduced at a Quiz Night when I went back to Banchory to visit relatives. Almost 20 years had gone by since that life-changing moment... some people have long memories.

I can tell you with absolute sincerity that there isn't a day goes by when I don't hark back to that dreadful experience. I guess it's a piece of heavy baggage I'm destined to carry with me until I go to my grave. In fairness, I do think that maybe it has reached the stage where it's possibly more to do with me failing to let it go than what other people are thinking. I cannot help myself. Whenever I meet a Scots person for the first time, I invariably start the conversation by saying: "I'm sorry".

I found it interesting when I was researching for this book, trying to remind myself of the order of events, that I kept coming across things relating to the World Cup that I didn't know. Then it dawned on me that I'd made a conscious effort at the time to completely turn my back on Argentina 1978. I was in such a bad state that I knew the only way I could get through it was to try and block it from my mind.

I'm not too sure where to start on this chapter of my life. I've already painted the picture of how things were with Tommy Docherty and my time at Derby and although I'd been selected for the Home International Championships, I didn't expect to be play. I did figure in the opening game against Northern Ireland at Hampden - we drew 1-1 when Derek Johnstone cancelled out a goal from Martin O'Neill - but I was left out three days later. Graeme Souness took over my central midfield spot as we also drew with Wales.

Ally MacLeod had rung the changes to give most of the squad some action but as the home game against England three days later would be our last before we launched the World Cup campaign, he went for what presumably he felt was his strongest line-up. I was back in for that fixture, lining up in midfield alongside Bruce Rioch and Asa Hartford. It had been a tried and trusted combination over the previous two years but our team performance that day was a sign of things to come. We just didn't function and an 83rd minute goal by Steve Coppell gave England a 1-0 win.

We hadn't played well and it was worrying - but I don't remember any post-match inquest. Throughout my time with Scotland there never was in any detail, regardless of whether we'd played well or badly. It was simply a case of: "That's gone boys ... let's get on with the next one." Bruce and I were very aware we'd caused a big problem for Ally. His captain and vice-captain, key men throughout the qualification period, were desperately short of form and confidence. We only had a fortnight to sort it out before we faced Peru.

Margaret and I went straight to Middlesbrough after the England game to spend the weekend with my parents - then I reported to Dunblane Hydro with the rest of the squad. Despite our poor efforts in the Home Internationals, the hype surrounding us was off the scale. Rod Stewart even flew in on his helicopter, wearing a Scotland strip, to ramp up the fervour even more. The television cameras and photographers were out in force as we had a little game of 'keepy-uppy' with him, then went down to the games room to play snooker.

For months before that, Ally had been touring the country whipping up enthusiasm and in many respects it could only be a good thing to promote football. We were the only UK country to qualify for the World Cup Finals and it was a chance not to be missed. It did need to be done in a sensible way, though, and the players thought it was way over the top.

It was a different world back in the Seventies, of course, and I'm certain that what went on then would not have occurred today. For example, one big issue was that the Scottish FA was run by a committee, mainly made up of representatives from little clubs or regions of the country. There were loads of them - and we'd earned the majority an expenses-paid holiday of a lifetime. They were all loving the hype and reflected glory but the players were very uncomfortable about things. Ally had to take much of the blame for setting the bar so high. He kept telling anyone who would listen that we were off to win the World Cup but you never heard a single player suggest that. It was ridiculous. No European country had ever won it in South America and although we were confident of giving a good account of ourselves, it was unrealistic to think we could do more.

The fans were fantastic. On the day we set off, thousands crammed into Hampden Park to wish us luck. We toured the stadium on an open-top bus and the streets all the way from there to Prestwick Airport were lined with people. Of course we were grateful but to be honest, we found it embarrassing. We had good players and on our day, were a formidable team. But there was no way on earth that we could produce performances and results that would meet with their sky-high expectations.

It wasn't just Bruce and me that had problems. None of us was in the best frame of mind after our lack-lustre displays in the Home Internationals and we were definitely looking to Ally for some controlled leadership. This was his time. He was always a bubbly character, a born optimist, and there's nothing wrong with being positive. But it was going to take a lot more than that.

I'm very reluctant to criticise Ally. I liked him. He was always totally fair with me although I have to admit that nine years spent learning his trade as manager of Ayr United hardly qualified him for the huge task he was facing. What I really wanted from him at that moment in time was evidence that he'd used the previous eight months wisely. I desperately hoped he'd been plotting and planning, putting the building blocks in place to give us the best possible chance.

As I saw it, four main questions needed to be answered:
1. Knowing that the players were going to be cooped up together for a minimum of three weeks, were the facilities for living and working ideal for doing the job?
2. We already knew we would be facing Peru, Iran and Holland in our group games so did we have a thorough understanding of their strengths and weaknesses?
3. Knowing the conditions we were likely to find, with the climate and playing surfaces, did we have a style of play we could adopt that would get us the results we needed to reach the next stage of the competition?
4. And most important of all, did Ally know what was his strongest available team?

If you had posed those questions today, they would all be a 'given'. Of course the manager would have them covered. Highly-paid staff would have spent months ticking all the boxes and nothing would have been left to chance. Back in 1978, it just didn't happen. I'm sorry to say that the answer to all four questions in our case was 'No'. But then, maybe we need to go on and ask: "Why didn't it happen?" I'd stake my life on the fact that had Jimmy Sirrel or Dave Sexton been the manager, no way would things have turned out the way they did. I can only judge it against how they might have handled things.

We were staying at a base camp in the small town of Alta Gracia, not far from Cordoba, and when we arrived, all the locals came out to greet us. A lovely touch that we really appreciated and it would have been nice if we'd had the chance to meet them and find out more about their way of life. That didn't happen. We were banned from leaving the camp and guards were permanently on duty to make sure we didn't. The facilities within the complex were horrendous. They really were. There was even a swimming pool with no water and absolutely nothing that was going to keep us occupied during our down-time over the next three weeks or so. We were bored silly and I was probably one of the worst affected. I've always tended to be on the go all the time - I hate just sitting around.

Looking back, I think the management were very fortunate that there were no serious cliques within the squad. Obviously players spent more time with some than others but in general we all got on very well. Had that not been the case, it could have been a recipe for major problems. They could well have had a rebellion on their hands.

Typical of the state of things was that our bonus scheme had never even been discussed. I know there are some who will say money shouldn't have come into it - we should have been prepared to play for nothing. But we were professional footballers and in my case, within the next three years or so, my income from football would have dried up. That was our livelihood and the World Cup was the pinnacle. It was as big as it gets for us. The bonus scheme should have been sorted out long before we left Scotland. Instead of that, we had to set up a series of meetings when we arrived. We had a four-man Players Committee, of which I was one, and we had to thrash it out with Ally and the people from the Scottish FA. It was crazy to be doing it at that stage.

Every step of the way there just seemed to be a nasty taste. Nothing was as it should be. For example, our training facility was just a wide-open field located a short bus ride away. The whole thing was a shambles and at a time when we were trying to psyche ourselves up to do our country proud, those who should have been taking the lead appeared to be stacking obstacles in our way.

I didn't expect to be picked for our opening game against Peru, nor did Bruce, but Ally was incredibly loyal to us. There was certainly logic behind the decision because we knew that if we performed to our capabilities we were well worth our places. He was, though, taking a big gamble. I was very grateful to the manager and whatever problems I might have had, I was determined to put those aside and do everything in my power to justify his faith.

I thought back to four years earlier, when I was playing in the Second Division with Notts County. The local paper had asked me to do a World Cup preview article and everyone laughed when I said I'd be playing for Scotland the next time the World Cup came around. An outrageous predication? Maybe it was but it was about to come true.

The top two countries in our group would progress to the second stage. It was going to be tough but we felt it was 'do-able'. Why we felt that way I'm not too sure because we had no clear idea about what we were up against. We expected Holland to be favourites, simply because they were beaten finalists in '74. Peru had the benefit of being in South America - which would surely be a massive help - and Iran, in theory, should be there for the taking. How wrong could we be!

We totally underestimated Peru. We started against them in Cordoba and they were far better than we'd expected. They were skilful, with bags of energy and ideas, and what quickly became apparent was that they'd done their homework on us. Shame we couldn't say the same. In the end, that was to cost us very dearly. Ally had come in for a lot of criticism from the Scottish media because he'd spurned the chance to watch Peru in action against Argentina a few weeks earlier. He said he'd had a prior engagement. That was unforgiveable before a match of such importance. One of Peru's strengths was their imaginative free kicks. They executed them really well and scored a crucial goal from one. The feeling was that had we had a better idea what to expect, we would have defended them better.

I guess all that I've said so far in this chapter sounds like making excuses but it's definitely not my intention to do that. All I've tried to do is give an honest appraisal as I see it and highlight how ludicrous it was to suggest that a little country with a population of 5 million could win the World Cup. We lost 3-1 against Peru and from that day to this, I have blamed myself for that result. We began well enough and took an early lead when Joe Jordan finished off a fine move and although they equalised just before half time, we should have taken firm control in the period that followed. Joe wasted a couple of gilt-edged chances and then, on the hour, we got a penalty when Rioch was brought down.

I quickly made up my mind to repeat what I did against Wales. It had worked perfectly that night. Why shouldn't it do so again? I checked my run, as usual, and fired it towards the goalkeeper's right. But by the time the ball reached him he was already in position, waiting for it to arrive. They'd done their homework.

I was devastated. It ripped me apart and when Ally sent on Archie Gemmill and Lou Maraci after 70 minutes, to replace Bruce and me, it was actually a massive relief. The game was still poised at 1-1 when I came off but I just knew that I'd done untold damage. Teofilo Cubillas scored two brilliant goals after 72 and 77 minutes and we'd blown it.

Could things get any worse? Well, actually they could. We were told immediately before the game that two players from each side would be selected for a drugs test. What happened next has been very well chronicled over the years. Archie and Kenny Dalglish were selected but as Archie insisted he was dehydrated, he asked Willie Johnston to take his place.

I don't think I'd ever met Willie - or 'Bud' as we all called him - before we were told we'd be rooming together when I turned up to make my debut for Scotland two years earlier. Ever since, we'd always shared a room and although we were quite different characters, we got on great. He had a really short fuse that got him into all sorts of scrapes throughout his playing career. Off the field, though, that wasn't the 'Bud' we knew. He was a real livewire and great company. Put in the situation we were in - especially in Argentina where there was so little to occupy us - we really got to know each other. So much time was spent just lounging around and chatting. After three weeks of that, we had very few secrets left.

Anyway, we had no hint of the next bombshell that was fast approaching as a very subdued Scotland squad headed back to our complex. 'Bud' and I went straight to our room and were lying on our beds, trying to cheer each other up when there was a tap on the door.

Poised to take on Peru in the World Cup Finals –
with Ally MacLeod, Archie Gemmill and Alan Rough.
Little did we know what was just around the corner.

It was Ally, and I'll never forget the grim expression he had on his face. He told 'Bud' that he needed to go with him to the team doctor's room. He never came back.

The next thing I recall was being told I had to take one of the Scottish FA committee members with me to my room. I was totally confused. What was this all about? I showed him which was 'Bud's' stuff and which was mine and he started to pack his gear into a case.

"Enough," I said. I was getting really irritated. "Tell me what the hell's going on."

He explained that 'Bud' had tested positive and was being sent home immediately. What? How could that possibly be?

I actually have no memory of us being given a list of banned substances and told in no uncertain terms what the consequences would be if we were found to have taken any. However, other players have told me that did happen so I'm happy to accept that. It was one of the very few subjects I didn't get around to discussing with 'Bud' during the many hours we spent together.

I certainly didn't see him take any tablets but apparently he had taken Reactivan. You could buy that over the counter in any chemist in the country and it was supposed to act as a pick-me-up for anyone feeling 'low'. The crucial thing was that it contained a stimulant called Fencamfamin - and that was on the list of banned substances. This was all unknown territory for me because I never got involved in that type of thing. However, some of the other lads later told me it was fairly common for footballers to take Reactivan and some were even encouraged by their clubs to do so.

'Bud' was shown absolutely no mercy. He could hardly have been treated any worse if he'd been suspected of murder. He was bundled into a car with a blanket over his head and driven some 400 miles to Buenos Aires. After spending the night in the British Embassy, he was put on a plane home. As far as I could see, no one had lifted a finger to help him and I was really angry about that. He'd tested positive and had to take the consequences but the Scottish FA still had a duty of care. Anyone that knew 'Bud' would realise that at worst, he was guilty of being stupid and naïve.

It was the final straw for me ... I couldn't take much more. I was in a terrible state. I was inconsolable about missing the penalty and letting the lads down, and now my mate had been sent home in shame. I didn't sleep a wink and it was the longest night I'd ever known. I just kept going over and over the events of the day, wishing I could turn back the clock and deal with them differently. I didn't even have anyone to pour out my troubles to. I felt there was only one course of action and first thing in the morning, I went to see Ally. I begged him to let me go home. I knew that with the state I was in he couldn't possibly use me again and having me hanging around would do nothing to improve the morale of the others.

As if Ally didn't already have enough problems on his plate? He was in a state of total shock himself. I think he'd said so many times we were off to win the World Cup he'd become convinced we were going to do it. I wasn't the only one whose world was falling apart and in his case, he certainly couldn't walk away from it. He was brilliant with me. He said that after all I'd done to help get us to Argentina, I had nothing to feel ashamed about. He was very firm in saying I would not be allowed to go home but added: "I won't put you through any more."

I sat in the stand with Bruce for the game against Iran. Archie and John Robertson replaced us in midfield but freshening things up didn't have the desired affect. This was to be our 'formality' game. This was the one we were going to win comfortably and with two points on the board, and a respectable goal-average, there was still hope. Oh dear. The performance totally lacked inspiration against a very average team and even when a comical own goal put us in front, we didn't push on. It finished 1-1 and we looked very dispirited and disillusioned. The whole World Cup experience had fallen so far short of what we'd all dreamed about. Ally was totally distraught. He had a very expressive face anyway and the television pictures highlighted this as they panned in on him, muttering away to himself and squirming in pain and frustration. He was a broken man.

The fact was, though, that it was still possible for us to qualify and a monumental effort from the players four days later in Mendoza took us to the brink of doing so. The Dutch, who included the likes of Ruud Krol, Johan Neeskens and Rob Rensenbrink in their side, went ahead from a penalty midway through the first half. But Dalglish equalised just before half time and after Archie made it 2-1 from a penalty, the 'wee man' scored one of the finest goals ever seen at a World Cup. It was a magnificent example of controlled skill and composure as he cut in from the right and weaved his way past several defenders to score. Suddenly, there was a real chance of staying alive. Not for long, though. Holland scored again and a 3-2 defeat was good enough to send them through with a superior goal-average.

For an hour that day, we showed what we were capable of achieving. It was beyond dispute that we had a really talented batch of players. Had we been properly prepared in a better working and living environment and done ourselves full justice, who knows what we might have achieved?

There was a clever film made that starred Gwyneth Paltrow, called 'Sliding Doors'. I'm constantly reminded of that when I think back to 1978. It's all about what would have happened had she chosen a different direction when she arrived at various 'crossroads' in her day. Like that, it could have been oh so different for us. Had Joe Jordan accepted one or both of his good chances when it was 1-1 against Peru and had I converted the penalty, we would surely have gone on and won comfortably. That, I'm convinced, would have given us the momentum to see off Iran with no difficulty and the outcome of the Holland match wouldn't even have mattered. We would have already qualified by then and been in the driving seat. If only.

Once the word had got out to the press that I'd been sharing a room with Willie Johnston they were all after me, wanting to know what I knew. His failed drugs test was a massive story that had gone worldwide and the media were all over us. Unless you've been in that situation, it's impossible to understand how difficult it is to handle. They hunt in packs and can be unbelievably aggressive, demanding answers to their questions. I wasn't thinking straight anyway after all that had gone on and I didn't handle it well. I said things without really thinking them through - things that I wouldn't have said had the circumstances been different - and I was drawn into it by wanting to show support for 'Bud'. To put the record straight, though, once and for all, I want to make it absolutely clear that although it was by no means unheard of in the English leagues for players to take Reactivan, at no time did I ever take drugs of any sort.

The Sunday newspapers in particular were all desperate for a follow-up angle. I had very little to say on the drugs issue but did agree to do a more general piece with Mike Langley of the Sunday People. Basically, I just told it like it was. How the whole exercise had been a shambles, with no proper preparation and no thought given to how the players were going to live and work comfortably for a minimum of three weeks. The Scottish people had been built up into a frenzy. They were expecting so much from us and we hadn't delivered. There was bound to be a witch-hunt and the fans needed to understand it was not just the players who were to blame. They needed to dig deeper than that. I was one of the main culprits and I've always been quick to hold my hands up. But the players' side of the story had to be told and unlike the rest of the lads, I had nothing to lose. I was 32-years-old. There was no way I would be picked for Scotland again. I just told the truth and to be honest, I was glad to get it off my chest.

The reaction from the Scottish FA was predictable. A few weeks later, when I was back in Nottingham, a letter arrived saying I'd breached my contract by speaking to the media without permission and being critical of the Scottish FA. I was banned sine die. I knew it was coming. I'd made the decision easy for them. It was still a sad end to what had otherwise been an international career of which I'm proud. I had only won 17 caps after being picked for the first time at the age of 30, but I'd helped to win the Home International Championships twice in successive years, figured in some thrilling World Cup qualifying games, toured South America and captained my country on two occasions.

Pride wasn't on my mind when we landed back at Prestwick. Memories of the fantastic send-off we'd been given three weeks earlier were still fresh. The homecoming could not have been more contrasting. We had failed the country miserably. There was no getting away from that and as we all headed off in different directions, I was just as depressed as I had been on the night of the Peru game. Time was doing nothing to heal things.

Incidentally, it's an amazing thing that I never met up again with 'Bud' for 30 years. As often happened with footballers, we found ourselves playing in different divisions and even different countries and our paths never crossed. But when I was taking my new wife Brenda up to the Highlands to introduce her to Banchory, we did a little detour. I knew that 'Bud' had a pub in the Fife coastal town of Kilcaldy, and turned up unannounced. As it happened, his son was running the pub by that time but 'Bud' was there. It was brilliant to see him again. We'd been through a lot together and shared the evening with a pub full of great characters, re-living all the stories.

So, I'd certainly arrived at a crossroads in my life when I finally made it back to Burton Joyce and the first words I said to Margaret were: "That's me finished." I'd thought it through and decided I was going to settle for the quiet life, look to pick up where I'd left off as a 17-year-old and start a new career as a painter and decorator.

What I definitely couldn't face when I was in such a depressed state was another dose of Tommy Docherty. Eventually it had to be done so I drove across to Derby and explained to him that I wouldn't be back for pre-season training, I was packing the game in. "You can't do that," he said. "You're under contract for another year and we're going to hold you to it."

I didn't report back when I should have done so he fined me a week's wages. I couldn't argue with that but it was just the first of many things I got fined for. Every time I turned round there seemed to be a letter, informing me I'd been 'done'.

Then right out of the blue I got a call from Derby telling me I had to go to Norwich for transfer talks. John Bond was their manager ... and he just wouldn't give up! Margaret and I went across for talks and at long last, it was nice to actually meet 'Bondy' face to face. It was as if we'd had some sort of weird long-distance love affair for years and he still seemed determined to have me in his team. He was just as I'd expected. A real football enthusiast with a very positive outlook and after an hour with him, I was starting to get some enthusiasm flowing again. I was impressed with the set-up at Carrow Road and Margaret and I fancied the idea of a few years living in Norfolk. We told Bond in the course of the conversation that we wouldn't sell our house in Burton Joyce and would rent somewhere in Norwich.

He seemed really keen for me to go there. He was pushing the fact that Martin Peters had been a great signing for them, Martin Chivers had just joined them and how well we would work together. By the time we left, it all looked as if it would all go through smoothly.

Imagine my astonishment, then, when I picked up a newspaper and the headline from Docherty said: "We're not selling greedy Masson." According to him, I'd told Norwich that I wanted a house and a car as part of the deal and as a result, they had dropped their interest". It was just not true. I'd made no such demands. A couple of days later I got a call from Bond and he said: "I'm really sorry but The 'Doc' has pulled the plug on it." One of them was telling 'porkies'. I was so angry about it but by that stage, I had very little fight left in me.

I was back to playing 'guerrilla warfare' with Docherty and it wasn't getting either of us very far. I did turn out for the reserves in a couple of pre-season matches to try and keep myself in trim but basically, he kept making up reasons to fine me and I kept refusing to pay.

I was aware that my son Neil was getting some fearful abuse from school-mates which upset me. It wasn't easy for Margaret or Jayne, either. Every time I saw someone looking at me, I knew what they were thinking. I was feeling a little bit more positive after the trip to Norwich - someone still wanted to know me - and friends were doing their best to get me back on the straight and narrow. My mate Dennis came up from London for four days to help me lay a new patio and I remember how a night out with him and Arthur Mann really gave me a boost. They did a 'job' on me.

Something had to give though. I couldn't carry on the way things were and the turning point, not just in my football career but for my life at that time, was a phone call from Notts County chairman Jack Dunnett. He'd clearly spoken to Jimmy Sirrel and he wanted to know what my situation was. I explained it to him in some detail, including the fact that I was by then owing Derby thousands of pounds in fines. He said I should leave it with him. I told him it would be fantastic if he could organise for me to return to Meadow Lane but knowing how deep-seated my issues with Docherty had become, I didn't see how he could pull it off.

The following week he rang me to say: "It's all sorted ... and you don't have to pay Derby anything."

Notts County chairman Jack Dunnett, who had a profound influence on my life, became the most powerful man in English football when he was elected President of the Football League.

17

A FANTASTIC OPPORTUNITY – BUT I JUST WANTED TO PLAY
(1978-80)

Was it written in the stars that I should be reunited with Jimmy Sirrel for the final leg of my playing career? It was easy to think that because everything made absolute sense. Even so, nothing was a foregone conclusion when Jack Dunnett rang to say he wanted to meet. I couldn't escape the fact that I'd come back from Argentina in a big carton that was labelled: 'Damaged Goods'.

I still felt very strongly that my best option was to walk away from football. Margaret had been a rock. I'll be forever grateful for the way she stood by me and helped to re-build my confidence but she, and the kids, were being given a hard time because of my failings. Was it fair for me to subject them to the risk of more? No strings attached but I agreed with the chairman that he and Jimmy would come to my house in Burton Joyce to discuss the possibilities.

What immediately became clear when we started to chat was that Jimmy was not the man I knew. Something was missing. Possibly more than anyone I'd ever met, he always thought he knew best and what he said must go. He genuinely believed it was within his power to change anything and would often say that he should have been the Prime Minister because he'd 'get things sorted'. In his mind, he really believed that. He thought he was an expert at virtually everything and unless you knew him and understood how his brain functioned, it was easy to take a dislike to him.

Jimmy had made the same career move as me. He was desperate to prove he could manage successfully at the top level and less than a year after I moved to Queens Park Rangers, he was appointed manager of Sheffield United. I was shocked when I heard the news - not that he'd left Notts County because I understood very well that he needed to fulfil his ambition. But why had he chosen to go to Bramall Lane? United were cut adrift at the foot of the First Division at that time and turning them around would be an enormous challenge.

I don't know the ins and outs of it. Maybe it was the only top-flight job he could get but knowing Jimmy, I cannot imagine for one second that he believed he was taking a risk. He will have looked at the situation, taken account of the quality of the players at his disposal and told himself: "I shall sort that!"

It didn't happen. The players didn't respond to his quirky methods of man-management and they certainly didn't lock into his strange mannerisms. I explained earlier that Jimmy had a language all of his own. He spoke in riddles half the time but when the Notts County lads grew to understood what he meant, it added to the atmosphere for a team storming our way up through the lower divisions. The supreme confidence he had in himself was projected onto us and was definitely a factor in our success.

It just didn't work at Sheffield United and I wasn't surprised. He was dealing with vastly experienced players like Tony Currie, Alan Woodward, Len Badger, John Colquhoun and Jimmy Johnstone, who had a fair smattering of international caps between them. Jimmy needed to 'up' his game when working with them. Training and coaching methods that were successful in the lower divisions, and even the Second, wouldn't work for them. He struggled to adapt.

A couple of years later I went to America in the summer to play for Minnesota Kicks and one of my team-mates was Chico Hamilton, who had been with United when Jimmy first took over. He told me a story that I have to say, knowing Jimmy, I found totally believable.

Cec Coldwell was the United trainer and the normal procedure was for him to put the players through their warm-up at the training ground. By that time Jimmy would have arrived and he'd then step in and supervise the session. One morning they were hanging around for more than half an hour, waiting for Jimmy, and when he finally appeared, he was clearly very rattled. He pulled the players into a huddle and explained: "It was your fault Chico. I was driving along thinking more about your performance on Saturday than where I was going. I drove straight across a roundabout." He'd made a real mess of his car. Chico told me that the players all looked at each other and they were thinking: "Is he for real?"

He never did win them over in the way that he did the Notts County lads. Consequently, he didn't win many matches either and they gave him a hard time. It reached the point where he had to face the fact that he was not infallible after all - and that wasn't easy for him. I'm told that Jimmy did admit years later that the biggest mistake he made was not taking Ron Fenton with him to Sheffield. I'm not sure Ron would have gone anyway because Dunnett promoted him from reserve-team coach to become County's new manager but I do know what he meant. What he really needed in what was clearly a difficult environment, was an accomplice he could trust implicitly who would act as a go-between for him and the players.

Two years after joining Sheffield United in October 1975, Jimmy was back in familiar surroundings at Meadow Lane. As we sat in my dining room wondering what the future held, he and I both knew the truth of it. He was very aware of my situation while I couldn't believe the change in him. The cockiness had gone. He no longer knew all the answers but did he still have the same drive and ambition? If he did, maybe we could help each other to pull through the crisis of confidence we were both suffering. I felt I owed it to him to give it a try.

"Well? What do you think?" the chairman asked, after offering me the chance to return. Like I've said, it seemed on the surface that it was meant to be but the problem was that I was plagued with self-doubts for the first time in my life. I wanted County fans to remember me as I was during my first spell. I wasn't sure I could re-produce that form. I asked for time to sleep on it. If I said ''yes', it would mean that I could escape the clutches of Tommy Docherty and still remain involved in football. I had to be sure though, that I would be doing it for the right reasons. It wasn't just Jimmy's ambition that I doubted.

The following day, I moved back from Derby County in a straight swop that involved Steve Carter going the opposite way and incidentally, I was disappointed about that. I thought little Stevie was a really talented right-winger and had I not gone to QPR, I was convinced I could have helped to make him a better player. Now, we never would get to find out.

It was the strangest of feelings when I drove back into Meadow Lane. I don't think I'd been back at any time since moving to Rangers yet so much was just as I remembered it. Some of the stalwarts had gone, though. I kept looking around for Les Bradd and David Needham but they weren't there any more. County had banged on the door of the First Division a couple of times while I'd been away, finishing 5th and 8th under Ron Fenton, but Jimmy'd had to lead them through a relegation battle the previous season.

The player who instantly caught my eye was Iain McCulloch. He had moved down from Kilmarnock for a club record fee of £80,000 during the previous March but as the deal was clinched after the transfer-deadline, he wasn't eligible to play in League games until the 1978-79 season. What I saw was a classic example of a late-starter dedicating himself to making up for lost time. Especially today, the majority of professional footballers never get to sample the 'real world' in work terms because they get signed up at an early age. I've always felt you could spot a mile off the footballers who came to the full-time game at a later stage.

McCulloch was one of them. He'd been a heating-engineer as his main employment until he was 24 and used to tell me tales about how he had to work on a Saturday morning before going off to play for Kilmarnock against the likes of Celtic. Consequently, when he got the chance to go full-time with County he really appreciated the massive opportunity he'd been handed and was determined not to waste it. He was seen as a right-winger when I arrived and his pace and aggression made him such a handful for defenders. Full backs hate playing against wingers who kick them. It was always supposed to be the other way around. The more Iain got to understand the game, the more effective he became and he turned himself into one of the top strikers in the country. With the likes of him on board, we'd have a chance.

Maybe Jimmy would ease me back into things. I'd always been naturally fit and had kept myself in decent shape by doing plenty of running on my own since getting back from the World Cup but because of my situation at Derby, I'd missed the vital hard-yards of pre-season. I was conscious of not being properly 'football fit'. Maybe I'd be given a bit of leeway to catch up? No chance of that ... I was named in the team to play against Leicester City at Filbert Street a few days later.

The new season was already five games in by that stage and back-to-back 1-0 wins against Leicester and Leyton Orient made it the perfect start for me. There was no better way to boost my confidence - especially as I marked my first appearance back at Meadow Lane by scoring the goal that beat Orient with three minutes remaining. Happy days were here again!

Two months down the line, in the November, there was an unexpected development. The previous season Jimmy had taken on Colin Murphy as his assistant after he was sacked by Derby, but when Lincoln City approached him to become their new manager he opted to move on. For many years Jimmy had run the show on his own - apart from Jack - but he knew he wasn't physically capable of doing that any more. He had to find a replacement for Murphy.

A few weeks later, he and the chairman asked to see me. They had an interesting proposition to discuss and they made it sound very attractive. The plan was that I would become player-coach, work alongside Jimmy to learn the ropes and eventually become the manager. No timescale was discussed for that to happen but that didn't concern me. I wanted to continue playing for as long as I could so there was no great rush.

My confidence was gradually being restored and I was keen to take on the challenge. It certainly didn't frighten me but knowing how dominant Jimmy had always been in that area of the football club, I wasn't totally convinced that he'd be able to let go of the reins. I did him an injustice. He knew he had a batch of really talented young players coming through and he wanted to put my experience to good use, in matches and on the training ground. The following day he brought the players together and explained that I was the new player-coach and in future, I would be in charge of running the daily sessions.

Talk about tossing me in at the deep end! I had to think on my feet a fair bit in those early days and I loved it. Inevitably, I suppose, I introduced a lot of the training drills that I'd worked with under Dave Sexton and the players responded superbly. Seeing a gradual improvement in them - especially the youngsters - was immensely satisfying for me and I was conscious of how different my relationship with them had become compared to my first spell at Meadow Lane. In those days I would only have been deeply immersed in myself. Now I had much wider responsibilities and I was keen to carry them out to the best of my ability. For example, I remember organising a meeting to advise them about the importance of getting themselves involved in a pension scheme. No way would the Don Masson of old have done that.

Another thing that had definitely changed was my relationship with Jimmy. He was still very much 'the boss' and I had no issues with that. But I found it really interesting that the tone of our conversations was so different to what they'd previously been. Instead of him just dishing out the orders, my opinions mattered. We discussed things, almost as equals and I took it as a real compliment. His 'pupil' had grown up. I'd gone away and become an international and I sensed that he felt that qualified me to talk football with him on equal terms.

For quite a long period during that season we were right in the frame for promotion. We lost only three of my first 17 matches so there was a good level of consistency and when we strung together a run of five straight wins in March, I started to think the First Division was beckoning me again.

Ironically for Jimmy, it all started to fall apart when we went to Sheffield United. Why does football produce these amazing situations so often? We got smashed 5-1 that day and after that, we only managed to win one of our last eight games. Despite that, we finished the season in 6th spot and in today's world, that would have got us into the Play-offs, alongside Stoke, Sunderland and West Ham. The truth of it, though, as we clearly showed in the final weeks, was that we were not ready for the top flight. There was still work to be done.

In theory, everything was progressing nicely but I realised that I had a big decision to make. I cannot remember exactly when but I felt I had to share my mood with Jimmy. Although I was thoroughly enjoying the coaching role, I was far from happy with my own performances. I knew I wasn't doing myself justice. By then, I was just short of my 33rd birthday so there was a limit to what I could expect from myself. Even so, I firmly believed I could continue playing at a good level for another couple of seasons ... but only if I gave it my full attention. The way I saw it, I had the rest of my life to coach but every day as a player from now on would be precious. I explained to Jimmy that the best way I could help him - and Notts County - would be to improve my performances and be a leader for the young players coming through.

I'm not sure as he knew that was coming but he totally understood the point I was making. There were no guarantees, of course, that I could find an extra 10 per cent in my performances but we agreed that I should try. I told Jimmy I was happy to help out in any way I could - especially until he found a new assistant - but my situation wasn't the only thing on his mind at that time. Quite surprisingly, considering how close we had come to winning promotion, he was planning a major re-building programme during the summer of 1979.

His hand was forced to a large extent during the summer because that was the year the Independent Tribunal System was introduced. It meant clubs would no longer have total power over players. When contracts expired, they had the freedom to talk to other clubs with a view to joining them. If a fee could not be agreed between the clubs, it was set by an Independent Tribunal.

When you looked through the County team that had made a decent fist of trying to win promotion in 1978-79, three of our more influential players would have been Eric McManus, Arthur Mann and Mick Vinter. By the time we reported back the following pre-season, all three had gone.

Eric, our very likeable Irish goalkeeper, had just been voted 'Player of the Year' after appearing in every match and been the model of consistency. In the same vein, Arthur had only missed two matches and with his classy midfield performances and surging runs down the left, he was a big favourite with the fans. The thing was that in both cases, they thought they deserved a better contract than Jack Dunnett was offering them and under the new situation, they decided to call his bluff. He didn't 'blink' - and it reached the point of no return for both of them. Arthur moved to Shrewsbury while Eric, after being without a club for some time, eventually signed for Stoke. As for Mick, whose goals two years earlier had been a massive factor in keeping County in the Second Division, he was the subject of a club record £150,000 bid from Wrexham - and County surprisingly accepted it.

Was it good business to allow three key players to walk out of the door so easily? History says that it was - but I was far from convinced at the time, and was especially sad to see my mate Arthur moving on. The prospect of spending time with him again was one of the big attractions for returning to Meadow Lane, but it wasn't all bad. He and Sandra had already decided that wherever his playing career took him, they would continue to live in Nottingham so I still saw plenty of him.

I certainly wasn't the only one who was stunned by what happened next. In fact, I genuinely thought that someone must have added in an extra nought when I heard we had paid £200,000 for a new goalkeeper. That figure was more than double what we'd ever spent on a player before and it was so out of character for Notts County - and with their chairman. It was widely recognised throughout football that he ran a very tight ship and even with the Vinter money to spend, it didn't seem to make a lot of sense. It went against everything County stood for. At the very least, it was a massive gamble.

Actually, it took just one training session for me to realise that it wasn't a gamble at all. On the contrary, bringing Raddy Avramovic across from Rijeka was an incredibly brave yet shrewd move that was to be central to all that followed over the next four years. It wasn't so obvious at the time because we performed poorly in the 1979-80 season but he undoubtedly helped to lift us to a new level.

The fee was an absolute fortune by County's standards and Jimmy was clearly staking his reputation on that signing. You could never accuse him of rushing into a transfer deal. Goodness knows how many midweek trips he made to Scotland to watch McCulloch before finally getting the deal done so the mind boggles at how much time and effort he must have put into signing Raddy. In those days, of course, you couldn't just press a button on your computer to check out all you wanted to know about a player in Yugoslavia but he managed to pull it off. He managed to convince Raddy that it was in his best interests to sign for a mid-table Second Division club and I'm not sure whether Jimmy ever really got the credit he deserved for doing that.

Raddy had everything you could possibly want from your goalkeeper. A big presence in the penalty area, he was brave, decisive, had great reflexes, was a brilliant shot-stopper and was really positive at coming out to collect crosses. What's more ... he could play. If ever we were doing a keep-ball exercise in training, he was as good on the ball as any of us.

The one problem initially was communication. He didn't speak any English when he arrived but he soon conquered that. He was a really bright bloke. He'd given up studying law at university to become a footballer and it used to amuse me the way he played mind games with people. He wasn't too good at speaking our language but he was quick to grasp what we were saying to him. The clever bit was that only if it suited him did he let on that he understood what had been said. It cracked me up when he would put on the bewildered expression he'd developed and say: "I no understand".

When Raddy first landed in Nottingham, rather than go into a hotel he and his wife and young son moved in with Jimmy - just down the road from me. Margaret got on great with Bratislava and we became close friends. In fact, we used to room together on the away trips and I loved his company. He was such an interesting chap to talk to - not just about football but life in general - and had a brilliant sense of humour. There was one big drawback, though. He chain-smoked. The first thing he did when he opened his eyes in the morning was to reach for his fags but if ever I complained about the fog in our room, he just countered it by saying: "I no understand".

Trevor Christie arrived from Leicester to take over from Vinter up front but he wasn't a like-for-like replacement. While Mick was a 'sniffer out' of chances, a real livewire in the area, Trevor was an old-fashioned centre-forward. The big Geordie got his share of goals but you couldn't call him prolific and we really struggled that season for goals. In fact, embarrassingly, it was our left-back Ray O'Brien who finished the season as top scorer. He scored 11 League and Cup goals - eight of them from the penalty spot - and pleased as I was for Ray, that statistic reflected very badly on the rest of us.

That would have to change and I'm sure it was prominent in the thoughts of the man Jimmy had selected to become his new assistant. He opted for Howard Wilkinson and it spoke volumes for the confidence that Jimmy had in him that he was prepared to wait three months for him to join us.

Although nothing was said at the time, he was actually appointed in the September of 1980. But as the FA insisted he must serve his three-months notice as their staff coach for the North-East Region, Jimmy - and Jack Wheeler - had to continue running the ship by themselves through to Christmas. None of us had much of a clue about Howard. I was aware that he was a player at Sheffield Wednesday and Brighton and had been player-manager at non-league Boston United and bearing in mind that he had basically been brought in to fill the role I'd walked away from, I was fascinated to see what he had to offer.

I talked earlier about what a great signing Raddy was. Well, you have to bracket Howard alongside that because it was such a shrewd appointment by Jimmy. The fact that, throughout the period he was serving his notice, he watched us incognito every week was so Howard-like. He was meticulous in whatever he did and by the time he reported for duty at Meadow Lane, he knew everything about us.

It's fair to say that he didn't win over the players straight away. He definitely had to prove himself but he didn't take long to win me over. I could see so much of myself in him. He was very intense but had tremendous drive and ambition and was not the slightest bit bothered about upsetting people. His sole aim was to win football matches and if you weren't with him, he had no time for you.

I unwittingly handed Howard an opportunity to show his strength within days of him arriving. As per normal, we were staying overnight in a hotel on New Year's Eve before we played Cambridge United and it was traditional in that situation for the lads to come to my room for a midnight drink. We certainly weren't rowdy but must have made enough noise to prompt Howard to complain to the hotel management that his players wouldn't be able to sleep. "I'm sorry sir," came the reply, "but one of your players has the room you are talking about!"

Some people would have jumped straight in with both feet to assert their authority. Once Howard was satisfied it was just a quick toast to bring in the New Year and then off to bed, it was fine.

I loved his training methods. He'd clearly been to the same 'school' as Dave Sexton and everything was done with a purpose. He

Howard Wilkinson ... such a shrewd signing by Jimmy Sirrel.
His sole aim was to win football matches.

worked us hard, often two sessions a day, but as long as you could see there was a means to an end, I didn't mind. We were no where near good enough at that time to seriously think we could get into the First Division and stay there but very gradually, round pegs were being fitted into round holes.

One of those saw the emergence of Brian Kilcline, a 17-year-old central defender who already had the physique of not just a man but a giant. The thing about him was that he wasn't just brute force and ignorance. He could 'play' and it was obvious from the start that if he was managed properly and responded to it, he could go to the very top. He had a couple of 'tasters' in the early part of the season, then played the last 11 games. That was another round hole filled for next season.

We eventually finished 17th in 1979-80 - bitterly disappointing but as individuals and as a team, I knew we had made progress. The most important thing was that our very talented group of youngsters had spent the previous nine months learning their trade.

For example, they will have benefitted from the experience of being involved on the final day of the season, which turned into one of the most remarkable games I ever played in. A crowd of 33,883 had packed St Andrew's to see Birmingham City clinch promotion to the top flight. Jim Smith's team only needed a point and when they led 3-2 with not long to go, the celebrations were already underway. But big 'Killer' put them on hold when he equalised, converting my corner for his first League goal, and you could have heard the proverbial pin drop when Paul Hooks rattled the crossbar with seconds remaining.

It was an amazing afternoon. What were the chances, I wondered, of us emulating Birmingham and going into action on the final Saturday of the next season with a realistic chance of reaching the top flight?

Incidentally, that Birmingham result was no fluke - we were far more effective on the road than we were at Meadow Lane. Our seven away victories included some notable scalps - West Ham, Fulham and Swansea - and it was good to show the QPR fans I could still play when we went to Loftus Road and won 3-1.

18
CREATING MY OWN LITTLE PIECE OF HISTORY
(1980-81)

My burning ambition from a very young age was to captain Scotland and having ticked that particular box on one of the greatest football nights in our history, I was now free to focus on chasing my other highly improbable target.

In its own way, this one was every bit as ambitious as thinking I might one day lead my country into battle and as Notts County headed into the 1980-81 season, I reckoned I had one last chance to pull it off. I wanted to become the first player to captain the same club right through from the Fourth Division to the First.

At that stage, only two clubs had ever made that arduous journey up through the leagues - Northampton Town and Carlisle United - and both had changed captains along the way. There was an opportunity to make history and I wasn't going to pass it up lightly. Winning two promotions with Notts County before I moved to Queens Park Rangers was the easy bit. In comparison, completing the job of reaching the top would be a mighty big 'ask' and a lot of things would need to fall into place if I was to pull it off.

To start with, I'd have to stay fit, which was by no means a certainty at that stage of my career, and we would need to perform considerably better than we had the previous season if we were to mount a challenge.

Key to that would be whether or not the talented youngsters could raise their standards. Also crucial within that equation would be Howard Wilkinson's contribution. The coach had been given chance since Christmas to get his feet under the table and it was immediately clear when we reported for duty that Jimmy Sirrel intended to take a step back and give him some scope to pull the strings. He was always a man full of bright ideas - but what did he have in store for us?

Well, the first thing came as a shock and some of the players were less than happy about it. We were told we had to report back for pre-season training seven weeks before the first League game. That was unheard of and seriously ate into our summer break. Personally, I didn't mind. I loved training anyway and what could be better than being paid to keep fit? There was a rider to that, though ... I was reserving judgement until I was sure there was good reason for bringing us back so early. There was.

Howard wanted to completely change our style of play. He'd taken a long, hard look at what he had at his disposal and reckoned that by moving a few more round pegs into the holes they were best suited to fill, he could create a successful team. The most significant change involved Pedro Richards. The masterplan was to play the ball out from the back - and he was switched from right back to fill a major role as sweeper.

Pedro was a great lad, very popular with the players, but he did always seem to have a chip on his shoulder. He took some managing because he had a real 'rebel streak' in him and soon after Howard arrived, they had a big run-in. What was beyond doubt though was that he was a class player and he was particularly good at reading the game. You never saw him flying into tackles because he had a natural ability to spot danger early and his anticipation was superb. He was ideal for the new role but could he be trusted with the extra responsibility? All credit to Howard - and to Jimmy. They were banking on him responding to the challenge. The feeling was that he had a lot more to offer but before they could get chance to find out, there was an issue to resolve. Pedro was out of contract and was refusing to sign a new one. It was standing in the way of progress but clever management sorted the problem. He was sent with a young team to play at Shepshed - not at right back but as a sweeper. He was immaculate that night and when he said how much he'd enjoyed himself he was told: "Sign a new deal and you can play there for the first-team."

The big question was, if Pedro was to fill that role, where did that leave Brian Stubbs? Young Brian Kilcline had emerged from the ranks to establish himself in the centre of defence at the back end of the previous season with a series of mature displays and quite simply, three into two wouldn't go.

I found myself in one of the most difficult situations I ever faced in my life. Immediately after we reported back, Howard had asked to see me - along with youth coach Mick Walker - and he outlined what he had in mind. Then he dropped the bombshell that in order to put those plans into action, there would be no place for 'Stubbsy'.

It's debatable whether Notts County ever had a better servant than big Brian. He'd played more than 400 games in 12 years for his only League club. He was a massive part in moving us up the leagues and was a magnificent club man. The fans loved him, so did Jimmy - and that was potentially a major obstacle. Howard laid this out to me and said that if he was to get his ideas past Jimmy, and pair Richards and Kilcline at the back, he needed my support. I was incredibly uncomfortable about it. Brian and I had been through so much together and I knew it would be a life-changing decision from his point of view. I agonised over it but deep down I knew I had to do what was right for the football club. Very reluctantly, I told Howard I was with him.

Even so, none of us players could have imagined at that stage that 'Stubbsy' would never play again for County. In fact, it was the end of his League career because he didn't want to play for any other club. He was only 31 and could have gone away and done an outstanding job for another club for the next three or four years. He didn't want to do that. He was Notts County through-and-through. He hung around for a while but didn't figure in the first-team. It was such a sad end to an outstanding career.

The other big change involved Tristan Benjamin. Raddy Avramovic was pretty much banned from kicking the ball. His orders were to roll it or throw it out at every opportunity and in order to make that work, we had to have two full backs who had good 'touch' and were comfortable on the ball. No qualms about Ray O'Brien, who was voted 'Best Left Back in the Second Division' at the end of that season. The system suited him perfectly but with Pedro now operating in the middle, we needed a new right back. 'Benjy' slotted in there, played every game bar one in that position for the next two seasons, and he was superb.

I had so much time for him and in my opinion, he became good enough to play for England. He'd started out as an apprentice striker at Meadow Lane, spent a fair bit of time in midfield and also played as a central defender. It spoke volumes for his ability that he was comfortable wherever he played but it was an inspired decision to move him to right back. He had all the qualities Howard wanted in that role - plus genuine pace. He was a beautiful mover. He floated across the turf and I was totally in awe of the way that, whenever the need arose, he would suddenly move through the gears and accelerate away. You wouldn't meet a nicer lad than 'Benjy' and had he not been the most introverted professional footballer I ever came across, I'm sure he would have been a really top player.

Howard tells a story about 'Benjy' that really sums him up. One day, we were hanging around for ages, waiting to start training, and that was so unusual because Howard was a stickler for good time-keeping. It turned out that just as he was heading out of the changing room, 'Benjy' had asked to speak to him. It was such a rare occurrence for 'Benjy' to say anything that Howard didn't dare say: "No". Hence the fact that we were outside, freezing, while he said his piece. It's a fact of football life that the top players - and managers - all have a touch of arrogance about them, which stems from having a strong self-belief. You could never say 'Benjy' was arrogant. He just wasn't made that way and although it held him back to some extent, he was an outstanding footballer and person.

Vital cogs had been installed and as every day went by, I was getting increasingly excited about what was happening. We were developing a style very much along the same lines as we'd used at QPR when we finished runners-up and it suited me perfectly. Basically, I was going to get more touches than anyone as the ball was fed through from the back and that just played to my strengths. It did mean I was under pressure to perform but that didn't bother me. The more we worked on the system in training - often two sessions a day - the more confidence I got in the other players. They grasped what was expected of them within their respective roles and worked really hard to take it to the end product that Howard and Jimmy had hoped for.

We had two new recruits on board that summer and one of them was a former QPR colleague. Eddie Kelly had come from Leicester and we'd previously played together in the Rangers midfield for a few months before I left. Earlier in his career he'd helped Arsenal to win the League & Cup 'double'. His experience would be invaluable with our young squad. Rachid Harkouk was our other signing and what an interesting one has was. Although he came from QPR, I'd already left by the time he joined them from Crystal Palace so we didn't know each other. It only took a couple of training sessions for me to realise he was a player capable of having a massive influence on our season.

It was helpful that rather than play mundane pre-season games, we had something to aim for with three group matches in the Anglo-Scottish Cup before the League programme got underway. We managed to qualify for the knockout stages by winning at Fulham and drawing with Leyton Orient and Bristol City and there was a fascinating aside to that clash at Ashton Gate.

City had a midfield player called Gerry Gow, who was a combative Scot. In fact, I would say he was probably the most difficult opponent I faced on a regular basis and it was business as usual that afternoon. He never left me alone, kicking me from pillar to post and he wasn't the slightest bit interested in where the ball happened to be. "My orders are to stick tight to you," he said when I questioned what the hell he was playing at. Fair enough I thought, so I took him to all sorts of places where I knew he wouldn't want to go. I kept wandering back behind Ray O'Brien and it left a gaping hole in the middle of midfield. Although we only drew 1-1 the new system showed promise - but Gow wasn't impressed. "Play like that when the League games start and you'll get f***ing relegated," he said as we left the pitch.

I guess the jury was still out for a lot of people but our belief was growing by the day. To underline the point, when Iain McCulloch was told that a local bookie was offering 66-1 against us getting promotion, all the lads and coaching staff couldn't resist the temptation. We certainly didn't have a betting culture within our club - far from it - but we felt we knew something the bookie didn't.

Absolute priority when we kicked off the League programme against Bolton Wanderers was to get a proverbial monkey off our backs. We hadn't won at home since early November and that couldn't be allowed to continue. Another box was ticked as we won 2-1 and then came one of the most significant games of the season.

I scored the goal as we drew 1-1 in midweek with Newcastle United but the result was almost irrelevant. Our performance at St James' Park that night was superb. We demonstrated the full value of all those hours and hours of hard work on the training ground. Newcastle spent long periods chasing shadows. Okay, we didn't have an end product but they couldn't get the ball away from us. To some extent, it went under the radar and that was probably a good thing. Had it been at Meadow Lane and had we won the game, expectation levels might have gone through the roof. Instead of that, they were kept in check long enough for us to come to terms with what was happening.

I remember the players all getting into a huddle at the back of the coach on the way home and I stressed to them - especially the youngsters - that they needed to take on board what was happening. This type of situation didn't come along too often in the course of a career and if we stuck together and worked hard to ensure that the performance against Newcastle was just the start, we could be in for a life-changing year. We had some strong, really determined characters in our team. People like O'Brien and McCulloch were brilliant professionals who set a great example to the others and I could sense there was a real desire to be successful.

The next big crossroads came at the end of August when we went to West Ham and got spanked 4-0. On the evidence of that day, they would clearly be the outstanding team in our division but my big concern was how we would react to the defeat. The response was fantastic - and revealed so much about the lads. We won four and drew the other of our next five games. In fact, that West Ham game was our only defeat in the first 18 matches of the season, and by mid-November we were top of the table on merit.

There had been a little blip from a personal point of view along the way - thanks to my good friend Tommy Docherty. For some reason, it seemed to be his mission in life to make things as uncomfortable for me as he possibly could. By then he was managing QPR and from what I could tell of it, the key message he wanted to get across in his team-talk before we played them in the third round of the League Cup was: "Wind up Masson."

There was nothing subtle about it. They were all sniping away at me and although I was always very good at ignoring that type of thing, on this occasion I wasn't. Eventually I snapped and when I had a confrontation with Andy King a minute before half time, we were both sent off. It was the one and only time in my career that I was ever sent off. I was furious with myself for not showing more self-discipline but every bit as angry with Docherty. I was determined to have it out with him when the half time whistle sounded but Jimmy prevented me from getting down the corridor between the two dressing rooms.

It was probably just as well because I was so angry that I don't know what I might have done. We won that game 4-1 and it was difficult to escape the feeling that Docherty wouldn't have been bothered about that. He'd got the 'result' he wanted.

That win earned us an attractive League Cup trip to Manchester City. It meant yet another eventful meeting with John Bond, who was in charge at Maine Road by that stage. We lost 5-1 - Dennis Tueart scored four of them - and ridiculous though it might sound, we played very well. Raddy was in a state of shock. He'd only conceded one goal in the six League games before that and I remember him on the coach coming home. He just kept shaking his head and saying: "Six shots, five goals." There was a lesson to be learned from that. The biggest difference at the top level is the clinical way in which they exploit their chances.

We weren't scoring enough goals and if anything was going to derail us, I feared that would be the problem. Although the front partnership of McCulloch and Trevor Christie were doing well and were a real handful for defenders you wouldn't call either of them a natural goal-scorer. We had to work hard for every goal - and point - we got but if hard work was going to get the job done, we'd be fine.

We'd discovered how to win at home again - we won five and drew one of our first six games at Meadow Lane and I distinctly recall a four-day spell in October when we really looked the part as leaders of the Second Division. Leyton Orient and Oldham were renowned at that time as tough places to go to but we came away victorious from both grounds. That was a real boost to our confidence.

It's almost inevitable that at some stage during the course of a season you will have a bad patch but when ours came, it lasted for three months - from the start of November until the end of January. We didn't win a single League game in that period. Our saving grace was that we were in the days of two points for a win and one for a draw. We drew nine of our 12 games involved over that period, and managed to stay in touch with the leaders.

I missed three of those games in November because I was suspended and back in 1980, that didn't just mean you couldn't play in matches. You were actually banned from going to the ground, not just on match-days but throughout the period of your punishment. It was a ridiculous situation but I couldn't just sit at home and twiddle my thumbs. I went back and said to Margaret: "Pack your bags ... we're off." Jimmy had told me I couldn't go on holiday but for once, I took the law into my own hands. We went to Sorrento, the delightful cliff-top town that overlooks the Bay of Naples in southern Italy, and had a brilliant time. I know it's not what you normally associate with a Scotsman but it's always been the way of things that I only have to look at the sun to get a tan. I'd totally changed colour by the time I got back and when I went to the ground a startled Jimmy said: "Little fella, where have you been? I told you that you couldn't go on holiday." It was soon smoothed over and to be fair, I felt great. I was rarin' to go again and knew I would get the benefit.

The rest of the lads must have been incredibly envious because they were at full-stretch. Our small squad was severely hit by injuries and suspensions and I cannot stress enough what a great effort it was to keep ourselves in the promotion picture when the odds were so heavily stacked against us.

The situation was so serious when we went to Preston on the day after Boxing Day that we got involved in one of those romantic little football stories which were quite commonplace back in the day. We didn't even have enough players to raise a team and had to use the newly-signed Ian McParland as a substitute. He was a little right winger who had been working in the pits and playing for Scottish junior club Ormiston Primrose. In time, he turned out to be a fantastic signing. Just like McCulloch, he was all aggression and pace and he went on to become a prolific goal-scorer for County when he switched to playing through the middle. It was a far cry from that at Preston, though, when this little lad literally stepped off the train from Scotland and wandered into our dressing room.

We had to keep believing that the turning point was not far away and it finally arrived at the end of January, when we headed north to play Sheffield Wednesday. Hillsborough has always been one of my favourite grounds. The big pitch really suited me and I was right on top of my game that day. We emerged as 2-1 winners, inspired by a fantastic goal from Christie. I struck a 40-yard diagonal pass that dropped onto his favourite left-foot as it came over his shoulder and he smashed it into the roof of the net without breaking stride. People tell me that I just stood in the centre-circle with my hands on my hips, shaking my head in disbelief, and that doesn't surprise me. If I'm totally honest, I didn't believe Trevor was capable of scoring goals of that quality. Yet just to prove it was no fluke, we produced a carbon-copy goal between us a few months later that helped set up a crucial win at Cambridge United.

I lived for moments like that. Nothing I ever did on the football pitch was more satisfying that creating a goal. I scored 96 times in League and Cup games during my three spells with County and I'm very proud of that statistic. But what I'd really love to know is how many 'assists' I recorded? That would be the figure that mattered most to me. My biggest thrills came when I picked a pass and delivered, like I did with those two goals for Trevor, or played a little one-two in the box to set someone up.

Anyway, that win at Hillsborough did the trick and we started winning games again. Players were coming back from injuries and suspensions and we had a reinforcement - just the one - when Mark Goodwin arrived from Leicester. Eddie Kelly moved out at the same time so it was a straight swop in midfield and with Goodwin on one side of me and David Hunt on the other, I had two hungry lads who were very willing to do any running that I couldn't manage any more. 'Hunty' was an excellent team man. Maybe not the most talented of players but he more than made up for that with his high-energy performances and he did a colossal amount of work off the ball. The three of us quickly developed a good blend - and we kept pressing on.

In some respects, it was a distraction that we made good progress in the Anglo-Scottish Cup but you won't be surprised to know that I enjoyed it. Apart from Hampden Park, I'd played at less than handful of grounds in Scotland during the course of my career so I was really pleased to add Morton and Kilmarnock to that list. Glasgow Rangers were also in the competition but sadly they were eliminated before we could have a crack at them. In the end we made it all the way to the final and, with great respect, it was a massive anti-climax that our prize was a two-legged tie against Chesterfield.

We lost the first game at Saltergate but only 1-0. We'd be fine with that back at Meadow Lane, we thought, but it didn't turn out that way. I eventually managed to haul us level after 73 minutes with a glancing header - my first goal with a header since I'd scored past Ray Clemence at Hampden five years earlier - but although we bombarded Chesterfield in the closing stages, we couldn't get another goal. We had to go into extra time and lost to a goal in the very last minute. I was a runner-up again!

Greeting Chesterfield captain Bill Green and referee Pat Partridge before the first leg of the Anglo-Scottish Cup Final at Saltergate.

We had bigger fish to fry, as they say, and although a run of four straight draws kept the tension going until deep into April, it was all laid out in front of us on Easter Monday as we made our way back from a 2-1 win at Cambridge. Two more points - the equivalent to one win in those days - from our last three matches and Notts County would be back in the top flight after an absence of 55 years. Was it inevitable that we'd achieve that? Of course not ... but it was difficult to escape the feeling that it was meant to be. We had to play Watford and Cambridge at home with a trip to Chelsea sandwiched in between. We knew what had to be done.

Watford, under Elton John and Graham Taylor, were making their own journey up from the Fourth Division to the First at that time and although they had slipped out of the promotion race, they'd be tough opposition. Supporters were confident 'this would be the day' but we knew we'd have to work hard for anything we got. That was underlined when Luther Blissett put them ahead with a penalty and although Goodwin came up with an equaliser, we suffered a double-blow. Blissett scored again when Raddy made an error that was so out of character for him, and I had to go off late in the game because I was in so much pain after falling awkwardly.

It didn't take long back in the treatment room for 'Doc' Clarke to diagnose that I'd cracked a couple of ribs. I hit the roof when he jabbed a finger into my chest and I feared the worst as he stood there shaking his head. The only cure was rest ... my season was over. All those years, matches, goals and gaffs over two spells that I'd invested into hauling County up from the dregs of the Football League and fate had decreed that I wouldn't be there at the finish. I was mortified. Surely this couldn't be happening.

The supporters had planned their big end-of-season function for that night, hoping it would turn into a promotion celebration. Sadly it all fell flat and the winner of the 'Player of the Year' trophy - me - wasn't even there to collect it. I was at home in a lot of pain and feeling very sorry for myself so Raddy and Bratislava transported Margaret to the event and she went on stage to collect it for me. Incidentally, I'm very proud of the fact that I was - and still am - the only player to win that award three times.

I made up my mind fairly quickly that I simply wouldn't be able to face going to Chelsea the following Saturday. People to this day cannot understand how I could be anywhere other than Stamford Bridge but I just couldn't do it. I was never a good spectator at the best of times. That was a factor but there were also other things to consider. I desperately wanted to be out on the pitch, leading from the front, and if that wasn't going to be possible I didn't feel I could contribute anything worthwhile. I would just have been hanging around in the dressing room, adding to the tension. Howard and Jimmy wouldn't have wanted that, nor would the lads. They had to do it for themselves - and I was confident that they would. It would be agony but I was better off out the way.

Come the big day, I took Margaret and the kids up to Middlesbrough for a family visit. I wasn't going to be comfortable wherever I went. That would be as good as any. I guess younger people reading this will have difficulty understanding the full picture but basically, I could have been in a foreign land. I'd taken the decision to detach myself - and there was no way of keeping in regular contact with what was happening at Stamford Bridge. I remember watching the Rugby League Cup Final on television to try and take my mind off of events at Chelsea and I had no idea what was happening. Then, as I sat there trembling when they read out the final scores ... I couldn't believe it. They got to Chelsea v Notts County and said: "Result not yet in."

What had happened, of course, was that the Chelsea fans had invaded the pitch in protest about the way their club was being run and the players had to escape to the safety of the dressing room for at least 20 minutes. Consequently, there was a long delay before I finally got the news that the lads had won 2-0 and we would be promoted.

I don't need to dwell too long on the events of the day because every Notts County fan knows them chapter and verse. At the heart of the story was Rachid Harkouk, who was picked to replace me. Incredibly, he was actually born in Chelsea and it was pure romance for him to return to his roots and produce a 'Man of the Match' performance. He should have been man of every match he played in because he had so much ability and although I doubt whether it keeps him awake at night, he got no where close to fulfilling his potential. He'd had a very frustrating first season at Meadow Lane. He'd missed the first chunk of it through injuries and suspension and never got an extended run in the starting line-up. But Jimmy and Howard were banking on him to come up trumps in that massive game at Chelsea, and he didn't disappoint. It was from Rachid's corner that Christie put us ahead in the first half and he clinched the 2-0 win all on his own, carrying the ball almost half the length of the field before firing home from the edge of the box.

Within 10 minutes of hearing the final score, I'd bundled the family into the car and we were on our way back to Nottingham. I was determined to be at Meadow Lane when the team arrived back - so were several hundred supporters - and it was a memorable scene. Even though I'd missed out on the ultimate moment of glory, it was a life-changing day for me in more than one respect. I'd hit the jackpot. Our decision in July to back ourselves to win promotion had been an incredibly shrewd bit of business and I'd also agreed a 'tasty' promotion-bonus with Jack Dunnett when I was negotiating my return to Meadow Lane.

I remember laying in bed that night, slightly the worse for wear, thinking back to the day when Bob Worthington and I first set foot in the ground. It was just a silly dream, surely, to think that I could help this ailing old club into a position where we'd be lining up against the likes of Arsenal, Manchester United and Liverpool. Those sort of dreams didn't really come true. But this one had and I'd secured a little bit of football history all to myself. The first man ever to captain the same club right through from bottom to top. It was an achievement that Jack Dunnett, Jimmy Sirrel and Jack Wheeler could share with me. We'd made the journey together, our own 'Gang of Four', and it was such a satisfying feeling.

Howard Wilkinson's contribution certainly couldn't be overlooked. He'd found a way of developing a successful unit out of meagre resources, getting the absolute maximum out of us, and we'd stuck together to achieve our objective. I thought he and Jimmy managed me brilliantly that season. I still loved training, still loved pushing my body to the limit every day, but there were some things I just couldn't do any more. They recognised that and adapted things to accommodate me. I remember saying to Howard at one stage that if we'd worked together when I was in my prime, there was no telling what we might have achieved. That's how highly I rated him.

A 2-0 win against Cambridge rounded things off in style in the final game at Meadow Lane and, yet another one to add to my collection, we finished as runners-up to West Ham.

Time might be catching up with me but I'd done my bit. I'd played in 53 League and Cup games that season and I still had a few more to come, providing the ribs would let me, because I had a really exciting adventure lined up. The chairman had an interest in Minnesota Kicks and as part of the deal when I moved from Derby, he offered me the chance to go to America and play for them for four months.

I went to the ground the day after the season's finale with Cambridge and Jimmy said: "Little fella - what are you doing here?" I told him I'd come to collect my boots and it was immediately clear that he had no idea what was going on. It was a really strange situation. Howard knew I was going, so did the players and I took it for granted that the chairman would have talked it through with Jimmy. He clearly wasn't happy about it but it wasn't my place to get involved in that. He had to sort it with the chairman. Officially I'd been given a free transfer by County. It had to be that way in order for me to move to America but although nothing was certain, the plan - in the chairman's eyes - was that I would be back in August to try and play my part in getting us established in the top flight.

How lucky was I? I would be 35-years-old in August but was still going strong - and still had so much to look forward to.

All yours! Raddy Avramovic presents me with a cluster of end-of-season awards after we'd clinched promotion to the top flight. In just the mood to celebrate - with Jack Wheeler and John Mounteney.

Chapter 19
TORNADOES, RAPIDS AND CHICKENS
(1981)

I had an interesting relationship with Jack Dunnett. Would I say we were friends? I think we were. It was certainly more than a 'business arrangement' and in many respects he was like a father-figure to me. I could always rely on him for sound advice, whether it was football related, something to do with furthering my career prospects or getting the best from my money. One way or another, as I'm sure he'd be the first to admit, we scratched each other's backs very effectively. I played a considerable part in helping him to achieve many of his ambitions over the 11 years in which I worked for him at Notts County and he, in turn, was never slow to show his appreciation.

One of the biggest favours he did me was paving the way for me to go to America for four months during the summer of 1981. That was a perfect example of what I'm talking about. He was keen that I should go during the summer period to play for Minnesota Kicks in the North American Soccer League. The lucrative deal involved, plus the chance to experience a very different way of life were hugely appealing.

I've sung the chairman's praises at regular intervals during the course of this book and I have so much admiration for the way he ran his affairs. It was a phenomenal achievement to take little Notts County up to the top flight without throwing vast sums of cash at the

The Notts County history-makers. Back row (left to right): Trevor Christie, Eddie Kelly, Mick Leonard, Raddy Avramovic, Pedro Richards, Rachid Harkouk. Middle row: Jack Wheeler, David Hunt, Gary Wood, Brian Kilcline, Brian Stubbs, Ray O'Brien, Tristan Benjamin, Mick Walker. Front row: Don Masson, Paul Hooks, Gordon Mair, Jimmy Sirrel, Howard Wilkinson, Iain McCulloch, Jimmy Doherty.

project and I thought it was very revealing in the Eighties that he was elected President of the Football League and held onto that post for six years. He was the most powerful man in English football throughout that period and the support he got from his peers illustrated just how highly they regarded him.

A lot of people around that time were sensing big opportunities in America. Our brand of football finally appeared to have taken off on the other side of the Atlantic and was providing serious competition for baseball and American football. The off-shoot was that they wanted to bring in the best players, regardless of what it cost, and the whole scene was a massive lure to English-based players. Equally, businessmen were queuing up to get involved.

I never got to the bottom of Dunnett's actual involvement with Minnesota Kicks and I didn't need to. He left his close-friend Ralph Sweet to 'front up' on everything. Ralph was announced as the new owner when a consortium took over the franchise in October 1980 and three people put the cash together to buy it. There was no mention of 'JD' but reading very much between the lines, I fancy he had more than a passing interest. The way he talked to me about an exciting opportunity to go there and play, plus the deal he set up for me, certainly suggested there was more to it than met the eye.

Anyway, I didn't care about the whys and wherefores. I wanted a slice of what was on offer and it was all agreed that as soon as the season was over, I'd be off to Minnesota for four months with Margaret, Neil and Jayne.

The magnificent adventure began in great style when the chairman sent his chauffeur-driven Rolls-Royce to collect us from home, the day after our final League match against Cambridge. We piled on board with suitcases galore and Meadow Lane was the first stop, so I could collect my boots. Then Alex Gibson, a former County player who was the chairman's chauffeur, took us to London.

One of Dunnett's many 'caps' was that he was the long-serving MP for Nottingham East and he had a plush apartment just around the corner from the Houses of Parliament. We stayed there overnight with him and his wife Pam, who cooked us a fantastic meal, and then Alex took us to Gatwick early the following morning. Talk about five-star treatment. It didn't get much better than that and over the next four months, that standard was pretty much maintained.

I'd never been to America and I instantly fell in love with just about everything to do with it. The food, the people, accommodation standards and the big wide open spaces. Until you go there you don't quite realise what a vast country it is and I hate to think how many thousands of miles I travelled in my time with the Kicks. The Americans do things in a way that really appealed to Margaret and me and it was easy to understand why so many of my new colleagues had applied for the 'Green Card' that enabled them to become long-term residents in the country.

Ralph Sweet was there to meet us when we landed in Minneapolis, the major city of Minnesota, and so were Freddie Goodwin and Geoff Barnett. I already knew Sweet well from his time as Notts County's vice-chairman and I knew of Goodwin and Barnett. Freddie, a former Birmingham City manager, was President of the Kicks and Geoff, a former Arsenal and Everton goalkeeper, was the coach.

They sorted me out with a new Pontiac car and pointed us in the direction of Edina, a suburb to the south west of Minneapolis, where we would be living in a condominium on an up-market complex, complete with shared swimming pool. It was easy to get the impression that I was there on holiday ... but you know me. I only know one way to treat my football and it was a deadly serious business as soon as I got to work. I'd never knowingly sold anyone short and I wasn't about to start now.

Maybe they do speak English in The States but in most other respects, things were incredibly different. Being able to communicate from the 'off' was a massive help but every day was part of a learning curve. I couldn't put a price on the life-experience I gained from my time with Kicks. We wanted for nothing and although the players were a real mixture from here, there and everywhere, they were a brilliant bunch to work with. It was compulsory for every club to employ two Americans in their squad and we also had 'Tino' Lettieri, who was the Canadian international goalkeeper.

Most of the lads, though, had served their time in the Football League. People like Geoff Merrick (ex-Bristol City), David Stride (Chelsea), Stewart Jump (Crystal Palace), Ron Futcher (Luton), Chico Hamilton (Aston Villa), Tony Want (Spurs) and Steve Heighway (Liverpool). Add them all together and we formed a very useful team.

Standard procedure out there was that every now and again you went, what they described as, 'on the road'. It would have been a lot more accurate to call it 'in the air' because it was a five-day exercise that took in two away games. My first taste of that involved flying to Dallas on the Friday. The following day we drew 1-1 in front of a poor crowd in a fantastic stadium, then flew the next day to Canada. We played Calgary on their astroturf pitch on Day 4 of the trip, stayed overnight and then flew home the next day. Incidentally, Colin Harvey - a member of Everton's famous 'Holy Trinity' midfield, alongside Howard Kendall and Alan Ball - was in Dallas while we were there. His brother happened to be living there and as Geoff Barnett knew Colin from their days at Goodison Park, we arranged to meet up. We had a brilliant night in a traditional Texas bar and I even had a go on the bucking bronco. It only lasted for a few seconds!

While I was away, Ralph Sweet had organised to fly Margaret and the kids to Florida for three days, where they had a fantastic time in Disney World. The Kicks paid for everything. It was an incredible gesture. They were home again waiting for me when I arrived back ... and didn't stop talking about their experience for months.

Our first home game was quite something. Talk about razzmatazz. Everything was done in a calculated manner, designed to entertain the fans so royally that they went home craving for more. The whole approach was very different to how things were run at home. For example, the changing rooms at all the stadiums we used were massive by our standards and as soon as the final whistle went, the media got easy access. Clubs were desperate to get as much TV and radio exposure as they could and they weren't precious about the players like they are in England. If someone wanted to interview us straight after the game we were expected to make ourselves immediately available, and it was quite common for a near-naked player to wander past 'in shot' while it was happening.

I found it difficult at first to cope with the humidity, which could be incredibly draining. We were given salt tablets before we went out and although we didn't kick off until 8pm, the conditions still took their toll. It didn't help that the games often lasted longer than I was used to because of all the distractions. Gimmicks seemed to be part and parcel of the way of life in the States and you had to get used to that. For example, on one occasion, when we were playing San Diego, a chap dressed as a chicken kept running up and down the touchline. I've no idea what it was all about. As far as I was aware it wasn't a sponsorship thing but the crowd loved it and that's always the yardstick over there. If the crowd love it, you have to find a place for it - even if he keeps causing play to stop. I was less than pleased when he came and sat on the ball just as I was about to take a corner. But the fans thought it was hilarious so that was my cue to smile through gritted teeth.

Kicks had a proud tradition that they were looking to me to help maintain. They'd been the first team ever to win four straight divisional titles and had qualified for the play-offs in each of the six seasons since the franchise transferred to Minneapolis. While I was there we pulled in crowds of 25-30,000 every time we played and they gave us terrific support. Home games were a proper day out - especially as that was where 'tailgating' was invented. Thousands of fans would converge on the massive car park at the Metropolitan Stadium anything up to three hours before kick-off and set themselves up to eat, drink and socialise from the boots of their cars. By the time the game started, many of them were in proper high spirits and they loved their football.

I'll never forget the welcome I got at my first home game. The cheer-leaders were out in force, forming a tunnel for the players to run through and it took ages to get the game going because we were all introduced individually to the crowd. In my case, the announcer said: "And now, all the way from Ban-chory in Scotland, let's give a special super-Kicks welcome to Donny Masson!" It was great but I always wondered what the noise levels would be like when your name was announced if you'd had a 'stinker' in the previous home game. Fortunately, I never found out.

I was especially looking forward to our home game against Vancouver Whitecaps because Willie Johnston played for them. I hadn't seen him since he did his sudden disappearing act in Argentina. It didn't work out as I'd hoped because he missed the trip through injury but I did have some consolation. I got to meet Johnny Giles for the first time. He'd always been one of my heroes because I really admired what he and Billy Bremner achieved with Leeds United. I used to look at them and tell myself they were proof that if you can 'play' and have a big enough heart, size really doesn't matter.

One of the big plusses of the whole experience was that virtually every game we played created an opportunity to catch up with an old acquaintance or two and when we flew to Seattle to launch another spell 'on the road', it was great to see Willie Donachie again. We'd always got on well in our days with Scotland and when we'd finished our game against Portland Timbers, I went back to his place and we had a great night reminiscing.

I know it was only a whistle-stop tour that took in just a fraction of the vast area that makes up Canada and the USA but I was very conscious of the fact that I was being paid for doing what others saved up years to enjoy. We were just in and out of some places but got the chance to appreciate others. I was really taken with Toronto, for example, when we went on a sight-seeing tour of the city the day after we played them - then flew on to Montreal for our next fixture.

Spending so much time together in those situations meant you quickly formed a bond and I got particularly friendly with Steve Heighway, Chico Hamilton, Tony Want and David Stride. Our families enjoyed spending time together with regular barbecues and it was all about outdoor activities in the superb weather. I soon got up a regular golf foursome with Chico, David and Ron Futcher and you can get into bad habits over there. No one walks anywhere in America. It's always a 'given' with golf that you will play on a buggy and we used to load up a few six-packs and have a great time.

Minnesota is known as the 'Land of the Lakes'. Apparently there are almost 10,000 of them throughout that region and we certainly made the most of those close to where we were living. On one occasion the families got together to organise a white-water rafting expedition and we had a fabulous time. It took an hour on the bus to get us to the source of where the rapids began, way up in the hills, and a lot less time coming back! I was so pleased that Neil and Jayne got to experience it and from my point of view, it brought back great memories of my childhood days in Banchory when my dad used to pull me down the River Dee in the inner-tube of an old tyre.

Just about the only negative I can remember is that you were always at risk from tornados in the Minnesota area. Between March and November, they used to get around 30 a year. As soon as we arrived we were warned not to mess with them. As with all properties in that region, we had a specially equipped basement and immediately you heard the siren, you headed down there. On one occasion, I cannot recall why, I stupidly went back upstairs to fetch something just as a tornado was attacking a house along the road. I couldn't believe my eyes. It absolutely demolished the house in a matter of seconds. Never have I been more frightened.

I think you'll have got the message by now that it was an incredible way of life and Margaret and I were agreed that we would have taken very little persuading to follow the lead of so many of my colleagues and apply for a 'Green Card'. We even found a piece of land that we seriously considered buying. It was by the side of a lake, just down from where Tony Want lived, and we could have made a wonderful home there.

The problem was that I was beginning to smell a rat. Things were not quite going according to plan. Jack Dunnett came out twice during my time there and Ralph Sweet always used to introduce him to people as "my friend". He kept a very low profile but did have easy access around the place and it made me smile when he used to come in the dressing rooms. Jimmy Sirrel would never have allowed that to happen at Meadow Lane.

I was delighted during his first trip that he was keen for us to sit down and agree my new deal with County. We dealt with all the paperwork and he explained that as soon as I got my international release from Kicks and flew home again, I would need to go to the FA headquarters at Lancaster Gate to re-register as a County player. He was clearly convinced that I had a part to play in getting them established in the top flight and that was exactly what I wanted to hear. He didn't need to tell me it would be the last of many playing deals he'd agree with me but once that part of the agenda was complete, he brought up the possibility of me coming back to Minnesota to coach the team for the next two summers. What! I couldn't wait to share that news with Margaret.

By the time I met up again with the chairman, a couple of months later, we were seriously thinking of investing in that piece of land and setting things in motion to have our own place built. He advised me that would not be a good idea. The wheels were coming off for the great American adventure and I have to admit that I wasn't totally surprised.

I won't pretend to understand the financial workings of a football club on the other side of the world but knowing the way we operated, I just couldn't see how they managed to make the figures stack up. Those five-day trips on the road, for example, must have cost a small fortune because we had the best of everything. We were straight on and off the flights with the minimum of fuss and always stayed in the best hotels in town. Knowing the deals that some of the lads were on, the running costs of the club must have been colossal and it seemed that all clubs in the NASL were operating the same way.

Three of them had dropped out of the League in 1980 and the following year, seven more clubs folded. All 24 clubs lost money in 1981 and it was reported that Kicks had lost some $2.5million. Sadly, although efforts were made to sell the franchise, the Kicks folded as well in December that year. I felt very sorry for the lads who had opted to build a new life there. It was a very worrying time for them but many battled through it and continued to earn a good living with the re-formed structure. Others - like Steve Heighway - felt they couldn't take the risk and returned home. It proved to be a good decision for him because he became Liverpool's academy director.

We eventually finished second in the Central Division of the NASL, which again qualified us for the play-offs. Margaret and the kids very reluctantly went home at that point, so they would be ready for the new school year, while I stayed on to try and help mount a challenge for honours. We did manage to beat Tulsa Roughnecks in the regional play-offs but then went out against Fort Lauderdale, the team run by Rodney Marsh. By then, the rumours were swirling about the Kicks' financial troubles and it was such a shame that my association ended on a sour note because it had been a fantastic experience. I was really looking forward to going back and sampling some more but now, it wasn't going to happen. Ralph Sweet was clearly shaken by what was happening. He was in his element as the owner of Kicks and he took the collapse hard.

Jack Dunnett was there waiting for me when I arrived at Lancaster Gate. I took a taxi straight there as soon as my flight landed at Gatwick and as all the forms had already been completed, it didn't take long for me to sign for Notts County for the third time in my career.

I had to get my head - and my body - around the fact that it was going to be very different back in Nottingham, competing against the best players in the country, but I was confident that once I'd got the jet-lag out of my system, I'd be ready to go again. Jimmy Sirrel wasn't so sure and he came to my home as soon as I arrived back and suggested I should play for the reserves at Halifax a couple of days later, so he could check on my fitness. I thought he was joking at first but I soon realised he wasn't. I hadn't forgotten that the last time our paths had crossed was when I went to the ground to collect my boots immediately before I left for America and he was really put out that he knew nothing about it. I just had the feeling that he was trying to make a point.

Anyway, as I pointed out to him as respectfully as I could, I wouldn't be going to Halifax. I'd been playing non-stop for the previous 12 months, had hardly missed a game in all that time, and at my stage of life, I was as fit as I was ever going to be. I was back to do a job that would be as challenging as any I'd ever faced with Notts County and it was hugely important to me that I did it well. I just wanted to get on with it.

20
MISSION ACCOMPLISHED... I'D REACHED THE PINNACLE
(1981-86)

I made a huge mistake. I ought to have come off the pitch at Portman Road after our 3-1 win over high-flying Ipswich Town in January 1982 and announced: "That's it … I'm done."

It couldn't get any better than that. Lots of people have told me over the years that they thought my performance that day was as good as any I ever produced for Notts County. Many also thought they'd never seen the team play better. Put all the ingredients into the pot and you could certainly state a very strong case on both counts.

Bobby Robson's title-chasers had won nine games on the trot before we played them, and with players in their ranks like Arnold Muhren, Frans Thijssen, Mick Mills, Kevin Beattie and Paul Mariner, they were a terrific team. But we were no respecters of reputations. The lads had shown that while I was still in America by going to Aston Villa on the opening day of the season and beating the newly-crowned League champions. A lack of consistency did hold us back but we soon chalked up home wins against Coventry, Arsenal and Sunderland and then, on a very special day, made the short trip across Trent Bridge to beat Nottingham Forest 2-0.

We also played particularly well at Old Trafford in October, where we lost 2-1 but dominated for long periods. There's a nice little story attached to that game because Martin Buchan and I were the respective captains. We were born 18 miles apart in the north of Scotland and became good friends when we were in Argentina for the World Cup. We used to joke that we hadn't done too badly in the game for a couple of 'Teuchters' [an unflattering term for Scottish Highlanders] and at every opportunity when we were together, we'd lapse into our weird local dialect. We couldn't resist it when we met in the middle to spin the coin and the expression on the face of the referee once we got chatting was absolutely priceless.

After our performance that day you could also add United to the list of clubs who had 'come around'. We'd succeeded in forcing people to take us seriously. No one had given us a prayer of surviving in the top flight but when we went to Ipswich in January and turned on that scintillating display, the ITV 'Star Soccer' pundit Jimmy Greaves led the tributes. He particularly picked out Iain McCulloch and the emerging Brian Kilcline for lavish praise and our reputations - individually and collectively - went through the roof that weekend.

From my point of view, it was the absolute pinnacle. All along my dream had been that before I called it a day, I wanted to play a leading role in getting us into the top flight and then use my experience to help our youngsters prove they fully deserved their place among the elite. I cannot put into words how proud I was of them on that particular occasion. We didn't just look good enough to compete at that level, we played like a team capable of pushing on to have a real impact. Hardly anyone had heard of Tristan Benjamin, Kilcline, Pedro Richards, Paul Hooks and Gordon Mair - five home-grown youngsters who played the majority of games that season. When was the last time a top-flight club, even with a multi-million pound academy set-up, had five former apprentices figuring regularly in their team?

The highlight at Ipswich was a very special goal that we scored midway through the first half. I'd figured six years earlier when Queens Park Rangers scored the 'Goal of the Season' against Liverpool and this one was right up there alongside it. As with the QPR goal, the ball went from one end of the pitch to the other without the opposition touching it. Raddy Avramovic rolled it out to Ray O'Brien, who launched a series of one-touch passes down the left. McCulloch and Hooks were involved and the move eventually put Mair in the clear to fire the ball low past Paul Cooper.

Howard Wilkinson told me that while the game was still going on, Robson went across to him on the bench to shake his hand and congratulate him on the quality of that goal. It was a really classy thing to do but I can understand what prompted it. From a coach's angle it was the ultimate and no doubt that was a factor when Robson took over as England manager and decided to appoint Howard as his England Under-21 coach.

I'd done it. I knew that afternoon it was mission accomplished and after carrying out a series of post-match interviews on TV and radio, I should have walked away. Instead of that I appeared in 1-0 defeats against Swansea and Arsenal and then, after a period out injured, came back for a sad swansong against Manchester United.

We'd only played one League fixture during December because of the bad weather and Howard made really good use of the spare time we had. Many of the top-flight clubs flew out in search of better conditions to work in but not us. We used to train in those days at the Nottingham University sports ground and Howard persuaded the groundsman to roll the snow every day to give us the best possible surface, so he could work on giving us a Plan B. He was worried that many of the better coaches operating in the First Division had 'sussed' out our close-passing style and he felt we needed to develop an alternative. This involved playing the ball longer, often cutting out the midfield, and that was a problem to me. I wasn't physically capable any more of getting box-to-box as I had done five years earlier and that was exposed when I returned to the team against Manchester United at Meadow Lane.

United were particularly strong in central midfield with Bryan Robson, Remi Moses and Ray Wilkins and the game just passed me by.

Chewing the cud with Martin Buchan after a Scotland match. We did okay for a couple of old Teuchters from the Highlands! Pedro Richards, one of many home-grown Notts County youngsters who transferred successfully from the youth team to the First Division, tangles with Arsenal's Alan Sunderland.

We lost 3-1 and I hardly got a kick. The harsh reality was hard to accept, of course it was, but I didn't need Jimmy or Howard to tell me. My time was up - but it was a huge consolation to know that our youngsters didn't need me any more. They could stand on their own feet and they underlined that four days later when a hat-trick from McCulloch inspired them to a sparkling 4-2 win at West Brom.

That in itself was a great example of what I am saying. Iain has often reminded me over the years that I did him a massive favour when I gave him a simple piece of advice. I could see he was made of the same stuff as me and was desperate to squeeze out every last ounce of his ability. I told him that on the last day of the season he should bang on Jimmy's office door and ask what he needed to do during the summer to become a better player. He knew he would have to strap himself in for a long ride because that wouldn't be a quick job with Jimmy! But that became an annual meeting between the two of them and every year, Iain came back for pre-season a better player. It was a tragedy for him when he broke a leg while he was in his prime in a horrific collision with Manchester United goalkeeper Gary Bailey. He never played again and how typical of Iain, one of the most committed players I ever came across, that the injury occurred when he was chasing a completely lost cause.

I'd been awarded a testimonial in the 1981-82 season, having completed 10 years service in my first two spells with County, and in April a Don Masson Select XI played an International XI. John Hollins rounded up some London lads for me - Kenny Sansom, David O'Leary and Gerry Francis - to play in the International XI. Peter Shilton was in goal and my former Derby colleagues Gerry Daly and Roy McFarland also played. It was hardly a big success because the attendance was just 3,033 but you won't hear any complaints from me. It literally poured with rain all day and I was genuinely surprised that as many people as that bothered to come. I was really grateful to those who did.

Incidentally, I invited Rod Stewart to come and play in the game.

I vaguely knew him from my time with Scotland and although it was a 'long-shot', I thought it was worth a try. He seemed very sincere in saying he'd have loved to come but would be on his way to Australia on that date. He did, though, send me 10-signed LPs to use at fund-raising events. A nice touch that I very much appreciated.

I also had a black-tie testimonial dinner that featured Jack Charlton and Dave Sexton as the main speakers. I was sitting between Jack and Jimmy Sirrel when we were having the meal and Jack was very forceful in telling me he thought I was retiring too early. He insisted I could still do a good job for someone and when I told him I wanted to go out 'at the top' he suggested I should stay on with County and work with their young players. Jimmy had been listening intently and clearly decided at that point the time had come to get involved. "I don't think so Little Fella," he said. "I think it's probably best if you move on."

At the end of that season, I did. Eleven years, 440 League & Cup games and 96 goals for County - I'm very proud of those statistics. I'm also exceptionally proud to claim I was also the first man - and possibly the only one - to captain the same club from the Fourth Division to the First. Needless to say, the scene when I left was very different to the one I'd walked into when I moved down from Middlesbrough. For the record, County were 15th in the table at the end of the 1981-82 season. They also remained at the top level for another two seasons and had Howard not left to take charge of Sheffield Wednesday, I'm sure they would have stayed even longer.

You always knew where you stood with Jimmy and he'd made it abundantly clear that I had no future at Meadow Lane. He did, though have a special little farewell gesture up his sleeve. He came to my house a couple of weeks later to tell me he'd opened the way for me to get four months of very lucrative employment. Ron Wylie, the former Birmingham, Coventry and West Brom coach, was managing a club called Bulova in Hong Kong and he wanted to sign me on a short-term deal. There was a restriction on the number of foreign players they could sign but as Phil Boyer had just returned to England, Bulova had a vacancy. A deal was quickly agreed - from May until August - when I spoke to Ron on the phone and he said he'd send the flight tickets across the following week.

I had a terrific time. As with my spell in America, it was fantastic to experience life from a fresh perspective. It was such a vibrant place and although the culture was very different, I just found it all incredibly stimulating. As the locals were always quick to tell me, Hong Kong has the highest number of skyscrapers of any city in the world and considering its size, it has a huge population.

I've always enjoyed visiting new places and I'm so pleased I went there because I learned an incredible amount in four months. I loved

With dad at my Testimonial Dinner at Meadow Lane
- a special night for both of us.

everything about it - the place, the food, the people, the social life and even the traffic jams added a certain flavour to the experience. I lived in a hotel in Kowloon with the other ex-pats in our team and a 10-seater taxi used to pick us up every morning and take us to where we trained, in the middle of the racecourse. It was fine while we were on the eight-lane motorway but the interesting bit was when the road suddenly dropped to two lanes as we went into a tunnel. It was every man for himself but somehow we always lived to tell the tale.

I liked Ron Wylie. He was a great bloke who really knew his stuff. It can't have been easy working with a bunch of players who not only came from different countries but also had very different levels of ability but he found a way. We had a full-time interpreter attached to us but Ron preferred to physically show people how he wanted them to play.

Tommy Hutchinson, the former Blackpool, Coventry and Manchester City player, was the star of the show. He'd already endeared himself to the locals by the time I arrived and had sorted out what-was-what within the city. He was a bit of a Pied Piper character in Hong Kong. Tall and fair, he stood out in the crowd and when we were out and about, the locals would trail along behind him. All very weird. He used to play games, deliberately walking up one of the main streets in the city to see how many joined the queue!

While I was with Bulova I did my best to help him remove the tag that he'd been lumbered with in life, rather like me missing the penalty against Peru. It really niggled him that he was best known as a quiz question: Who scored for both teams in the FA Cup Final between Manchester City and Tottenham? Tommy thought that when we got to the Hong Kong Cup Final and caused a major upset by beating Seiko, who were the strongest team at that time, it would give people something else to remember him by. No chance of that. He's still the answer to a popular sports quiz question.

We also won the prestigious Viceroy Cup while I was there and as it was the first time Bulova had won either trophy, it was great to be part of helping to make history. I think I was very fortunate to see Hong Kong at its best. Politics is not my game but I'm very sad to see the way life has changed there in recent years.

My four months with Bulova absolutely flew by and I made loads of good friends. They were really friendly people, who couldn't do enough for me and I came away with many happy memories - plus a case-load of handmade silk shirts and suits. It's true what they say about Hong Kong's tailors. You turn up in the morning to be measured and then go back a few hours later to collect your order. It's top-quality stuff and ridiculously cheap.

I decided when I got home that I really was finished with football. I was going to do something else with my life and would take a few months off to decide what that would be. I played lots of tennis and golf and also took on a project to build a snooker room in my loft at Burton Joyce and develop a sauna area in the garage. It took me the best part of a year to complete that and I enlisted the help of Arthur Mann and his joiner-friend Steve Gutteridge. It was a fun project. We really enjoyed our time together and half-jokingly, we said that we ought to start a development business. Eventually we did but not for a few years because football got in the way again.

Right out of the blue I got a call from Jack Dunnett in March 1983. He'd got me the job as player-manager of Kettering Town, one of the top non-league clubs in the country at that time, but there was more to it than that. He saw it as an opportunity for me to serve my apprenticeship over the next two to three years with a view to me becoming the manager at Meadow Lane. Did I really want to get back on the bandwagon? I wasn't convinced but I agreed to meet with their chairman.

Tom Bradley was the Labour MP for Leicester East, hence the fact that he knew Dunnett well. Born and bred in Kettering, he was keen to see his local club progress and struck me straight away as a good man. Ron Atkinson and Derek Dougan had cut their teeth in management at Rockingham Road - even the great Tommy Lawton started there - so it was a proven career path. But although they'd finished as runners-up in the Alliance Premier League in 1980-81, they narrowly avoided relegation the following year and were in trouble again. They were third from bottom with six games to go and the chairman reckoned they would need to win three of those to stay up. I said I would take it on. Although I hadn't played all season, I was still in good shape and as Arthur Mann knew plenty about the Alliance Premier League scene from his time with Boston United, I thought when he agreed to come with me that we could make it work.

Away to Barnet was our first fixture and I got my first 'taste' that day of Barry Fry and his chairman Stan Flashman. We won 3-2, so it was a great start for me, but one of the things I remember most about that day was going into the Boardroom afterwards and Barry greeting me with: "Aw wight my son?" We did what was required. In fact, we did slightly better because we eventually finished 19th, four points clear of the drop zone, but I was really struggling with the job. It just wasn't football as I knew it. We were training Tuesday and Thursday nights with players who had already done a hard day's work and my brain didn't function that way. I only knew how to be ultra-professional and give it my total focus. It just wasn't possible in that set-up and I very quickly lost interest.

I'd persuaded Les Bradd and David Needham to come and join me and although I thought we were well short of having a team capable of mounting a challenge for promotion, I did feel we were well-equipped to win the FA Trophy. When I shared that thought with the chairman, he said: "Providing we don't get relegated, that will do me." I didn't get chance to find out whether it would work out as planned. Bradley stepped aside very early on the following season and I immediately felt that I wouldn't be able to work with the new chairman. He clearly felt the same way. That became evident when he asked me one day to come in early for training, so we could have a chat. We mutually agreed that evening that I would finish.

Dunnett was straight on the phone the following day to ask: "What the hell are you doing?" I don't think there was ever an occasion during my time working for him as a player when he expressed disappointment in me but he wasn't happy with me then. He thought he'd got things neatly sorted out for the future and I'd thrown his plans into disarray.

Notts County were down in the relegation zone of the First Division and speculation was flying around that he was about to change the manager. I urged him to let me take over straight away but he said he couldn't do that. He insisted that I didn't have enough experience to do the job that had to be done. Basically, I'd blown it. He'd set me up with a great opportunity to develop a career in management and I'd made a mess of it. I should have worked harder to try and adapt to a very different way of doing things but my age-old intolerance problem reared its ugly head. The part-time game didn't allow me enough time to work with the players to bring about the improvements I was looking for and that wasn't going to change. It was down to me to change - and I couldn't.

Fortunately, I didn't annoy 'JD' so much that he decided to wash his hands of me and not long afterwards, I again got the benefit of his amazing 'match-making' skills. He was a good friend of Don Burris, a wealthy American lawyer who had worked on the Watergate case. He was based in Los Angeles and numbered among his clients many of the rich and famous in the Hollywood area. In fact, he even had his Head Office on Sunset Boulevard, as I discovered when I went there for a meeting. 'JD' knew how much Margaret and I had enjoyed our time in Minnesota and an introduction to Burris could just pave the way for me to get involved in an exciting new long-term project in the States. He'd invited him to a game at Meadow Lane and told me I should come and meet him. I must have made a good impression because he outlined what he had in mind, then told me I should go over with the family and see where it led.

It all revolved around the fact that he was a football 'nut'. He couldn't get enough of it but since the virtual collapse of the North American Soccer League, there was a big gap in the structure. He insisted that there was great enthusiasm for soccer among both the men and women. The population alone suggested there must be massive potential but although there were loads of amateur leagues across the region at various levels, the professional game was non-existent.

Of particular concern to Don was that there was no place to go for the talented youngsters when they finished college. They were playing the game to a very good standard but as soon as they left college, they were lost to football. He wanted to launch a new league, based in Los Angeles, and thought I could be the man to spearhead the project. I saw it as a dream job and Margaret and I were blown away by the prospect of setting up home in that sprawling city at the southern end of California. It was very different to Minneapolis but with its brilliant climate and all the charismatic connections with the movie industry, how could you not want to live there?

Don was a big man, a real larger than life character who believed in getting things done. He specialised in business litigation issues in California and was a named Super Lawyer, which meant he was one of the top-rated lawyers in the country. More to the point, he was my sort of bloke. I knew I could work with him. As I said earlier, he was a total football 'nut' and during his time in England, he was desperate one night to go to a game - wherever it was. When I looked through the fixtures, the only game on within anything like reasonable travelling distance was Scunthorpe v Halifax. "Let's do it," he said. As luck would have it, my old County midfield partner Mick Jones was the manager of Halifax at that time so I contacted him and organised tickets in the Directors Box. Now, even someone with a vivid imagination could not pretend that the Old Show Ground was a glamorous venue but Don thought the whole experience was brilliant. We got to meet Mick after the game and Don was like a big kid on the way back to Nottingham, he was so full of it.

Not only was he a keen football follower, he was also a huge fan of The Beatles and one of the reasons he'd come to England was that he'd somehow fixed up a meeting in Liverpool with Pete Best, who was the original drummer with the Fab Four. They got on brilliantly - as most people would with Don - and it ended up with him inviting Pete and his wife across to Los Angeles for the same fortnight I would be out there. He put the Bests up in a plush hotel and I stayed with Don.

Pete was great company and needless to say, I was fascinated by stories of his time with The Beatles in the early Sixties, before John, Paul and George famously sacked him. He was with them working in Hamburg when they were just in the process of taking off, and if he was bored by having to keep telling the same tales wherever he went, it didn't show.

Taking Pete to Los Angeles at that time was a very clever move on Don's part and he made him 'sing for his supper' - as he did with me. Don had organised a football competition in Santa Monica involving top amateur teams from various parts of the world and while I refereed some of the games, Pete's role was to work with Don to promote the event. I had the most fantastic fortnight's 'holiday' but in the end, Don's dream scheme didn't get off the ground. From what I understood of the situation, he had loads of wealthy contacts who were interested in pumping in some cash as sponsors but it was going to take a lot more than that to establish a professional League and set up the clubs to compete in it. He just couldn't get things to stack up financially the way he wanted. It was a real shame but I'd lost nothing - and gained a lot.

It certainly wasn't the end of the world. By then, I was pretty much financially secure and happy to take my life in a different direction. I was so fortunate to be in a situation where I was under no pressure to make quick decisions. Just as a little aside, I was contentedly painting my front gate one morning at Crow Park Drive in Burton Joyce when a car screeched to a halt alongside me. It was Asa Hartford. Unbeknown to me, he was signing for Nottingham Forest that day and was being driven around the area to look at houses. We'd always been good mates and it was a brilliant surprise.

Still the phone kept ringing, I'm pleased to say, and it wasn't long before I took a call from Dennis Roach. He was a leading agent who I vaguely knew from my time in London because he worked with Frank McLintock. "Do you want to go and play in South Africa?" he asked. Before I had chance to answer he said: "The problem is that I need to know straight away."

It was at the time when a variety of international boycotts were in force in protest over apartheid in South Africa and FIFA had ordered a worldwide ban on all football contact. People were finding ways around it though, notably the cricketers, and a football tour had been organised as well. The invitation was for me to join it - at very short notice. The tour was hugely controversial and on the back of lots of negative publicity, Ossie Ardiles and his Argentina team-mate Mario Kempes had pulled out. Roach wanted me to fill one of the holes they'd left but I told him I couldn't just give him a spur of the moment decision. I needed to know more about what was involved and I certainly needed to talk it through with Margaret. She had got herself a little part-time job and I said I'd ring him back when she got home. As soon as I told her what they were going to pay me, she raced upstairs and found me a suitcase!

Like I said earlier, politics is not my game but when I discovered more about what the tour entailed, I didn't see a major problem. The plan was to play six games in six weeks and all of them involved playing against black players. In fact, three of the games were scheduled to be played in Soweto. Jimmy Hill was fronting up the tour as 'consultant' and strongly believed that what we were doing would help sport to triumph over politics. World Cup referee Jack Taylor was the tour referee and John Barnwell was managing the team, which was just called The International XI. If people of that calibre were involved, I was willing to trust that they were doing the right thing.

When I rang Roach back to say I was 'in' he said he would organise for a taxi to come to my house and take me to Heathrow, where my flight tickets would be waiting for me. I was booked on a night-flight to Johannesburg, where I would be met and accompanied on an internal flight to Durban. By the time I arrived at the hotel I'd been travelling for the best part of 24 hours and I collapsed straight into bed, knowing I was expected to play in a match that night.

It didn't take too long to realise that things were not working out as planned. I was sharing a room with Dave Watson, the former England central defender, and he was still operating in the First Division at that time with Stoke City. He got a call while I was with him from Ted Croker, the FA Secretary, warning that he would almost certainly be subject to sanctions if he played in any of the matches. He decided to pull out of the tour.

We still had loads of star names in the squad, players like Mick Channon, Brian Greenhoff and the former Aston Villa captain Ian Ross, and we gelled quite nicely when we drew the first game 0-0 in Cape Town. We were up against a team managed by Johnny Byrne, the former West Ham and England centre-forward, who was working at the time with Durban City. It passed off largely without incident and after a memorable visit to Table Mountain, we flew to Johannesburg to prepare for our series of matches in Soweto. We were told to expect crowds of 50,000 but the first of them - we beat AmaZulu 1-0 - attracted just 3,000 people. In fact, there was a far bigger crowd outside the ground protesting very loudly. They were incredibly hostile, to the point where it was actually frightening. They couldn't have made it any clearer that they didn't want us there. We got the game played and went straight back to the hotel. None of us was prepared to go through that again and the organisers took no persuading to cut-short the tour.

There couldn't have been a bigger contrast in every respect when we flew off to spend a few days in Sun City, which is South Africa's answer to Las Vegas. One of the highlights of the tour for me was that I got to play the Gary Player golf course, which had only just opened, and another was getting prime seats for an Olivia Newton-John concert. Dave Watson regularly boasted that he had good contacts in the entertainment business so we put him to the test. He came up trumps.

We also played a game against Transvaal Province but the tour was eventually abandoned because the other teams we were due to play pulled out. It was a relief for all of us to head for home. We had clearly made a mistake by going but that was with the benefit of hindsight. We went there with the very best of intentions, naively thinking that in some way it would have a positive influence on apartheid in South Africa. The issues went far deeper than could be solved by a group of rebel footballers.

Margaret and I flew out to Tenerife on holiday as soon as I returned. We had it in mind to invest in a couple of apartments and that was 'the' place to be at the time. Strange how little things stick in your mind. I can't remember the full address but it was definitely 26A and 26B.

It was a perfect opportunity for us to consider the next stage of our lives and of all the available options, we decided the way forward was to form a development business. I'd got to know David Sale, a successful Nottingham estate agent, when he dealt with renting out my house while we were in America for four months. I turned to him for help and his advice was invaluable. I re-mortgaged my house to raise the capital to set up the business and started doing the rounds, looking for derelict properties.

As soon as I found one and bought it, I brought the old team back together. I loved working with Arthur Mann and Steve Gutteridge. It was laugh a minute and every day was a pleasure. Steve really knew his stuff and what he didn't know, he knew where to turn to find someone who did. I just ran the business side of things and worked as the labourer. We did the first house up and sold it on, then used the money to purchase a piece of land on which we built four houses.

It was all going great and lots of former colleagues dropped by from time to time to give us a hand and share a 'builder's brew'. One of those was Jack Wheeler, our old physio at Notts County. He always used to go on about the fact that he did his apprenticeship as a bricklayer before going off to keep goal for Birmingham City so I called his bluff. We needed a wall building. I mixed the cement, he laid the bricks and seeing how much pleasure that gave him was so rewarding. What a lovely man!

One day everything was perfect and the next, my world had fallen apart. Margaret and I had just got back from a break in Tenerife, celebrating her 39th birthday, when she complained of a headache. She often suffered from migraines so I didn't think too much about it. This one was different. She couldn't shake it off and when the doctor arrived, he immediately called for an ambulance. After a spell in intensive care, she went back to the ward and remained there for two weeks for tests and observation.

We were so relieved when she was finally allowed home but within a couple of days, she was rushed back by ambulance, straight to intensive care. We couldn't see her for two days because she had to undergo an operation to relieve the pressure on her brain and it was such a shock when we were allowed in. She was on a life support machine, fighting for survival.

I got a call from the hospital in the early hours of the following morning, telling me that I should get there as soon as possible with Neil and Jayne. Mr Hope, the neurological surgeon who'd performed the operation, met us and he gave us the worst possible news. There was nothing more he could do for Margaret. Neil instantly fainted and had to be put into a bed and Jayne went hysterical and needed to be sedated. I wouldn't wish the experience on anyone. As I explained in the opening chapter of this book, Margaret - unbeknown to any of us - had been born with a venous malformation in her brain and it was something of a miracle that she survived as long as she did.

We'd been told she was brain-dead and we needed to make a decision about turning off the life support machine. I couldn't do that. I phoned Tom and Jessie - Margaret's parents - to give them the terrible news and they immediately set off from Middlesbrough.

We knew what had to be done but it was important for us to all be together to say our final goodbyes.

I had everything going for me and suddenly I had nothing. It's a big cliché to say that my world fell apart but it really did. There were numerous occasions when I didn't think I'd be able to carry on but my faith got me through it. I knew I had loads of support and was overwhelmed by the amount of sympathy. People came from all over to the funeral, like Pat and Lynne, the wives of Dave Clement and Phil Parkes, and I appreciated it so much.

At the end of the day I had to deal with it and face up to my responsibilities with Neil and Jayne. I completely dedicated my life to them and for the next four months, I hardly ever went out. I'd always enjoyed playing backgammon and every night I used to just sit there playing against myself. It was a difficult situation because I knew that it reached a stage where Neil and Jayne felt obliged to stay in with me. That couldn't be allowed to go on. They were starting to make their way in the world and had to get on with their lives. Jayne was working as a hairdresser, Neil as an apprentice draughtsman and I had to encourage them to try and move on. The trouble was that I couldn't see any way forward for myself and whatever advice I gave them, it seemed so false.

I did occasionally play tennis without going on to socialise afterwards and eventually - several months later - Arthur Mann got me to join him for a drink. He and his next-door neighbour, Ian Wilson used to go and watch Nottingham Panthers playing ice hockey, then drop off for a drink on the way home. I said I would meet them.

That was the day I got my life moving again although it took me many years to come to terms with the loss of Margaret. In fact, I don't think I ever will. She will always have a very special place in my heart. We'd been together since we were teenagers and I cannot start to find the words to explain what she meant to me.

21
FINDING BRENDA – AND 'OUR BANCHORY' AT BELVOIR
(From 1986)

Sometimes you need a little bit of help and I admit to having had a fair bit to drink before I rang my girlfriend Brenda and asked her to marry me. To be strictly accurate, I didn't actually make the call. I was sharing a room in Brazil at the time with Martin Buchan, the former Manchester United captain and my old Scotland colleague, and he set things up. He dialled the number and told Brenda that I wanted to speak to her.

Martin and I were in Sao Paulo as members of the Great Britain 'has beens' squad, competing in a tournament between former World Cup-winning nations. Only six countries had ever lifted the trophy at that stage - Brazil, Uruguay, Argentina, West Germany, Italy and England. So what were Martin and I doing there? Well, only players who had taken part in the World Cup Finals were supposed to be involved and as England had failed to qualify for the later stages in 1974 and 1978, they didn't have many options. Consequently, Martin and I were drafted in as part of a GB squad, and so were John Robertson and Kenny Burns.

It was 2am back in the UK when Martin made the call and as Brenda instantly realised when we woke her, we'd been on the red wine all evening. We'd had a great night celebrating 'Robbo's' birthday but I just about managed to string my words together and was delighted when she said: "Yes".

It had been a long and rocky road to get to that point. My life had been in tatters after Margaret died three years earlier and it took me ages to start thinking straight again. As I've already explained, I didn't go out socially for months. My one and only concern was doing what had to be done to make sure that Neil and Jayne came through the horrible experience as unscathed as possible. Believe me, absolutely the last thing I had on my mind at that time was starting a new relationship.

Every day I needed a boost and I got one when I helped the local tennis club in Burton Joyce to win promotion for the first time to the top division of the Notts League. Quite rightly they were keen to celebrate and they persuaded me to join them on a night out. We went tenpin bowling, played some snooker and then went on to the Arriba Nightclub in Nottingham. That's when I met Brenda. There's no big romantic tale to tell. She was there with her cousin. I tapped her on the shoulder, asked her if she wanted to dance and when we chatted afterwards, we agreed to meet for a drink the following Saturday.

My mate Denis Frith had been my 'minder' ever since we met up on my first day at Queens Park Rangers and I rang him in a panic. Knowing how grief-stricken I'd been, he couldn't believe it when I told him I'd met someone. I said: "I can assure you that you're no more surprised than me!" I told him to get himself up to Nottingham the following Saturday to give me some moral support and when Brenda turned up she also had a chaperone. Right from the start we got on well. She was divorced with two children - Mark and Claire - who were similar ages to my two and although she'd worked in the Nottingham Forest commercial department in the days when they won trophies for fun, she'd moved on and had her own business. It was a grocery shop in the Carlton area of Nottingham and she also did outside catering.

I told Brenda straight on the first occasion we were together that she shouldn't have anything to do with me because I wasn't a nice person. I was weighed down with guilt from the way I'd conducted myself during much of my time as a player and an overwhelming feeling that I should have done more for Margaret. That wasn't going to disappear overnight and as we soon discovered, there would be other issues to contend with.

Even though we were nothing more than friends at that stage Brenda was subjected to all sorts of hostility from people who had known Margaret. Quite frankly, it was horrible. I'm not going to go into details but I really don't know how she put up with it. I don't think I could have done. On top of that, Neil and Jayne made no secret of the fact that they were very unhappy about me taking up with someone else only six months after their mum had died. It was such a difficult situation. I hadn't set out to make this happen. It just had and I had no idea how to handle it. In the end, I guess, I chose to run away from it.

The obvious option would have been for me to simply say this wasn't going to work and end my friendship with Brenda. I didn't want to do that, nor did she but it was very clear to both of us that there was no way we would be able to stay together if we remained in Nottingham.

On the spur of the moment, I rang Don Burris in Los Angeles and arranged for us to go out there. He was unbelievably kind and the fact that Brenda and I have been very happily married for more than 30 years is due in no small measure to him. We went to London to pick up our visas and then, in my usual impetuous manner, I suddenly decided to drive straight up to Middlesbrough to introduce Brenda to my sister Joan. It was daunting for Brenda and she was really nervous about it. Although Joan took time to accept what was happening, they have since become very good friends.

I made plans for someone to move into my house to keep an eye on Neil and Jayne while I was in the States. They were old enough to look after themselves but it was important for me to know there would be someone instantly available if they needed them. Strictly speaking, it wasn't ideal for anyone but Neil and Jayne understood my predicament. Somehow I had to find out where this might lead. Brenda and I had not been living together and were not really a couple. We were two strangers who enjoyed each other's company and a spell in America would tell us whether we had a future together.

We didn't have any firm plans when we arrived in California. Maybe we would be there for a fortnight, maybe we'd stay for years. We had completely open minds about it. The way Don handled the situation was that he gave us both a job - but didn't pay us. Instead, he set us up to live in a very pleasant condominium, where we stayed free of charge. That was the deal.

Brenda worked in the reception area of his high-powered law firm and it appealed to his sense of humour that she had the title of 'English Receptionist'. As he used to say, how many law companies in the States can claim they have a specialist English receptionist? For my part it was easy for Don to find me a role. He was still trying really hard to get a decent standard of football established in the Los Angeles area and had set up a team of part-timers called California Kicks. My job was to train and coach them. We played our home games at the University of Los Angeles and the policy seemed to be that we would go wherever we could get a game. We even flew to Seattle for one match.

Don was amazing. I went to see him 'in action' on one occasion, conducting a defence case at Orange County Court and it was an unforgettable experience. He had such presence and command of the language. I can only thank my lucky stars that I got the benefit of his obsession with soccer, as the Americans insist on calling it. What he did for the California Kicks must have cost him a personal fortune and he was brilliant at using his considerable influence to promote them. There was always a gathering of star-names at home matches and I was particularly pleased when Neil Diamond came and agreed to kick-off a game against the All Stars. It was special to meet him, as I'd always been a big fan.

We had some very decent players with the Kicks. I'm sure that given the right opportunities, many of them could have gone on to make a living from the game. They showed that by the way they acquitted themselves when Hearts and Norwich City flew out at different times to play us. Most of them had graduated from the local colleges and universities and the problem was - as I discovered in my first spell in California - there was no professional pathway for them to progress onto.

It was all very strange, doing a 'voluntary' job and living in a rent-free home, but the change of scenery was doing me good. Life was not without its hitches though, and I certainly hadn't bargained for spending a night in Santa Monica jail. The Kicks had been playing a match about 90 minutes drive away and I'd borrowed Don's top of the range people carrier to get me there and back. Needless to say, it had all the mod cons imaginable - it was the first time I ever came across a car phone - and that's probably what made the police suspicious of me.

I was halfway home when I stopped to get petrol and just as I pulled out again, the siren sounded behind me. I was ordered to get out of the car and put my hands behind me and a split second later, I was handcuffed. When the police asked me for my ID, I didn't have any on me. I was dressed in a brown tracksuit and I'm sure it didn't help that they were struggling to understand my Scottish accent. I wasn't sure what I was supposed to have done wrong and it quickly became clear that their policy was to deal with me first and ask questions later.

It turned out that they thought this scruffy individual in a tracksuit must have stolen the expensive car and they also suspected me of being an illegal immigrant. I was driven straight to the Police Station, where 'mug-shots' were taken from all angles and they detained me overnight. I was put in a communal cell with about a dozen others and it was an experience I never want to repeat. I didn't sleep a wink. I was allowed to make one phone call and when I rang Brenda, she thought at first that I was joking. She was also really worried because I'd rung her from the car, just before I pulled in for petrol, and said I was 20 minutes from home. For some reason, we'd taken a scrapbook with us to America and Brenda brought that to the police station, thinking it would help convince them of my identity. They were not the slightest bit impressed by the fact that I'd been an international footballer and we had to get Don involved in the end. Fortunately, he employed a woman who specialised in illegal immigration cases and with her help, I was bailed to appear in court the following week. By that time, they'd got all the answers they were looking for and although I still had to appear, the case was instantly dismissed. I put that one down to experience.

We decided after five months that it was time to come home. Brenda and I were getting on fine but she's very perceptive. She knew that I still hadn't completely got over the loss of Margaret and I needed some space. I wasn't ready to commit to another permanent relationship and I had to go back and give time to Neil and Jayne. We agreed when we got back that we wouldn't see each other for a while.

I felt it was important if I was to move on that we leave Crow Park Drive and having talked it through with the kids, we moved to Church Road in Burton Joyce. It was fine there, except for the fact that we got burgled. Jayne, who was working as a receptionist at that time, came home to find the glass broken in the front door. All my medals and stuff had gone but strangely, they left my international caps. A week later, we got a call from the police to say that my possessions had been found in a letterbox in Nottingham. I got most of it back ... it clearly couldn't have been very valuable!

So what was I going to do now? Well, as he so often did throughout my life, Jack Dunnett came up with the answer to that question. He had a penthouse suite in The Albany, Nottingham's top hotel on Maid Marion Way, that he used for his weekly overnight stays when he was up from London and he called to say he wanted me to go and see him. He had a proposition to make to me. Notts County had re-developed one end of Meadow Lane when they got promoted to the top flight and it included a fairly extensive sports centre with good facilities to accommodate the likes of badminton, squash and volleyball. The club had been running it themselves but decided they wanted to lease it out. He thought it might be ideal for me.

It was. In fact, it was just what I needed at that time. I took it on in September 1987 and although it was never going to be a big money-spinner, I got a lot out of it on a personal level. Part of that was the fact that I employed Jayne as our receptionist and I really enjoyed having her around to share the experience with me.

Being based at Meadow Lane, as almost an extension to the football club, was great from my point of view and kept me in regular contact with the players and staff. Iain McCulloch was working in the commercial department and it was a regular thing that we would take on Paul Hart and Wayne Jones - two of the coaches - in a lunch-break game of head-tennis. They were highly competitive and brilliant fun.

Brenda and I were back together by then and it was in January 1989 that I flew out to Brazil as part of the Scottish contingent for that World Cup makeover. The matches were played at the home of Santos FC, Pele's club, and involved a Who's Who of world football. Germany, for example, included Franz Beckenbauer, Uwe Seeler and Paul Breitner, Claudio Gentile and Romeo Benetti were in Italy's line-up and I loved watching Roberto Rivellino playing for Brazil. He looked just like he did when he was in his prime and still did exactly the same tricks.

I can't recall much about the games but it was certainly a marvellous experience and we had a great time with lots of laughs. One of my highlights of that trip was putting Gordon Hill in his place. The Manchester United winger always had plenty to say and really fancied himself at tennis. He asked me if I was any good at it and although I played hard to get, I told him I'd give him a game. We didn't hear much more from him after I beat him 6-0, 6-1.

The absolute highlight, however, was hearing Brenda agree to marry me. We'd been back together for a while and were ready to move it on to the next stage. I took it upon myself to make all the arrangements for the wedding and it was the perfect day. We were married in St Andrew's United Reform Church in Nottingham, with

Brenda's son Mark giving her away and my brother-in-law Dave as my Best Man. We went to Ibiza for two weeks on honeymoon and when we rang our accountant while we were there, he told us everything had gone through smoothly to set up the next chapter of our lives.

By then I'd moved out of the sports centre. Jack Dunnett wanted me to take on a five-year lease when my original one expired but it just wasn't viable to do that. No matter - he'd done me yet another massive favour and the time I spent there helped to restore my confidence.

Brenda and I had discussed the possibility of running a hotel together and when I got back from Brazil, we headed up to Scotland to look at some potential places. I'd always had it in my mind that I would eventually go back to Banchory but Brenda wasn't convinced. Deep down she's a home-loving girl and I had no issues with that. At just the right time, we got to hear that The Gallery Hotel on Radcliffe Road in West Bridgford was up for sale. Location-wise, it couldn't be better. It was right at the heart of the Nottingham sporting scene. Just down the road from Trent Bridge and the City Ground, and within 10 minutes of Notts County, Nottingham Panthers and Nottingham Racecourse.

We did a deal with Alan Waplington, who I already knew because he was a big Notts County fan, and Brenda and I sold our houses to finance it. Neil, at that time, had gone travelling and was living and working in Australia. Jayne moved into The Gallery with us in June 1989, a month after we'd got married.

It was a whole new experience for me - a real adventure that I found very daunting at first. We had only been running the place for a couple of weeks when Nottingham Forest hosted a Jehovah's Witness Convention that attracted thousands. Thirty-eight of them filled every bed in our hotel and the following morning, they all came down for breakfast at the same time. We couldn't accommodate them all in the dining room at the same time and had to organise two sittings. I was running around in circles. It was a classic Fawlty Towers situation and I eventually went through to the kitchen, where Brenda was doing the cooking, and said: "I can't do this - I'm a footballer!"

She flew straight back at me saying: "Not any more you're not. You're a waiter ... now get back in there and sort it."

For much of the next 15-years I did that and we loved the life. We worked incredibly hard but made a great partnership and were determined that we would enjoy it. I'm one of those people who only

With Brenda on our wedding day.

ever needs four or five hours of sleep per night so the fact that we had to start early and finish late seven days a week was not a problem to me. There was always something to do but I've never been afraid of hard work. Those decorating skills I'd learned during my days on the groundstaff at Middlesbrough were put to excellent use and we added en-suites to every bedroom that didn't have one. It was really satisfying to see the hotel develop. Within a year or so we were full to capacity most of the time and built up a great list of repeat business. The vast majority were really nice people who came from all over the UK, and various other parts of the world, and although I've never been comfortable in situations where I needed to do 'small talk', I tried really hard.

Our location and my sporting connections were hugely important to the success of the business. Both Nottingham Forest and Notts County regularly pointed people in our direction and over the years, many of their young players stayed with us - so did parents when they used to come and visit. A steady stream of celebrities also passed through. Famous umpire Dickie Bird always stayed with us when he was at Trent Bridge and he used to tell people it was the "Best B&B in Britain". We also enjoyed the company of the likes of Fred Trueman, Sir Garry Sobers and former Australia captain Ian Chappell. In fact, I got to play tennis with Ian on one occasion. I often used to play with Chris Frake and Bill England and Chappell was friendly with Chris. I made up the four when they were organising a game and then they came back to The Gallery for a session.

We used to find ourselves in some amazing situations and we even got an invite to the wedding of the former Australia batsman Michael Slater, who is now a top TV presenter 'Down Under'. He had to delay his wedding because he was making his debut in the Trent Bridge Test and several of the players' wives and girl-friends were staying with us at that time. We got on great when the players came to visit them and it ended up with them sending us an invite to their re-arranged wedding! Unfortunately, we had to decline.

We entertained so many top sports celebrities in our time at
The Gallery Hotel - including the great Sir Garry Sobers (pictured
with Basher Hassan) and former Australia captain Ian Chappell.

Plenty of football celebrities stayed with us - including World Cup winners Nobby Stiles and Alan Ball. They both had speaking engagements at Forest and as Les Bradd was working at the time as assistant to the club's commercial manager Dave Pullan, he often pointed people in our direction. Our bar area could be a lively place in the evenings, sometimes into the following morning, and one of the best nights was when Frank McLintock came to see us. My old QPR colleague was acting as Teddy Sheringham's agent and had just helped to negotiate his move from Forest to Tottenham. What a night that was!

The best drinkers though, by far, were members of the Southern Irish Branch of the Forest Supporters Club. They came to us every year on their annual trip over and no matter how much 'booze' I got in, they always managed to drink us dry. I would add that we never had a single problem with them. On one occasion, when they had voted Stuart Pearce as their 'Player of the Year', I contacted him and persuaded him to come and receive his award. The Irish lads couldn't believe it. It gave them another reason to celebrate.

I actually developed a bit of a bond with Stuart. He was a West London lad who supported QPR when I played there and had lots of happy memories of those days. I wrote to him when he missed the World Cup penalty with England because very few people understood better than me how he would have been feeling. He really appreciated it and asked if he could come to see me. I hope that our chat helped him to come to terms with the situation, and move on.

I still got to play plenty of tennis and I loved the fact that my games often involved Neil. I marked out a tennis court when I had the sports centre at Meadow Lane and it became a regular event for Neil and I to lock the doors on Sunday night and take on Tim Phillips and Rob Cree, often going through to the small hours. Neil was a talented all-rounder. He played for the county at schoolboy level at football, tennis and golf and had great potential at all three sports. We entered the National Father & Son Tennis Championships in 1990 and having fought our way through the early rounds, we then went to

Coventry and won the regionals. That was supposed to get us a dream trip to the Algarve to compete in the finals but because of problems over sponsorship, we ended up playing at Eastbourne - in the middle of February! We weren't there for long. Standards once we reached that stage were incredibly high.

Tennis, incidentally, remains a huge part of my life and I still play at least twice a week to a good standard. Every Tuesday I get together with Dave Hilton, Edward Benson and my partner, Trevor Ross-Gower for an hour of table tennis and then we join up with the eight or so other members of our 'oldies' group for two hours of tennis. One of those is John Poxon, who is 82 and an inspiration to us all. We issued a challenge to anyone living in Nottinghamshire and the stipulation was that they must have a combined age of 154 or over!

Another member of that brilliant gang of old-timers is Karel Dvorak, a Czech gentleman who is the subject of one of my favourite 'small-world' stories. He was living in Newcastle in the Seventies when I helped Scotland beat the Czech Republic en-route to the World Cup Finals. Karel tells a lovely tale about how he travelled across the border, armed with a portable TV, so that he could watch the match and support his native country. Amazingly, I just happened to have a recording of that game because a cassette arrived in the post last year, totally unexpected, from a fan living in Australia. I was delighted to receive it, not only because I reckon that was my best performance for Scotland but it also meant that I was able to give Karel a copy. In return - goodness knows where he got it - he gave me a cutting about me from the Newcastle Journal dated October 1977. Plastered across the back page was a story saying that Newcastle had agreed terms with QPR for my transfer and were waiting for Rangers' chairman Jim Gregory to get back to them. I was totally unaware of this. It's yet another example of players in that era having absolutely no say about their futures.

Football opportunities still kept coming my way and one that I was quick to sign-up for cropped up in 1989 - to play in an England v

> **A smash hit**
>
> Evening Post, Saturday, May 7, 1988
>
> NEXT STOP the Algarve — after proving a smash hit at Croydon!
>
> That's the aim of Don Masson and his son Neil (pictured right) who are in the finals of the Tennis Times father/son competition at Croydon this weekend.
>
> It's the second time they have reached this stage of the tournament — but Masson senior, the former Notts County and Scottish World Cup captain, had a prior date in the States and was unable to attend two years ago.
>
> "We play the quarter-finals and the semis over the weekend," said Masson.
>
> "If we get through to the big final, the prize is a week at the Roger Taylor Tennis Centre on the Algarve."
>
> Masson has been keeping fit and putting son Neil through a few strokes at his own Sports Centre on Meadow Lane.

Scotland 'oldies' match at Goodison Park in aid of the Hillsborough Disaster Fund. I was actually at Hillsborough on that dreadful day. Within a week or so of Brenda and I arriving back from California, Forest rang her to ask if she was interested in going back to take on the job she used to have in their commercial department. She accepted and on the back of that, I found myself on a staff coach heading to Sheffield for the FA Cup semi-final against Liverpool. There's nothing I can tell you about the disaster that you don't already know but I couldn't believe my eyes as I sat there watching the sad events unfold. We were situated not far from the television gantry and Jimmy Hill was there with the Match of the Day crew. He came down for a chat when he spotted me and I was so upset about what was happening that I told him I didn't think I would ever go to watch another football match.

Dave Watson organised that match between England and

Scotland and it attracted a good crowd. It was obviously a sombre occasion in many respects but I did enjoy lining up again alongside the likes of Alan Rough, Martin Buchan and Lou Macari. I also really enjoyed the company of Ian Storey-Moore. We travelled up together because he was based in the Nottingham area and I was fascinated that this former star of Forest and Manchester United was genuinely embarrassed about being included in such company. Strange how some people perceive themselves, isn't it? In his prime, Ian was a real star.

On the back of that, and with considerable input from Watson, matches involving the 'has-beens' suddenly became fashionable. He organised another England-Scotland clash at Wembley and drove Neil and I down in his Rolls-Royce. We provided the pre-match entertainment before England took on Yugoslavia in a full international that night, not that the Scottish lads showed much interest in the main event. We preferred to take advantage of the free bar. The 'free' sign was taken down as soon as the final whistle went. In true Scottish tradition, that was our signal to hit the road.

I also got an invite to play in Lisbon for an International XI to help mark the Centenary of the Portuguse FA. It was a lovely occasion with the game being staged on the ground where football was originally launched in that country. There was no crowd to speak of because it was just a park pitch but they organised it really nicely. Mario Coluna and the giant striker Jose Torres, two of the biggest stars of Portugese football, figured in their team and after the match, we all went on to a lavish reception at the British Embassy.

Time was catching up with me but I did manage one last hurrah, and I was delighted to have the opportunity to sign off my playing career in style. When Umbro announced they were sponsoring a competition for Over-35s we put together a strong team and entered under the name of Nottingham Knights. The attractive carrot being dangled in front of us was that the final would take place at Wembley. We had a real mixture of players and at one stage or another, plenty of former Forest and County stars turned out for us. People like John

Robertson, Kenny Burns, Archie Gemmill, Les Bradd, Arthur Mann, Brian Stubbs, Ray O'Brien, Iain McCulloch and Seamus McDonagh.

The idea was for ex-pros across the country to help promote the game among over-35s with a series of matches against local amateur teams and we had to see them off before we could progress to the later stages. We did manage to work our way through those early rounds, then beat Leyton Orient at home and Blackpool away to set up a semi-final at Everton. I didn't play in that one but Everton put out a strong, experienced team for a game they badly wanted to win. It turned into a tasty affair that boiled over at one point but the lads came through in the end to book our place at Wembley and what a weekend we had.

Local businessman David Tye, a big County fan and a lovely man, generously agreed to sponsor our trip and surely must have wished he hadn't! It was especially generous of him because his daughter was getting married that weekend so he wasn't even there to share it with us. We went to London by coach, stayed overnight at a hotel just off Hyde Park Corner and I have to admit that we were less than professional. We went to a nightclub and didn't get to bed until well into the early hours. Stan Bowles joined us. He'd become very friendly with 'Robbo' during his brief spell at Forest and ended up sharing his hotel room.

Our match was to provide the pre-match entertainment before the 1992 FA Charity Shield clash between Leeds United and Liverpool and although we were limited to 20 minutes each way it was still special. Incidentally, we had to do a detour on the way from Central London to Wembley to drop Stan off near his home in Brentford. You couldn't make it up! There was no happy ending because we lost 1-0 against West Bromwich Albion but at least I was able to boast that my last-ever appearance on a football pitch took place at Wembley. By then, I was 45-years-old.

I went back a very long way with most of the players involved in that competition. Over the years we'd shared so many of the highs and lows that football always throws at you and it was a delight to sample the very special camaraderie again. It's so important to treasure such times because the old adage is absolutely true ... you never know what tomorrow might bring.

I was devastated when I got the call to tell me that Arthur Mann had been killed in an accident at work. I was speechless, in a state of complete shock, but I had to somehow pull myself together. It was left with me to find his wife Sandra and break the tragic news. The call had come from Ronnie Mann, who was not related to Arthur but had worked closely with him as chief scout at Grimsby Town when Arthur was assistant-manager to Alan Buckley. He'd taken the call from Arthur's company, saying they couldn't find Sandra, and he asked me to deal with it because he couldn't face it.

When I rang Arthur's home number it was their daughter Georgina who answered and she said that Sandra, who worked as an assistant to a physiotherapist was not at home. I said: "Can you find her, please," and Georgina realised by my tone of voice that something was wrong. "Uncle Don what is it ... tell me," she said, getting increasingly more agitated.

I had a split-second to make a decision. Do I tell her that she has just lost her dad or wait to speak to Sandra? When she pressed me for more information, I explained that Arthur had been involved in a serious accident. Georgina reacted in the only way she could and I felt so sorry for her. It was an utterly, utterly horrible moment. The family were living by then in Sutton Coldfield and I drove there the following day to try and offer some comfort. The truth is that there's nothing of great value you can do in that situation but I did understand how they were feeling. I'd 'been there' with Margaret.

Arthur was the best friend that anyone could ever have. He was loyal, reliable and full of fun. He was one of the world's great enthusiasts, on and off the football pitch and it was impossible not to like him. I shared everything with him and I knew that my secrets were safe. I owed him so much for helping to pull me through the dark days after Margaret died and aside from that, he figured prominently in so many of the good things that have happened in my life.

Only a few days earlier he had called in to see me at The Gallery, and Sandra was with him. He was scouting for Nigel Worthington at Blackpool and they had just been to a game in our area. He was in great form as usual and it was a pleasure to see him and spend time in his company. He was my best pal and I still miss him.

Arthur had done well for himself on the other side of the football fence. After our spell together at Kettering he became Alan Buckley's assistant at Grimsby, where they won two promotions. They moved to West Brom, hence the fact that he was living in Sutton Coldfield and although Buckley wanted Arthur to go with him when he returned to Grimsby, he wasn't so sure. He'd got himself a job with a company of builders' suppliers and was enjoying it. But then, while he was reversing to move clear of an oncoming lorry, the fork-lift truck he was driving toppled over and crushed him. He tried to jump out of the way as it began to turn over but fell straight into its path. He was killed instantly. He was only 51.

There was a huge turn-out for his funeral, as there was always going to be. He made friends wherever he went and all of his former clubs were well represented. There was certainly a good turn-out from his colleagues at Meadow Lane and that was the day when the Former Notts County Players' Association was born. Arthur's funeral turned into a big reunion for us and the question was so obvious as we stood there reflecting: "Why does it have to take a sad occasion like this to bring us all back together?"

On the back of that, the Association was formed. Bob Worthington became the chairman, David Needham was the secretary/treasurer and the committee included Jack Wheeler, Jon Nixon, Les Bradd, Bobby Tait, Brian Bates, Gerry Carver and me. Also involved from the start were Colin Slater and Terry Bowles, our two long-term media men who were always closely connected to the club and the players, no matter what they might have said or written about us on match-days, while Dave Tye was our incredibly generous benefactor.

Committee meetings, hosted by Dave Tye, were an absolute treat. The official business took about 10 minutes and the rest was an evening of pure nostalgia, mainly devoted to retelling the Jimmy Sirrel stories that became increasingly embellished over time. Basically we only staged two events each year, a Tribute Dinner at which we honoured stalwarts like Jack Wheeler or long-serving groundsman Peter Thompson, and a Golf Competition that was brilliantly supported in the early days. We played for the Arthur Mann Trophy and Sandra always came to present it. Two events was enough. It meant that twice a year we all came back together and those occasions, full of fun and great memories, became Arthur's legacy.

I'm not too sure what the future holds for the Association because its core is our group of players who served County from the late Sixties to the early Eighties. In those days, the majority stayed together for 8-10 years and developed a real bond with the club and supporters. Players these days are in one door and out the other and the majority don't even live in the area where the club is situated. Neil Warnock's group that won back-to-back promotions - the likes of Tommy Johnson, Mark Draper, Dean Yates and Steve Cherry - have been very supportive over the years but getting interest from those who have played more recently is a struggle.

Middlesbrough also have an active former players' group, run by Gordon Jones and Alan Peacock. I've thoroughly enjoyed going back for their reunion events but sadly Queens Park Rangers don't have one. I've returned to Loftus Road several times as a guest and have been made incredibly welcome but strangely I don't recall there ever being a reunion of the 'Runners-up' team. There was going to be one a while back but then Dave Sexton died and it was decided to call it off.

I don't get to too many football matches these days but I do enjoy occasional visits to my former clubs. The burst of nostalgia they provide helps to keeps me going. It's a very long time since I gave up playing and I'm amazed at what long memories the fans have.

It was the ultimate for me when Notts County supporters voted me their 'Best Ever Player'. How good was that? It's so humbling to think that they put me at the top of the list out of all the players that represented the Oldest League Club in the World. I was also really honoured when the club decided to name one of their lounges after me. The sign for the 'Don Masson Suite' came down when former owner Alan Hardy decided for some reason that he didn't like being reminded of successful times at Meadow Lane but he cannot take away from me the fact that I was inducted into the Notts County Hall of Fame. What made it extra special on the night the award was delivered was that my good friend John Mounteney, such a huge influence at the club over many years, was inducted at the same time.

Neil and Jayne both live abroad these days. We keep in very regular contact and I'm delighted to say that they are both nicely settled. Neil has based himself in Koh Samui, an idyllic island in Thailand, and Jayne is living the dream in Spain with her husband Stephen and lovely children Sophie, Ben and Maddie. They fell in love with a place in Albatera, a small town close to Alicante, but couldn't quite bring themselves to go through with the move in 2006. After they'd stopped off to see my sister Joan in Middlesbrough, on the way back from a visit to Stephen's folks in Newcastle, she rang me to say they'd just decided to pull out of the deal. By the time they arrived home in Nottingham, it was back on again. Sophie, who was only about 11-years-old at the time, had persuaded Jayne and Stephen that it was right to go.

Anyway, the plan was that I would drive their transit van full of furniture to Spain. I went to Heathrow to pick up Neil, who had just landed from Thailand, and away we went - through the Channel Tunnel and down past Paris, Clermont Farrand, Toulouse, Perpignan and into Spain. We drove along the coast through Barcelona, Valencia and Alicante and on to Albatera. It was a journey of about 1,500 miles and we only stopped a couple of time for a quick nap and to fill up with petrol.

Neil kept ringing Brenda to say: "This man is crazy - he never sleeps!" We made it in two days and had no problems along the way. But then, just as I pulled into the driveway of their new home, I caught the near-side bumper on the gate and made a right mess of the van. Fortunately, Stephen is a body-repair specialist and he restored it as good as new.

Brenda and I eventually ran out of steam at The Gallery. We'd had 15 years there, looking after some fantastic people but we knew it was time to go. We loved the life but it was so demanding that you can only do it for so long.

The hotel was on the market for just three weeks before we sold it and that put us under pressure to find somewhere to live. Brenda took the initiative, as she so often has in our 30-plus years together. She's a get-things-done gal and having quickly identified five possible new homes, she found a real 'winner' in the Vale of Belvoir village of Elton-on-the-Hill. Against my better judgement she could see the potential to develop three of the bedrooms and turn the property into an ideal guesthouse.

One of my favourite pictures! Bob Worthington and I have aged a bit since we arrived together in Nottingham on a package deal from Middlesbrough - but we're still going strong.

I thought we were going there to retire but as Brenda insisted, that wasn't the way we lived our lives. It's very low key compared to running The Gallery but we've turned it into a lovely place that was not only awarded five-stars by the AA but also appeared for eight years in the prestigious Michelin AA B&B Guide. I refer to it as my Banchory in Belvoir. As I've pointed out before, I always thought I'd end up back in the wide-open spaces of the Highlands but I now have the next-best thing. We live in an old farmhouse, full of character that sits on a hill overlooking fields as far as the eye can see.

Some of our regular Gallery clients followed us across but we don't look for new business these days. I'm just happy pottering around, keeping the gardens looking nice and doing the decorating and maintenance when required. I have a stock answer if anyone calls. I just tell them I'm the gardener: "Go round the back and deal with the boss!"

I took it upon myself some 10 years ago to make sure that the grass areas of the local churchyard and the approaches to our village are kept in good order and these days I share the duties with my neighbour and friend, Robin Clarke. As he likes to say, he looks after the West Wing and I do the East Wing! If ever you are passing through, I'm the one with the woolly hat and goggles.

I also hold the keys to the church and at least a couple of times a week I go in there to do odd jobs and spend time by myself. Brenda says that if ever she can't find me, she always knows where I am. I really value the solitude - the chance to be alone with my thoughts and reflect on all that has happened in my eventful life.

'Be the Best You Possibly Can' was the motto I adopted very early in my career and whatever I've done I've always strived to live my life with that in mind. Maybe that was a big part of making me the person I became - totally driven to make the most of any talent I had. It undoubtedly helped to shape my character and I take great satisfaction from being able to look back and say that I did become the best footballer I could be.

I consider myself to be the luckiest person in the world to have spent 20 years with Margaret and 30-plus with Brenda. I've had a fantastic life. Do I have regrets? Yes, of course I do and many of those I've shared with you in this book. But I've tried very hard in my later years to make amends and people regularly tell me I'm a very different person compared to the one they knew in my early playing days.

I really hope that's the case.

DON MASSON

Career Highlights

1967	Promotion to the Second Division with Middlesbrough
1969	Notts County 'Player of the Year'
1970	Promotion to the Third Division with Notts County
1973	Promotion to the Second Division with Notts County
1974	Selected in the PFA Second Division 'Team of the Year'
1974	Notts County 'Player of the Year'
1976	Runners-up in the First Division with Queens Park Rangers
1976	Runner-up for PFA 'Footballer of the Year'
1976	Selected in the PFA First Division 'Team of the Year'
1976	International debut for Scotland v Wales
1976	Won the Home International Championships with Scotland
1977	Reached the UEFA Cup quarter-finals with Queens Park Rangers
1977	Won the Home International Championships with Scotland
1977	Captained Scotland v East Germany and v Wales
1978	World Cup Finals with Scotland in Argentina
1981	Promotion to the First Division with Notts County
1981	Runners-up in the Anglo-Scottish Cup with Notts County
1981	Notts County 'Player of the Year'
1982	Won the Hong Kong FA Cup and Viceroy Cup with Bulova

THE DON MASSON 'FAN CLUB'

The following people have expressed their appreciation of Don's significant contribution to British football by pre-ordering a copy of this autobiography.

Our sincere thanks for your support.

Phil Adcock Nottingham
Rob Anderson Bedford
Stephen Anderson Girton
David Armes Nottingham
David Armstrong East Leake
Richard Ashford Nottingham
David J Astill Nottingham
John S H Astill Nottingham
Ian Aston Long Eaton
Terry Atkin Bunny
Chris Atkins Florida, USA
Dean Atkinson Melbourne, AUS
Neil Austin Hermitage
Glenn Bacon Nottingham
Dave Badder Penrith
James Baguley Nottingham
Aubrey Bailey Scalford
Paul Batchford Bo'Ness
Vincent Bates Nottingham
Martin Bayley Ingleby Barwick
Stephen Beal Burton Joyce
Carol Beattie Banchory
James Beattie Peterculter
Paul Belshaw Nottingham
Adrian Bennett Nottingham
Edward Benson London
Jeffery Beresford Beeston
Murray Biddle West Bridgford
Mary Binnie Falkirk
Nigel Blackman Wells
Richard Blaney Beeston
Tom Bond East Leake
Andrew Boruch Whatton-in-the-Vale
Paul Bowmar Arnold
Dr Michael Bramley Towcester
Chris Bramley Hucknall
Peter Branch Bottesford
David Braybook Olney
Paul Breffitt Nottingham

Michael Briscoe Weymouth
Kevin Britnell New Ollerton
Simon Brodbeck London
Keith Brown Four Elms
Mark Brown Nottingham
Terry Brown Bestwood Village
Scott Brownson Bingham
Chris Brownson Nottingham
Broxham Family Wollaton
Kevin Buchan Inverurie
Fiona Buchan Banchory
Colin Bull Toton
Tony Bull Nottingham
Nigel Burnell Carshalton
Elsie Burnett Banchory
Alan Burrell Peacehaven
Joyce Burrows Nottingham
Ron Burton North Lincs
Chris Butler Ripon
Steve Carter Carlton
Elizabeth Carter Swindon
Justin Cast Carlton
Katherine Catherines Worksop
David Chapman Peterborough
Dr Mick Chappell West Bridgford
Chris Cheetham Kent
Bryce John Clare The Meadows
Simon Clark West Bridgford
David (Sid) Clarke Radcliffe-on-Trent
Robin Clarke Elton-on-the-Hill
Sylvia Clarke Nottingham
Steve Clay Wakefield
Tony Clay Scarborough
David Clayton Nottingham
Loz Clough Nottingham
Margaret Cobb Nottingham
Chris Coldwell Nottingham
John W. Collings Spondon
Richard Fredrick Collings Weymouth

Geoff Collins Halesowen
John Collins Newthorpe
Gary Cooke Tadworth
Jim Cooke Edwalton
Dave Cooper Nottingham
John Cooper Ilkeston
Conor Cotton Nottingham
Barrie Cousins Melton Mowbray
Bryan Coverdale Brighton
Neil Coy Grantham
Michael Croome Nottingham
John Cunningham Thornaby
Chris Curtis Hucknall
Chris Curtis East Leake
Paul Cuthbert Nottingham
Martin Dabell Birmingham
Justin Daley Mursley
Lynne Davidson Banchory
Jim Dawkins Nottingham
Pete Dawn West Bridgford
Peter Dennis Arnold
Alvin Denovellis Carlisle
Russell Dexter Quorn
Richard Di Mambro Aberdeen
Natalie May Dickinson New Hartley
Alan Dodson Nottingham
Doug Dowthwaite Sawley
Richard Draper Granby
Paul Drew Mansfield
Steve Dring Nottingham
Ian Driver ESP
Helen Drummond Nottingham
Barry Duffield Burnham on Crouch
Malcolm Dunmore Wokingham
Robert Dunn Hemel Hempstead
Karel Dvorak Prague
Steve Eastwood Notts
Brian Eavis London
William Eley Poulsbo, USA

Simon Elliott Purley
Steve Elwis Selles-sur-Cher, FRA
Christina Fearon Nottingham
David Fells Shepshed
Peter Fish Nottingham
James Fisher Hucknall
David Fitzpatrick Eastwood
Austin Flanagan Rushden
Joseph Flanagan Faversham
Malcolm Fletcher Godmanchester
Norman Fletcher Hucknall
Keith Flint Guisborough
Andrew Foss Ruddington
Ian Fraser Banchory
Sandy Fraser Banchory
Ian Fuller Beeston Rylands
John Gadsby Whatton
Neil Garratt Nottingham
Kevan Gaunt Daybrook
George Gee Nottingham
Jim Gee Nottingham
Duncan Gething Hucknall
Paul Gething East Bridgford
Geoff Gibbs Long Eaton
Paul Gibbs Nottingham
Richard Gill Sibson
George Goddard Balderton
Alex Goodfellow New Hartley
Ben Goodfellow Albatera, ESP
Brian Goodfellow New Hartley
Jared Goodfellow New Hartley
Maddie Goodfellow Albatera, ESP
Mary Goodfellow New Hartley
Sophie Goodfellow Albatera, ESP
Stephen Goodfellow Albatera, ESP
Ron Goodley Berry Hill
Sean Gordon Ireland
Kathleen Gordon Arbroath
Jim Gowan Yaxley

Jeffrey Grain Breaston
Russell Grande Nottingham
Albert Greenaway Nottingham
David Greenwood Thrumpton
Chris Gregory Mapperley
Mike Gyles Alfreton
Tony Hales Carlton
John Hallam Mapperley
Jurgen Halligan New Ollerton
Scott Hamilton Wandsworth
Geoff Hammond Manchester
Pete Harby Sutton in Ashfield
David Hardy Nottingham
Robert Hardy-McBride Nottingham
Michael Harley Notts
Darren Harper Derby
Paul Harper Nottingham
Scott Harrison Nottingham
Emma Hartley Stockton-on-Tees
John Hassell Castle Donington
Paul Hawksworth Wollaton
The Hawksworths Marlow
Steve Hayden Netherfield
Jim Haywood Stoke on Trent
Andrew Head Harpenden
Phil Hearson Arnold
Terry Henderson Ruislip
Jon Henderson Elton-on-the-Hill
Chris Hewitt Greenford
Richard Higginbottom Nottingham
Nicholas Hill West Sussex
Ron Hill London
Ron Hill Nottingham
Roger Hill Nottingham
David Hilton Kinoulton
Simon Hobbs Nottingham
Phillip Holland Bulwell
Duncan Hollick-Cooper Swanwick
Keith Holness West Hallam

Grant Hopkinson Hucknall
Andrew Horne Rochford
Stephen Hornsby Nottingham
Jas Hundal Nottingham
Keith Hurst Market Deeping
Les Hurst East Leake
Dale Huskinson Chapel-en-le-Frith
David Huskinson Nottingham
John Hutchinson Mansfield
Hazel Hutchison Aberdeen
Callum Ingle Loughborough
Rob Jackson Nottingham
Alan Jackson Keyworth
Malcolm Jaffe Nottingham
Andrew James Long Eaton
Steve Jayes Calverton
Dave Jenkins Thornaby
Michelle V Jennison Cropwell Bishop
Matthew Johnson Burton Joyce
Michael Johnson Nottingham
Gerald Johnson Nottingham
Bill Jones Dorridge
David Jones North Hillingdon
Michael Jones Arnold
Peter Jones Bolton
Martyn Joy Nottingham
Jez Kearney Nottingham
Rob Kearney Nottingham
Martyn Kelk Owthorpe
Brian Kemp Bramcote
Richard Kerry Nottingham
Graham Kershaw Arnold
Derek King Southwell
Roger King Harrogate
Rob King Guernsey
Jane Kirk Plungar
Paul Kirk Beeston
Rod Kirkham Arnold
Karen Knight Nottingham

Marco Benedikt König Batenhorst, GER
Nigel Lacy Basford
Derek Laidman London
Alexander Laidman London
Graeme Lamb Nottingham
Jamie Lamb Elton-on-the-Hill
John Lamb (R.I.P.) Nottingham
Malc Lambourne Bury St Edmonds
Chrissie Larkin Brookenby
Pete Lawson Calverton
Tony Leach Elton-on-the-Hill
Mick Leafe Arnold
John Leighton Bulwell
Steve LeMottee Nottingham
Jeff Lewis Manchester
John Leyson Kingswinford
Jeff Long Nottingham
Steve Long South Ruislip
Alan Lowe Corby
Eleanor Lowe Middlesbrough
Chris Loydall Nottingham
Jason Loydall Nottingham
Andrew Ludlow Hucknall
Clive Lynch Torquay
Gordon Macey (in memoriam) Woking
Mark Maltby Palmerston North, NZ
Alison Marriott Nottingham
Paul Marriott Basford
Rob Marshall Cambridge
Steve Marshall Nottingham
Stuart Marshall AUS
Anthony Martin New York, USA
Ian Martin Lincoln
Tony Martin Kimberley
Gregg Matthews Nottingham
Andrew Mattison Ilkeston
Tony Mattison Langley Mill
Reg Mayer Nottingham

Alan Maynard Nottingham
Ian McCondach West Yorkshire
Rob McDonough Elton-on-the-Hill
Julian McDougall Birmingham
IL & CL McLaughlin West Bridgford
Colin McLeary Thornaby
Iain McQuillan Nottingham
Mick Mellors Sneinton
Alan Middleton Wollaton
Ross Miles Nottingham
Howard Miller Horsham
Kevin Millington AUS
Andrew Millward South Normanton
Pete Minkley Moorgreen
Graham Moore Woodthorpe
John Morehen Nottingham
Simon Morehen Nottingham
Graham Morris Ripley
Joy Morson Nottingham
Richard Murfet Stevenage
Barbara Mutch Banchory
David Naylor Bramcote
Barry Nelson Nottingham
Susan Ness Portlethen
Clive Newman Melton Mowbray
Alan McCully Nicolson Motherwell
Alan Shaw Nicolson Cambuslang
Ricky Norris Arnold
Michael Patrick O'Dwyer Harrow
Mick O'Regan Nottingham
Richard Ogando Nottingham
John Okroj Nottingham
Stephen Oldham Woodhall Spa
James Oliver Nottingham
John Olney Selston
Michael Orton Nottingham
Dan Osborne Inberkithing
Dean Oswin Nottingham

Keith Page Nottingham
Brian Palmer Nottingham
Colin Parker Nottingham
Steve Parkin Grantham
Chris Parr Nottingham
Stewart Partridge Newark
Michael R. Patterson Farndon
John Payne Solihull
Tony Pearce London
Jonathan Pears Nottingham
Simon Peeks Epsom
David Peeks Gedling
Barbara Perry Newark
Tim Phillips Nottingham
Grant Phillips New Hartley
Neil Pike Nottingham
Stuart Powell Nuthall
Pam Powell Elton-on-the-Hill
Timothy Powell Nottingham
John Poxon Lowdham
David Prest Colwick
Barry Prettyjohn Long Eaton
Ken Pryer Hadleigh
Ian Radwell Milton Keynes
Glenn Raven Nottingham
Malcolm Raven Nottingham
John Rawle Newark
John Reynolds Hemel Hempstead
Paul Rhoades Sutton-on-Sea
Tom Rhys Jones Silkstone
Graham Rixon Eynsford
Malcolm Rixon Chesham
Andrew Robinson Nottingham
Dean Robson Windsor
Mick Robson Thornaby
Kathy Rogers Ingleby Barwick
Chris Roper Nottingham
Trevor Ross-Gower Nottingham

Clive Rowe Nottingham
Alan Rudd Nottingham
Heinz Ruelker Lette, GER
Philip R Russell Northwood Hills
Stephen Rutter Thornaby
David Sadler Banbury
David Selby East Bridgford
Paul Sexton Retford
Ian Shanks South Ruislip
Ian Shaw Chorley
Martyn Shaw Nottingham
Peter Robert Shaw Chew Magna
Richard Sheldon Heanor
Richard Shelton Cambridge
Steve Shepherd Derby
David Shipston Wollaton
Paul Short Nottingham
Stephen Short Nottingham
Paul Kenneth Short Nottingham
Mark Warwick Short Nottingham
Andrew Michael Short Nottingham
Jeff Silverman San Francisco, USA
Ashley Silverman Nottingham
Phillip Simpson Nottingham
David Sirrel Lincoln
David Skinner Hornchurch
Brian Slater Nottingham
Howard Smalley Sutton in Ashfield
John Smalley Sutton in Ashfield
David Smedley East Leake
Stuart Smedley Stickford
Neil Smith Nottingham
Malc Smith Shepshed
Steven B Smith Langar
Dean Smith Nottingham
Paul Smith Chipping
Brian Smith Haanor
Kevin Smith Nottingham

Iris Smith Nottingham	Julian Tyers Nottingham
Andy Smith St. Davids	Gary Upton Broughton
Nick Smith Nottingham	John Victor Gibraltar
Jeff Smith Hemel Hempstead	Rob Wagstaff Nottingham
Abbili Smith Ilkeston	Alan Wakelin Nottingham
Dave Smith Nottingham	Wakelin Family Guernsey
Zach Smith Bottesford	John Wakerley Nottingham
Samuel Smith Bottesford	David Walker Westwood
Kailem Smith Newark	Tony Walster Nottingham
Ian Solloway Rutland	Ian Warbrick Aylesbury
Stan Solloway Beeston	Graham Ward Nottingham
Philip Squire Snaith	Richard Ward Ashbourne
David Squires Nottingham	Kevin Ward Nottingham
Brian Squires Nottingham	Ashley Waterfall Bottesford
Simon Staples Chaddesden	Alastair Watson Banstead
Neil Stewart Great Missenden	Laura Watson-Dar Nottingham
Paul Stokes Middlesbrough	Gordon Watt Sherwood
Caroline Stokes Motherwell	Steve Wesby Radcliffe on Trent
Pete Storey Loughborough	Trevor West Bingham
Barry Strong London	Phil Weston Holmfirth
Mark Swaby Nottingham	Terry Whiting Allestree
Donald Swann Fiskerton	Vic Whiting West Bridgford
Gary Tacey Chilwell	Tim Whiting West Bridgford
Jeremy Taylor Gotham	Grant Whitt Radcliffe on Trent
Brian Taylor Banchory	David Whittaker NG8
Michael Thatcher Burton Joyce	Clark Whyte Alloa
David Thorpe Sudbrooke	Andrew Wighton North Hykeham
DKM Thorpe Edingley	Trevor Williams Plumtree
Callum Timms Bo'Ness	Steven Williams Carlton
Tommy Timms Bo'Ness	Arthur Wilson Sandiacre
William Towers Nuthall	Bill Winfield Nottingham
Alan Tunnicliffe Nottingham	Ian Wood Nottingham
Simon Tupman NZ	Terence Woolhouse Nottingham
Paul Turnbull South Norwood	Christopher Woolhouse Nottingham
Bruce Turnbull Brighton	Alan Wright Nottingham
Martyn Turner Kirkby in Ashfield	Andrew Wright Knaresborough
Philip J Turner Kenton	Ian Wright Brackley
Jacqui Turton Bingham	Peter Wright Nottingham
Lucy Tweedie Elgin	John Wright Glasgow